Cultural Analysis

Cultural Analysis

Jim McGuigan

Los Angeles | London | New Delhi
Singapore | Washington DC

First published 2010

SAGE Publications Ltd
1 Oliver's Yard
55 City Road
London EC1Y 1SP

SAGE Publications Inc.
2455 Teller Road
Thousand Oaks, California 91320

SAGE Publications India Pvt Ltd
B 1/I 1 Mohan Cooperative Industrial Area
Mathura Road, Post Bag 7
New Delhi 110 044

SAGE Publications Asia-Pacific Pte Ltd
33 Pekin Street #02–01
Far East Square
Singapore 048763

Library of Congress Control Number: 2008933210

British Library Cataloguing in Publication data

A catalogue record for this book is available from
the British Library

ISBN 978-1-84787-019-3
ISBN 978-1-84787-020-9 (pbk)

Typeset by C&M Digitals (P) Ltd, Chennai, India
Printed by MPG Books Group, Bodmin, Cornwall
Printed on paper from sustainable resources

Mixed Sources
Product group from well-managed
forests and other controlled sources
www.fsc.org Cert no. SA-COC-1565
© 1996 Forest Stewardship Council

To Graham Murdock, an excellent mentor

CONTENTS

INTRODUCTION: CULTURAL ANALYSIS

The perspective on cultural analysis presented in this book aims to be multidimensional in its approach to scholarship and orientated towards the critical study of issues that are of public interest.

A multidimensional analysis seeks to make sense of the ontological complexity of cultural phenomena – that is, the many-sidedness of their existence. It is concerned with the circulation of culture and the interaction of production and consumption, including the materiality and significatory qualities of cultural forms.

There are innumerable possible topics that might be studied in such a way, none of which would necessarily be lacking in value. Choices have to be made, however; decisions have to be taken as to priority. That is why questions of public interest are privileged in this account.

Questions of public interest refer to issues that are, for one reason or another, salient and contested for the citizens of a polity – a polity defined in inclusive rather than exclusive terms. We live in an interconnected social world and natural environment where cosmopolitan values are sorely needed. These questions of public interest become matters of debate that may have consequence for democratic decisionmaking in not only local, national and regional contexts but also continentally and on a global scale.

This perspective on cultural analysis might be controversial. Yet, some position-taking is required, it has to be said, on practical grounds and in order to distinguish the approach to cultural analysis under consideration from other kinds of analysis. That is not to say the perspective adopted here covers all which could reasonably be named 'cultural analysis' in the sense of studying symbolic process. There are many disciplinary specialisms that would come within a broader definition of cultural analysis. These are too broad and all-encompassing, though, for the purposes in hand, such as art history, literary criticism, musicology and – to cite another example that comes quite close to the present agenda – social anthropology. In any case, attempting to catalogue every conceivable strand of cultural analysis in a single book would be lunatic – comparable to the futile quest of the mythologist Casaubon in George Eliot's *Middlemarch*.

This book draws largely and specifically on the British tradition of cultural studies and the European tradition of critical social theory. Each of these has a particular history, established canon of work and pantheon of leading thinkers – none of it beyond question and settled forever. These are fluid traditions that are similarly characterised by a certain disrespectfulness for tradition as such. They are both interdisciplinary, as is this book. Both, however, had disciplinary points of departure – literary history and political philosophy, respectively.

My own disciplinary background is mixed, covering sociology, literature, the history of ideas and the multidisciplinarity of mass communications research. Programmatic interdisciplinarity is given much lip-service in the academy but seldom practised securely since it is always vulnerable to the criticism of superficiality from the point of view of disciplinarity. Still, public issues of consequence in 'the real world' do not fit comfortably into disciplinary categories and, for that reason, interdisciplinary research is worth the try.

The distinguishing feature of British cultural studies was the project to democratise our understanding of culture. It therefore encouraged, in effect, the synthesis of what in English can be referred to as 'Culture' with a capital C, on the one hand, and, on the other, lower-case 'culture' as the medium of social communication. That synthesis has been problematic in that it blurs some important distinctions that are still relevant – for instance, those between art and speech. Most importantly, however, it challenged elitist assumptions and promoted appreciation of the popular.

This move in the game was progressive, though it did have troubling results when questions of value (which is one way of defining 'culture' – that it is about values), paradoxically, became, in some quarters, impossible to pose. It is a matter of common record that the moment of British cultural studies was instrumental in establishing a new field of study – Cultural Studies – that long ago expanded beyond its British 'origins'.

The tradition of critical social theory is less easily located and summed up since, in some ways, it represents the distinguishing feature of European political philosophy as a whole – albeit intermittently since 'ancient' times – not all of which, incidentally, is actually critical of the existing state of society.

In the modern era, the critical tradition of social theory developed from German historicism, the critique of the political economy of capitalism and the ideology critique of capitalist culture, while retaining the critical rationalism inherited from the European Enlightenment that was centred on France in the eighteenth century. It was the counterpoint to positivist social science and, also, the sheer banality of much empirical sociology. European social theory of a critical persuasion anticipated many of the themes developed somewhat independently by British cultural studies. There were, however, some striking differences.

The European tradition favoured avant-garde culture and was critical of mass consumer culture. For that reason, it met with a measure of resistance and, indeed, opposition in Britain, where the cultural activity of 'the people' – even under highly commercialised conditions – was treated with greater respect, to the extent that it was increasingly contrasted favourably with 'elitist' high culture. Still, both traditions had much in common, motivated by emancipatory interests, and, while the British tradition emphasised concrete detail over abstract thought, continental rationalism was a vital corrective to the empirical verging on empirist mode of separatist Britain.

Older forms of cultural analysis tended to study the past – largely because it was assumed that time had to pass in order for posterity to do its work of selecting texts that were worthy of serious academic scrutiny. In contrast, newer forms of cultural analysis – pioneered by British cultural studies and the continental tradition of critical social theory – typically studied the present conditions of culture, which was refreshing. They had something to say about now, albeit in a historical framework.

The present is itself a moment in time within a particular configuration of history. Moreover, it became permissible to study mass popular culture – the culture of most people – not just the culture of a refined minority that had been inherited from the past. Thus, in the 1960s and 1970s, cultural studies in Britain was *contemporary* cultural studies.

There was disquiet at the way literary methods were used to interpret what sociologists had regarded jealously as their disciplinary subject matter. On the other side, it was feared that the sociological turn was in danger of reducing culture to society.

Cultural analysis is methodologically pluralist as far as this book is concerned, drawing freely on methods as and when appropriate to the analytical problem under investigation. In this sense, it is parasitic on a wide range of disciplines and a bit of a pest, rather like a magpie. It also offends against a disciplinary methodism whereby correctly prescribed technique is reified over and above the subject matter of the enquiry. To a considerable extent, cultural analysis remains insufficiently serious according to a pristine disciplinarity and, at the same time, it is deemed an impractical and unrealistic sideshow to the serious business of solving research problems defined and funded by capital and the State.

Moreover, since cultural analysis – in the sense that I am using the term – is so much concerned with current developments, it is likely to cross over with journalism. There is a curiously unexamined relation between cultural analysis and cultural journalism.

For much of academia, journalism is anathema because it is focused on the fleeting and all too transient features of life, forever chasing novelty and discarding yesterday's story. Academic work is much slower – tortoise-like in comparison with the haring about of journalism. Xeno's paradox and its version in Aesop's Fables is relevant here because academics do generally believe that their slower, painstaking work is of greater value than the flotsam and jetsam of day-to-day news. Indeed, it is not unusual for academics to hold a disparaging view of journalism.

Of course, journalists have little patience with the complex detachment and what they may perceive as the pedantry and sheer lack of urgency of academic work. When they draw on research findings, journalists are apt to reduce them to overly simplistic bullet points.

Academics persistently complain, with good reason, about the journalistic misuse and misrepresentation of their arduous work. Still, however, there is a relation.

When studying current events and unfolding developments of one kind or another, academics do have to draw on journalistic source material. Such material has to be treated with the kind of caution that historians apply to archival documentation – that is, being cognisant of textual features, the author–reader relation, the political context and the time–space conjuncture in which the evidence is produced.

Seen more positively, however, much journalistic writing – especially in some feature journalism and book form – is better as a means of communication than academic writing, which so often seems to the lay reader like the secret code of a mysterious sect. Inevitably, in a book of this kind, academic work strays occasionally into the territory of journalism and at least aims to be as communicative as the better examples.

It is not surprising that academics should be inclined to shy away from topical matters, avoiding them because they are apparently the sole preserve of journalists. The work of this book, though, takes a risk by addressing current issues of public interest and debate (much of it published too long after the event to be still newsworthy, however). It is interesting to recall now, for instance, that the controversy over the Millennium Dome was the biggest news story of the year 2000 in Britain as the gigantic tent has since become an everyday commercial venue after being abandoned wastefully by the New Labour government to murky business interests. Yet, the story was never just about an ill-conceived exposition. It was always about murky business interests, promoted with public money by governmental authority. Indeed, as I argue in Chapter 3, the Millennium Dome controversy was about something much deeper and more consequential than a poorly managed exhibition and not just for the 'sceptred isle' – to whit, the neoliberal turn of social democracy, which, in fact, has become a global phenomenon.

Such topical analysis, then, aims to make sense of a particular case in its significant detail at a specific moment – in effect, representing a flashpoint that is quite possibly symptomatic of deep-seated and longer-term processes of cultural and social change. In that sense, it is an exercise in critical-realist analysis. If journalism is the first draft of history, this style of cultural analysis is one sort of second draft.

This book is concerned with methodology in cultural analysis but it is not a nuts-and-bolts textbook on methods. There are rules and technical procedures that should indeed be observed for analysing culture in the humanities and social sciences. As many researchers – though not all, unfortunately – know, however, a great deal of research effort, in practice, involves imagination and invention. It is necessary to draw on established theories, appropriate and adapt techniques, to be sure, but, sometimes, we have to fashion new ones – in problem-formulation, data-gathering and analysis appropriate to the object of enquiry – so as to produce original interpretations and adequate explanations. It is not just a matter of following an already prescribed set of rules. It is as much art as science.

The opening chapter spells out my formulation of the concept of a *cultural public sphere*, by which I mean the affective – that is, aesthetic and emotional – aspects of the public sphere. Research on the public sphere as the forum for debate in a democracy has generally neglected affectivity, sometimes dismissing it as a spoiling agent for what should properly be an exclusively cognitive means of exchanging information and arena for open communication. Such a neglectful attitude fails to grasp the role of art and popular culture in articulating public issues that capture not only people's attention but also their imagination. An example of the operations of the cultural public sphere is addressed in Chapter 2 – the extraordinary response to the death and funeral of Diana, Princess of Wales in 1997, when issues of symbolic authority and relationships between men and women were articulated. This was an especially notable phenomenon in Britain but also around the world.

The third chapter, on the controversy over the Millennium Dome, is a case study in multidimensional cultural analysis, whereby the intersection of determinations is examined in order to make sense of a complex phenomenon in the round, so to speak. It looks at how the exposition was produced – its social construction – and mediated by broadcasting and the press and interpreted somewhat differently by actual visitors. This process involves giving due consideration to the ideological framing of the Dome's representational meanings within a specific political and economic context.

The Dome case study also begins to address questions of national identity that are taken up in Chapter 4 in connection with multiculturalism. There, I discuss a report on multicultural Britain that met with near unanimous hostility throughout the news media, despite the remarkable good sense of its carefully constructed arguments and recommendations. In that chapter, the notion of a 'community of communities' – formulated admittedly in a particular national context – is contrasted favourably with the celebrated 'clash of civilizations' thesis that takes the whole world at its canvas, but, strangely, on close interrogation, turns out to be more parochial in its purview, emanating from a narrow-mindedly American context.

Chapter 5 takes the argument concerning multiculturalism further, considering national and ethnic identities in the British Isles. It notes an illiberal drift in public culture, bound up with issues around migration, religious differences and geopolitical tension, countered by some progressive developments in popular culture but, at the same time, underscored by a fashionable derision of the weak and marginalised in popular culture, as exemplified by the counter reaction to 'political correctness' seen in one of the most popular television programmes of the 2000s – the comedy sketch show *Little Britain*.

The following chapter on the mobile phone shifts register from discussion of topical issues that have been especially newsworthy to consideration of the advent of new communications technology and increasingly mobile sociality. It is primarily methodological in focus, looking at various sociological methods for studying a rapidly changing and ubiquitous technology. This provides the opportunity to not only map out ways of investigating the relations between technology and social change but also clarifies the range of multidimensional cultural analysis in a predominantly anthropological mode that is, in addition, related to economic and political process.

Chapter 7, on risk and individualisation, looks at the implications of the risk society thesis for cultural analysis, which are many and varied. Risk consciousness is itself a notable cultural phenomenon that may or may not represent the actuality of risk in the world. This is a matter of considerable dispute and controversy, ranging from doom-laden alarmism – particularly concerning industrialism's impact on the natural environment – to Panglossian complacency and irresponsible political inaction.

How we understand ecological, societal and personal risk is mediated in all sorts of arguably faulty and inadequate ways by the major media of communication. It is very difficult to be sure of anything in the risk society. That is so at the level of individual self-identity and personal relationships, too – a level of existence that is illuminated immensely by the concept of individualisation.

The chapter looks specifically at the individualisation of work and the insecurity of careers in 'the creative industries' – a topic taken further in the next chapter, which addresses urban regeneration and cultural policy.

It is curious how 'culture' has come to be a panacea for social woes, so that somehow cultural policy can do the job of social policy. This is particularly strange considering the sheer dominance of economic reason today, that everything is ultimately reducible to economy. These are twin reductionisms, with cultural reductionism now accompanying the more familiar economic reductionism.

Logically, they seem to contradict one another, yet they are so often found together, as in the idea that culture – whatever that means – may solve the economic and, indeed, social problems of deindustrialised cities in the former industrial heartlands in the North, now that so much manufacturing has been transferred to cheap labour markets in the South.

This strange combination is a feature of hegemonic neoliberalism, successor to the social democratic consensus that prevailed in the mid-twentieth century. The idea is that capital and 'enterprise' should be released from the stultifying regulation of the State and public subsidy – in effect, the dead hand of socialism. Yet, what we find in projects of urban renewal through cultural policy (exemplified in Chapter 8 by the annual European Capital of Culture festival) is that the State – through local, national or international arrangements and finance – is required to provide the largesse needed to let business rip while fostering illusory hope with delusions of grandeur in beleaguered populations.

We are often told today that the era in which ideology was a prevalent force in the world has ended. Yet, at the same time it is quite evident that neoliberal ideology is massively dominant in the world, not only in business circles but also throughout commonsense reasoning and everyday conduct. Still, it is most nakedly present in business, though not simply as a set of economic nostrums but as a whole way of being, a way of being that in my work I have found it necessary to call 'cool capitalism', the incorporation of disaffection into the capitalist way of life, the effect of which is to neutralise criticism.

Chapter 9 takes a very obvious instance of cool capitalism and the popular appeal of business enterprise in contemporary culture – the television show *The Apprentice* – and produces a critical discourse analysis of its ideological mode of representation. This chapter is also meant to exemplify the value of close textual analysis of cultural form – a practice that has been rather undervalued by an emphasis on differential reading of texts that denies any preferred meaning in audience research. The chapter stresses a certain determinacy of textual meaning in the construction of popular knowledge and public culture.

The concluding chapter looks at the coalescence of the academic field known as 'cultural studies' with the popular face of neoliberal ideology that I have named 'cool capitalism'. This involves a survey of the development of cultural studies from its best-known place of origin – Britain from the 1950s and 1960s – to the latest rationale for the field a decade into the twenty-first century.

It is important to appreciate that cultural studies is diverse in both its formation and extant strands of education and research. Having said that, Chapter 10 is principally concerned with tracing a certain pragmatic reconfiguration of the field that moves it towards becoming useful and applied instead of merely critical. Something is gained in such a trajectory, but a great deal is lost.

In the chapter, I reiterate my own version of cultural analysis – irrespective of its location in cultural studies, sociology or elsewhere – that it should be multidimensional in methodology and orientated towards the critical study of issues of public interest. Along the way an assessment is given of the drift of cultural studies that might possibly be read, I recognise, as an obituary, but I hope not.

1 THE CULTURAL PUBLIC SPHERE

Introduction

The public sphere is both ideal and actual. The actuality is a good deal less perfect than the ideal of free and open debate that has policy consequences in a democratic polity.

Jürgen Habermas's *The Structural Transformation of the Public Sphere*, originally published in 1962, identified the formation of a bourgeois public sphere in eighteenth-century Europe, especially in Britain and France. Prototypically, the London coffee houses were sites of disputation where everyone present – middle-class males, for once on a par with aristocrats – had their say, in principle, on the issues of the day. Thus, the bourgeoisie found its voice in the transition from feudalism to capitalism; and this was represented in the press and other forms of public communication, including the arts.

There was always a contradiction, of course, between the ideal and the actuality. Universalising claims were made for equality and freedom of expression that were not realised in practice. It was not self-evidently in the immediate interests of bourgeois men to extend disputatious citizenship to women and subordinate classes. As it turned out, however, from the emergence of capitalism and liberal democracy onwards, the demands of the working class, women and colonial subjects for citizenship and self-determination were framed to practical effect by that contradictory amalgam of the ideal and the actual. They claimed for themselves the same rights as bourgeois men. Such claims not only involved bitter struggle but were, in a sense, logical and, therefore, difficult to argue against with consistency: this is the force of the better argument.

Young Habermas (1989 [1962]) told a tragic story about the rise and fall of the bourgeois public sphere. Press freedom and open debate were, he argued, diluted and distorted by commercial considerations and public relations by the middle of the twentieth century. Moreover, radical demands had been incorporated, to an extent, by the welfare state. This resulted in a generalised quiescence, according to the disappointed Habermas. Grievances had been partly ameliorated, thereby neutralising conflict, politics had become detached from popular struggle and the masses were becoming amused consumers, indifferent to the great issues of the day and preoccupied with their own everyday lives. That is exactly the kind of elitist imaginary that cultural populists are inclined to contest. For them, the meaningful practices of mundane existence are not signs of alienation but, instead, empowerment and 'resistance'. To what precisely I am not quite sure.

It is important to note that Habermas (1996 [1992]: 329–87) was later to revise his earlier pessimistic conclusions. His latter-day 'sluice gate' model of the public sphere awards primacy to social movements and campaigning organisations in forcing issues on to the public agenda that might not otherwise be there at all. Big business and big government would not of their own accord have addressed, for instance, environmental issues to anything like the current posture forced by public protest. Taking the argument further, the field of action for a social justice movement networked across the globe is the public sphere in its various forms and configurations, however much it is distorted by mainstream communications media and politics. Furthermore, inspired by Mikhail Bakhtin's (1984 [1965]) celebration of the carnivalesque, Habermas (1992) came to appreciate popular cultural subversion of hierarchical relations and, in so doing, also registered his belated recognition of the feminist 'personal is political'.

The theoretical value of the public sphere concept as a measure of democratic communications, then, is somewhat more complex than its use in the critique of news as propaganda (Herman and Chomsky, 1988). The news is indeed frequently, routinely and structurally propagandistic. This is undeniably so in many respects and must not be set aside by sophisticates as too familiar a problem to interrogate persistently. To take the most obvious contemporary example, the American and British news media's role in obscuring the reasons for invading and occupying Iraq remains an issue.[1]

Still, however, it would be grim indeed were there no space for dissent and disputation. Yet, because disputation is so often deflected on to questions of who said what to whom instead of addressing why something happened, it is vital to appreciate that argument alone is not evidence of an actualised public sphere in operation. Much of the time we are witnesses to what is rightly called a 'pseudo' public sphere, where politicians and docile journalists act out a travesty of democratic debate. No wonder, as Jean Baudrillard (1983) suggests, the masses are generally turned off by such 'serious' politics and turned on to something else that is much more entertaining. Nevertheless, it is necessary for 'subaltern counter-publics', as named by Nancy Fraser (1992: 109–42), to keep up the pressure. Otherwise the spin doctors will have it all to themselves and there is then a frighteningly fascistic closure of discourse.

Every now and again a really big issue does capture popular attention: famine, GM food, questionable reasons for pre-emptive war, global warming and so forth. It must be said, though, these are seldom the most compelling attractions for mass popular fascination. The ups and downs of a celebrity career, minor scandals of one kind or another, sporting success and failure – these are the kinds of topic that usually generate widespread passion and disputation. Such topics may, on the one hand, be viewed as trivial distractions from the great questions of the day or else perhaps, on the other hand, as representing deeper cultural concerns.

The literary public sphere

In *Structural Transformation*, Habermas distinguished between the literary public sphere and the political public sphere. Although not separate from one another, their functions diverged in a significant manner. Speech and writing went hand in hand, but certain kinds of writing and literary comment transcended fleeting topics of conversation. The Parisian salons, for instance, were important sites of the literary public sphere, somewhere that women were at least present and writers could try out their ideas before committing pen to paper.

Consider, for example, the Lisbon tsunami of 1755 in which in excess of 20,000 people lost their lives. This was news indeed, a conversation topic and the object of what we might now think of as disaster management. Voltaire, however, went further in reflecting on the reasons for such an event in his picaresque novella *Candide*, which was effectively an attack on both religion and uncritical rationalism. For the complacent ideologue Dr Pangloss, the earthquake was 'a manifestation of the rightness of things, since if there is a volcano at Lisbon it could not be anywhere else' (Voltaire, 1947 [1759]: 35). Candide was left none the wiser by this explanation.

Ruthless questioning of conventional wisdom, whether in the guise of theology or what would become public relations in a later period (in effect, ideology), was at the heart of the Enlightenment project and was more likely to be found in an eighteenth-century novel than in a newspaper. Moreover, disquisition on the social role of literature and philosophical reflection in the broadest sense, according to Habermas, prepared the ground for legitimate public controversy over current events. The very practice of criticism was literary before it was directly political (Eagleton, 1984).

The literary public sphere was not about transient news – the stuff of journalism – that is the usual focus of attention for the political public sphere. Complex reflection on chronic and persistent problems of life, meaning and representation – characteristic of art – typically works on a different timescale. Critics tend to have a better memory than the producers of distorted news events. Journalists are often agents of social amnesia, only interested in the latest thing. Old news is no news.

Social-scientific research must address treatment of the event while also putting it in the context of patterns of representation over time as a necessary corrective. Such research, however, is largely confined to cognitive matters and is neglectful of affective matters. It is concerned with the political agenda, selection of information and the framing of issues. The aesthetic and emotional aspects of life may be used to distort the news, but otherwise they are of little concern to critical social scientists. This is unfortunate as public culture is not just cognitive; it is also affective.

Should you wish to understand the culture and society of Victorian Britain, would you be best advised to read its newspapers, such as *The Times*, or its literary fiction, such as George Eliot's *Middlemarch* (1871–1872) and Anthony Trollope's *The Way We Live Now* (1875)? Admittedly, this is a rhetorical question. The great realist novels of the nineteenth century display sociological insight and enduring appeal unmatched by any *Times* editorial. It would be difficult to make the same claim for novels in the early twenty-first century. Again, however, *Times* editorials are unlikely to provide better insight. In any case, the value of affective communications is not confined to great literature. Perhaps television soaps are the most reliable documents of our era. Affective communications are not only valuable, however, as historical evidence; they are themselves sites of disputation, an idea to which the history of the arts in general would attest.

Art and politics

Plato wanted to banish poets from the republic whereas Shelley claimed that they were the unacknowledged legislators. So, the overpoliticisation of art goes back a long way in the European tradition, not only on the Left but also on the Right.

Since twentieth-century cultural politics is normally recalled as left wing, it is important to remember that it figured on the right wing of modern struggle as well. Indeed, in the 1930s, Nazism promoted the Aryan ideal in Germany, especially in its bodily form, and attacked 'degenerate art'. Adolf Hitler, himself a failed artist, hated modernism and sought to establish an eternal classicism modelled on Hellenic culture as the official art of the Third Reich (Grosshans, 1983). Artists were bullied into compliance, sacked from their teaching jobs and forced into exile. The 1937 Exhibition of Degenerate Art (Entartete Kunst) in Munich held modern and Leftist art up to ridicule. After the exhibition had toured the country, 'degenerate' pieces of art were sold off at international market prices, including major works by 'Auslanders' such as Pablo Picasso, as well as exiles such as Paul Klee.

It is particularly striking how successful the Nazis were at co-opting intellectuals to enact their cultural policies and organise and justify a massive theft of visual art works for the greater glory of Germany (Petropoulis, 2000).

Curators, dealers, critics and artists themselves were in the main prepared to do the Nazis' bidding. It was not only Josef Goebbels's media propaganda in news, documentary and fiction film, denouncing Jews and others in the name of German purification, that convinced many ordinary Germans of Nazism's ideological superiority. The Nazis also believed that Germany had the right to actually appropriate and possess the great European heritage of art since the Third Reich represented the pinnacle of civilisation.

In Walter Benjamin's (1970 [1955]) estimation, the Nazis had aestheticised politics with their showy displays and affective appeal. In this they left a lasting legacy, as anyone who saw Bill Clinton's rock star presentation on television at the Democratic convention that adopted the hapless Al Gore as his successor might have recognised; and which ironically may have been a minor contribution to the election of George W. Bush. As they say in politics these days, presentation is everything.

For Benjamin, the point of oppositional art was to reverse the process, to politicise aesthetics. There is a bad history of that project on the Left, culminating in Stalin's socialist realism and a suppression of experimental art and artists comparable to that of the Nazis. Yet, there was also an unorthodox – indeed heterodox – tradition of Western Marxism (Anderson, 1976), preoccupied with cultural questions and a quite different trajectory to orthodox Marxism-Leninism. It was much more open to new ideas and remains to this day residually influential.[2] Debates in the 1930s about form and media of communication, subject matter and political stance, historical contexts and institutional settings were to inform the resurgence of left-wing cultural politics from the 1960s and 1970s.

There was a very pessimistic side to that Western Marxist engagement with art, culture and politics articulated by Habermas's own mentors, Theodor Adorno and Max Horkheimer (1979 [1944]). The great refusal of authentic art was eclipsed by the mid-twentieth century's burgeoning culture industry and mass standardisation, according to the Frankfurt School pessimists. In so arguing, they set themselves up as the perpetually elitist fall guys for populist cultural studies. Their insights, however, inaugurated lines of enquiry into the relations between culture and business that are vital to understanding the operations of the cultural field now.[3] One of the distinctive features of recent development is not so much the marginalisation of the artistic refusal but its incorporation. Just think of the appropriation of surrealism and other avant-garde art into contemporary advertising, not to mention the commercial nous and profit-making patronage of 'Young British Art'.[4]

The commercialisation of art is not, however, a novel phenomenon. Since religious, monarchical and aristocratic patronage were superseded by the art and literary markets – one of the salient features of 'modernity' – much of the great work of that comparatively recent past was produced in a commercial context. This is quite a different matter from the observation made by Raymond Williams (1980 [1960/1969]: 184) as long ago as 1960 that advertising had become 'the official art of modern capitalist society'.

Despite the incorporation of art into advertising, it did seem as though everything was still up for grabs during the hegemony of social democracy in Britain; and not only on the counter-cultural margins. Public service broadcasting, for instance, as represented by the BBC in the 1960s and 1970s, provided some space for experimentation and critical argument. This was particularly so in the 'progressive' drama of *The Wednesday Play* and *Play for Today*. Williams (1977: 61–74) himself commented on one such production: Jim Allen, Tony Garnett and Ken Loach's *The Big Flame* of 1969, which imagined a Liverpool dock strike turning into a political occupation.

With the lurch to the Right in the 1980s and 1990s, such exceptional work was considered outdated, the remains of a failed Leftism, and became increasingly rare. Already it had been argued that radical interventions from the Left were less significant than what was going on in the very heartland of television. An exemplary statement of this kind was Richard Dyer, Terry Lovell and Jean McCrindle's (1997 [1977]: 35–41) paper 'Women and soap opera', originally delivered at the Edinburgh Television Festival of 1977, where both Williams and Dennis Potter also delivered papers.

Williams and Potter, in their different ways, wanted a further radicalisation of television drama in the single play slot. Alternatively, Dyer and his colleagues wanted appreciation of the actually existing television serial from a feminist perspective. The most popular programme on British television, the archetypal British soap opera *Coronation Street*, made by the commercial company Granada, put into the foreground the problems and capacities of women in everyday life. Was this a site of the cultural public sphere?

The cultural public sphere

Soap opera is a melodramatic genre. It deals with personal crises and the complexity of everyday relationships. In the form of a continuous serial of overlapping and fragmented narratives, it artfully corresponds to the haphazard flow of events and messy irresolution in lived reality. The genre offers multiple subject positions for men as well as women to identify with.

In order to amass huge and heterogeneous audiences, there is usually something on offer for everyone. Viewing may be a casual distraction from domestic labour or of passionate intensity, a special and sacred moment. You can keep up without paying much attention. Alternatively, the current episode may be the highpoint of the day in some households. Above all, for the lonely, physically or mentally isolated viewer – such as single parents, widowed elders and anguished teenagers – soap opera produces a vicarious sense of urban community, a mundane albeit degraded utopia (the rural setting of Yorkshire TV's *Emmerdale* is a comparatively rare exception to the general rule). This is especially notable in the leading and long-running British soaps – *Coronation Street* (1960–) and *EastEnders* (1985–) – that conjure up the nostalgic myth of the 'traditional' working-class neighbourhood, set ostensibly in actual places, respectively Salford in Greater Manchester and Cockney London.

The makers of *Coronation Street* were originally inspired by Richard Hoggart's (1957) founding text of cultural studies *The Uses of Literacy*. Idealised representations of working-class community maintain a residual yet powerful appeal for the British television viewer. Latterly, in Britain, the genre has evoked multicultural harmony and downplayed racial tension. Soap opera typically ignores public controversy in the world beyond the immediate context of imagined community.

Jostein Gripsrud (1992) has commented on the historical role of melodrama in the public sphere. He points out that nineteenth-century theatrical melodrama dealt with moral dilemmas and problematic social life. These are also characteristic features of twentieth-century Hollywood melodrama – 'movies for women' – and the variants of television soap.

Melodrama performs not only an entertainment but also an educational function, which is true of tabloid journalism too: 'Today's popular press … teaches the audience a lesson, everyday' (Gripsrud, 1992: 87). The lessons taught are not so much cognitive – to do with knowing – but, rather, emotional – to do with feeling. It is a sentimental, rather than a critical, education that is thus provided. According to Gripsrud, sentiment has its place in the public sphere.

This argument is perhaps offensive to the more solemn Habermasian who is concerned with rational-critical debate and just as much troubled by distracting sentiment and 'infotainment' as selective distortion. It is not unknown to figure the difference in attitude as between feminine and masculine sensibility, that there is a communicative gulf between women's heart-felt emotion and men's cold logic; as a popular advice book puts it, 'men are from Mars, women are from Venus' (Gray, 1992).

That difference is theorised with much greater depth and sophistication in feminist psychology. Carol Gilligan (1993 [1982]) has questioned Lawrence Kohlberg's cognitive and ethical universalism, which influenced Habermas's own discourse ethics. She invokes the notion of an 'ethic of care' that is sensitive to particular life experiences and is more typical of feminine than masculine responses to personal and social problems. Gilligan treats the difference as contingent and socially constructed, not essential and naturally given.

As Gripsrud argues, however, it is a mistake to simply map the difference between feminine and masculine sensibility onto the difference between the affective and cognitive dimensions of the public sphere. After all, there is nothing particularly feminine or caring about the discourse of tabloid journalism.

While consideration of the conventional polarities of femininity and masculinity may illuminate the gender differentiation of dramatic genres, it does not account satisfactorily for what distinguishes the cultural public sphere from the political public sphere.

Gripsrud identifies the provenance of the contemporary cultural public sphere as popular alienation from public life. This argument is consistent with Habermas's (1987 [1981]) binary opposition between lifeworld and system. Habermas was worried that the instrumental and strategic rationalities of capital and the State were colonising the lifeworld, which is the site of communicative rationality, mutual respect and understanding. On the other side of the divide, it is understandable for people to turn inwards, to cocoon themselves, out of a sense of powerlessness. Preoccupation with the dilemmas of everyday life and personal satisfaction is undoubtedly more pronounced than active citizen engagement with the systemic processes of business and government.

In a similar vein to Gripsrud, Peter Dahlgren (1995) has called into question the division of labour in media research between attention to cognitive communications with regard to the public sphere problematic and attention to affective communications with regard to the pleasures of popular culture. He says, 'rational communication is necessary, but if our horizons do not penetrate beyond the conceptual framework of communicative rationality and the ideal speech situation, we will be operating with a crippled critical theory' (Dahlgren, 1995). Furthermore, Dahlgren suggests that no representational form is entirely cognitive and rational, not even television news, in spite of its pretensions. The whole array of television genres across fact and fiction programming, in practice, combines affective and cognitive elements in variable mixtures.

Accuracy of information and conditions favourable to dissent and dialogic reason are normative requirements of genuine democracy. Nevertheless, a solely cognitive conception of the public sphere has serious limitations. If democracy is to be more than a legitimising myth in a highly mediated world, then citizens should indeed be properly informed about serious issues and be able to participate in rational-critical debate that has policy consequences.

That is not the whole of life, however. Why should people be expected to treat official politics, where they have so little power to influence what happens, with the same passion that they devote to their own personal lives and lived or imagined relationships with others? In actual fact, though, keen popular engagement in something like a public sphere, when it does happen, more often than not takes a predominantly affective mode, related to the immediacy of lifeworld concerns, instead of the cognitive mode normally associated with experience of a remote, apparently unfathomable and uncontrollable system. The concept of a cultural public sphere may go some way to explaining what is going on in this respect.

In the late-modern world, the cultural public sphere is not confined to a republic of letters – the eighteenth century's literary public sphere – and 'serious' art, classical, modern or, for that matter, postmodern. Rather, it includes the various channels and circuits of mass popular culture and entertainment, the routinely mediated aesthetic and emotional reflections on how we live and imagine the good life.

The concept of a *cultural* public sphere refers to the articulation of politics, public and personal, as a contested terrain through affective – aesthetic and emotional – modes of communication. The cultural public sphere trades in pleasures and pains that are experienced vicariously through willing suspensions of disbelief; for instance, by watching soap operas, identifying with the characters and their problems, talking and arguing with friends and relatives about what they should and shouldn't do. Images of the good life and expectations of what can be got out of this life are mediated mundanely through entertainment and popular media discourses. Affective communications help people to think reflexively about their own lifeworld situations and how to negotiate their way in and through systems that may seem beyond anyone's control on the terrain of everyday life. The cultural public sphere provides vehicles for thought and feeling, for imagination and disputatious argument, that are not necessarily of inherent merit but may be of some consequence.

One such vehicle was the death of Diana, Princess of Wales, in 1997 (see Chapter 2). The public response was extraordinary in terms of extravagant expressions of grief and loss. Most significantly, the eventful life and sudden death of 'the People's Princess' engendered public debate on the role of the monarchy and, also, more generally, as Beatrix Campbell (1998) argued, relationships between men and women.

Diana's estrangement from the Royal Family and her divorce from Prince Charles provoked much popular disputation. Her glamorous celebrity and charitable reputation contrasted sharply with the Windsors' haughty noblesse oblige. The Royals survived that moment of recrimination but, as Campbell put it, sexual politics had shaken the very institution of monarchy in Britain. The Royal Family was revealed, yet again, to be a distinctly inadequate model of personal conduct and intimate relations, which had been its ideological, if not constitutional, raison d'être.

In this way, the popular debate around Diana manifested what Anthony Giddens (1992) calls 'life politics', whereby people try to work out how to live in a detraditionalised moral universe where the old conventions are in question. Ulrich Beck and Elisabeth Beck-Gernsheim (1995 [1990]) have similarly discussed the negotiated relationships and chronic decisionmaking of personal life under the disconcerting conditions of reflexive modernity. These are not just theoretical issues for social and cultural analysis but also ordinary features of everyday life in 'Western' culture and society today.

The popularity of even the *Big Brother* television series can also be explained as a vehicle for reflecting on appropriate conduct when traditional assumptions are no longer taken for granted and people are confused about how best to carry on. Contestants are judged in weekly nominations for eviction within the house and by the voting public outside with greater enthusiasm than is usually evident in casting votes for candidates to public office. This has encouraged some to argue light-headedly that official politics should learn from game shows like *Big Brother* and adopt their popularising techniques. Still, there is a political point to these shows. The appropriateness of the contestants' behaviour in an artificially constructed situation is under perpetual surveillance, dull moment by dull moment, and, in the drama of narrative summary, providing the material for critical interrogation. In effect, *Big Brother* is a modern morality play.

Spaces of action

In conclusion to this chapter, I want to identify three broad stances regarding the politics of the cultural public sphere:

- uncritical populism
- radical subversion
- critical intervention.

I associate *uncritical populism* with populist cultural studies, the credibility of which derives not so much from its intellectual acuity but its affinity with currently conventional wisdom.[5] The domain assumption here is that consumer capitalism is culturally democratic. Consumer sovereignty goes unquestioned. What we get is what we want. The consumer is consulted and permitted to speak. In any case, consumption is an active phenomenon. Consumers are not the passively manipulated recipients of commodity culture and mediated experience: they choose; and woe betides any business that fails to respond efficiently to its customers' demands.

I read in the *Guardian* (Ward, 2003: 13) of a conference on 1950s culture at which a young academic remarked of the coffee bar scene so bemoaned by Hoggart at the time: 'It provided both male and female sites for dress, dance, display, discussion and democratisation.' Was the coffee bar of the 1950s, then, a democratic advance on the eighteenth-century coffee house as a site for the public sphere? The idea of the coffee house or, in latter-day nominations, the coffee bar or the coffee shop as places of cultural subversion and critical questioning has been revived in a bizarre manner recently by the pernicious Starbucks' hosting of public debates in association with the Royal Society for Arts. Postmodern or what?

It is an established protocol for populist cultural studies to endlessly seek out instances of really existing cultural and consumer democracy, not only in the past but also now. Occasionally, such discoveries are even related to the problematic of the public sphere, though rarely in cultural studies as narrowly defined. The work of social psychologists Sonia Livingstone and Peter Lunt (1994) on the much-derided television genre of audience participation talk shows is exemplary. Incidentally, it is also much more successfully grounded in empirical research than most cultural studies in this vein.[6] Political theorist John Keane (1998) has argued a similar case for really existing cultural and consumer democracy in contemporary civil society when he distinguishes between micro (subcultural), meso (national) and macro (global) public spheres.[7]

The value of uncritical populism – the kind of position that would regard *Big Brother* as a vehicle of the public sphere – is its debunking of the critical idealisation of a public sphere that is never present but always absent in favour of a 'realistic' attention to what actually goes on. As with *Big Brother*, public controversy today is very much associated with questions of identity, celebrity and scandal. Chris Rojek (2001) suggests that celebrity culture is a manifestation of the paradox of egalitarian democracy, the promise that everyone can make it but few actually do so. Public figures are the source of incessant fascination – in particular, their achievements and their failures. Nothing is so fascinating as a soaring star as a falling one. Manuel Castells (2004a [1997]) argues that public interest in official politics is largely mediated by scandal. The conduct of political leaders is constantly under scrutiny, their moral failings amplified and sometimes secretly admired. Interestingly, observes Castells, '[c]orruption per se seems less significant than scandals (that is, corruption or wrongdoing revealed) and their political impact' (2004a [1997]: 395).

Radical subversion finds all this deplorable. From such a perspective, the democratising claims of uncritical populism are part of the problem rather than part of the solution. Currently, radical subversion is most closely associated with the cultural practices of the global movement for social justice, especially in its anticapitalist and antiglobalisation manifestations. Parts of the movement draw on the kind of DIY culture that came to prominence in the 1990s with roads protests and raves in Britain.

Radical subversion has complex roots in the 1960s American counter-culture, French situationism and older traditions of international anarchism.[8] Such radicalism places special emphasis on symbolic contest, acting out various forms of carnivalesque subversion in order to disrupt, for instance, the City of London in June 1999 and the meeting of the World Trade Organization in Seattle towards the end of that year (Cockburn et al., 2000).

Kalle Lasn's (1999) manifesto for radical subversion *Culture Jam: The uncooling of America* is representative of this form of cultural politics. The remedy for the American cultural malaise is, according to Lasn, 'a rebranding strategy – a social demarketing campaign unfolding over four seasons' (Lasn, 1999: xvi). In the autumn, the question is asked: 'What does it mean when our lives and culture are no longer shaped by nature, but by an electronic mass media environment of our own creation?' (Lasn, 1999: xvii) In the winter, 'the media–consumer trance' of 'our postmodern era' is criticised and a further question posed: 'Can spontaneity and authenticity be restored?' In the spring, the fundamental question is put: 'Is oppositional culture still possible?' In the summer, 'the American revolutionary impulse reignites'. All of this – theory and practice – is meant to lead to a Debordian 'detournement – a perspective-jamming turnabout in your everyday life'.

Culture Jam is a book inspired by the critique of 'the society of the spectacle' and the subversive tactics of French situationism (Debord, 1994 [1967]). It also derives inspiration from the USA's own revolutionary tradition of independence and participatory democracy. It wishes to challenge the value and values of the most powerful culture and society in the world: the American consumerist way of life and its global reach.

Culture jamming is a form of 'semiological guerilla warfare', in Umberto Eco's phrase. As Eco (1987 [1967]: 135) argued in the 1960s, 'Not long ago, if you wanted to seize political power in a country, you had merely to control the army and the police. ... Today a country belongs to the person who controls communications.' Culture jammers, however, are unlikely to take control of the communications media in the USA. Their tactics in producing 'subvertisements' that attack capitalism, and in anti-media campaigning generally, are those of guerilla skirmishing in the space of signification, which on their own are unlikely to bring the whole edifice of postmodern culture and consumerism tumbling down. The battle is conducted at the level of signification, ridiculing the dominant system of meanings with the aim of rendering 'cool' uncool. In a volatile culture where fashion is constantly overturning itself and sudden reversals of meaning occur, counter-discourse may act like a virus entering the symbolic bloodstream of the body politic. Well, that's the theory anyway.

Radical subversion is the exact obverse of uncritical populism. Instead of apologetics, it offers total transformation whether people want it or not. In this sense, it is elitist and, to many, either downright offensive or simply unintelligible.

The third position regarding politics and the public sphere – *critical intervention* – combines the best of uncritical populism – an appreciation of the actually existing cultural field – with the best of radical subversion, producing a genuinely critical and potentially popular stance.

Television is at the heart of contemporary mass popular culture. It remains central to everyday life despite the Internet, though digitalisation does indeed bring about a convergence of media and there are many more channels of communication these days, including interactive media. Most people still, however, turn to the box in the corner – or perhaps now the screen on the wall – for information and entertainment. Public service principles have been seriously eroded in recent years. Even such an august institution as the BBC mimics commercial populism in order to justify its licence fee in 'a competitive market'. Yet, occasionally, even now, television – at least in Britain – affords a space for critical argument. This is a precious space and one that should be cherished and safeguarded.

For example, every two years, the BBC turns its resources over to Red Nose Day – the telethon organised by the Comic Relief charity. What is very significant about Comic Relief is not just the money it raises for projects in Africa and Britain – though that is not insignificant for the people who benefit – but also the combination of entertainment with critical agitation concerning poverty and deprivation. This mass popular television event is made up of comic turns and documentary material on the parlous conditions of life in African villages and British inner cities. The audience is, of course, guilt-tripped into donating a few pounds over the phone with their credit cards.[9]

Comic Relief is hardly the cutting edge of critical intervention in the mainstream. Other examples from British television are closer to the edge, such as Channel 4's satire show *Bremner, Bird and Fortune*. In the run-up to the latest Gulf War, impressionist Rory Bremner and the two old-stagers of British satirical television – John Bird and John Fortune – poured mockery on the British and American governments and examined the real reasons for bringing about 'regime change' in Iraq. When official hostilities ceased, a special edition of *Bremner, Bird and Fortune* (following on from the earlier *Between Iraq and a Hard Place*) devoted to the issues of war (this programme entitled *Beyond Iraq and a Hard Place*) was transmitted (11 May 2003). It examined the current and historical background to the USA's neo-imperialistic agenda and the human costs of the war. The programme offered a much more radical analysis of the meaning of the assault on Iraq than you would have found anywhere else in British mainstream media. Perhaps it was permitted because comedy is not serious.

Around the same time, the BBC televised *The Day Britain Stopped* (13 May 2003), a successor to a great tradition of British documentary drama stretching back to Jeremy Sandford, Ken Loach and Tony Garnett's *Cathy Come Home* in the 1960s and including Barry Hines's *Threads* and Rob Ritchie's *Who Bombed Birmingham?* in the 1980s.

Set in the near future, *The Day Britain Stopped* imagined what might happen if a disastrous chain reaction occurred in Britain's decrepit transport system. It started with a one-day rail strike in response to a crash at Edinburgh's Waverley station. Safety on the railways has been severely undermined over several years as a result of profiteering privatisation, which is, to say the least, common knowledge. *The Day Britain Stopped* told a 'What if …?' story, tracing gridlock on the roads to a mid-air plane crash at Heathrow. It told the story through individuals and families caught up in the chaos, interleaved with expert opinion and documentary-style footage.[10]

It is troubling that there was no great outcry against Bremner, Bird and Fortune's seditious comedy or the plausible but alarmist *The Day Britain Stopped*. Nevertheless, these are critical interventions in public debate from which there is much to learn. It is especially important to value such interventions and be clear about what actually constitutes a critical intervention. This is not necessarily measurable in terms of social impact. Neither of the two examples given here had much direct impact on contemporary politics, but they did articulate widespread dissent and, in so doing, contributed to an enduring tradition of independent criticism of dominant power and ideology in the cultural public sphere.

Notes

1. See, for instance, Curtis, 2003; Rampton and Stauber, 2003; Miller, 2003.
2. See, for instance, Bloch et al., 1977.
3. See, for instance, Miège, 1989; Björkegren, 1996; Hesmondhalgh, 2007 [2002]; Steinert, 2003.
4. See, for instance, Stallabrass, 2006[1996]; Hatton and Walker 2005[2000].

5. I have noted the correspondence between populist cultural studies and free-market ideology on several occasions; see, for instance, McGuigan, 1992 and 1997a. Also, see Frank, 2001.
6. See my discussion in McGuigan, 2002.
7. See my discussion in McGuigan, 2004b, pp. 54–8.
8. See, for instance, McKay, 1996, and McKay, 1998.
9. See McGuigan, 1998a for in analysis of Comic Relief.
10. In my opinion, *The Day Britain Stopped* was a more incisive intervention in the cultural public sphere than David Hare's much celebrated National Theatre play that was also broadcast on BBC Radio 3 (14 March 2004), *The Permanent Way*, for a number of reasons. Hare's play looked specifically at trouble on the railways and was a form of theatrical journalism or documentary based on interviews with various interested parties, their words spoken by actors. Rather than a dramatised documentary, *The Day Britain Stopped* was a documentary-style drama, which combined factual material with a fictionalised and tragic dramatisation of a chain reaction throughout the whole transport system – trouble on the railways, gridlock on the roads and a mid-air plane collision. It represented what might happen through typical characters and experiences, where chaos suddenly engulfs everyday life in a hypothetical and interlinked set of circumstances. The presence of *The Day Britain Stopped* in a popular medium – terrestrial and public service television – also attracted a larger and probably much more diverse audience socially than would normally be so of the National Theatre and Radio 3's audiences.

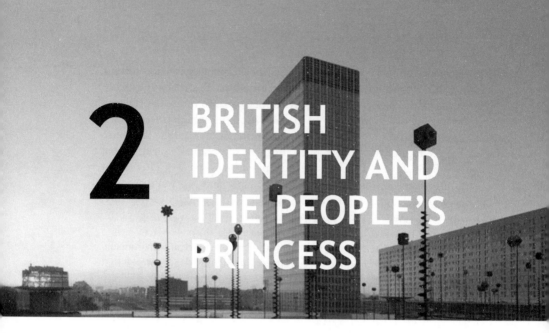

2 BRITISH IDENTITY AND THE PEOPLE'S PRINCESS

Introduction

This chapter treats the popular response to the death of Diana, Princess of Wales, in 1997 as a manifestation of the cultural public sphere, by which is meant a symbolic space for affective communication and an emotional sense of democratic participation.

The Diana phenomenon did not produce a 'revolutionary moment' but neither was it insignificant. Rather, it represented a vehicle for public debate on British identity, the role of the monarchy and, more diffusely, the conduct of personal relationships. New Labour and feminist appropriations of Diana are examined in detail and related to a general consideration of the diverse and contested meanings of her life and death.

We have now passed the tenth anniversary of Diana Windsor née Spencer's death. It was followed by Mohammad al Fayed's failed final attempt to pin the blame on a British State conspiracy, sanctioned by the Royal Family itself, to rid the country of a troublesome divorcée and her Muslim consort, al Fayed's own son, Dodi.

The first anniversary nine years previously was a bit of a flop, too. The media events of early September 1998 only partly rekindled what many people had apparently felt the year before. Writing shortly afterwards, the therapist Susie Orbach linked the general climate of indifference to disappointment with the New Labour Government. Somehow, the general election result of May 1997 and popular response to the death of Diana in September that year were connected together and had, according to Orbach, signalled the emergence of a culture of participatory democracy in Britain, a different, non-deferential Britishness. Her scanty evidence for this was, first, that voters had changed the government, which is rather more a sign of representative than of participatory democracy; and, second, emotion had been admitted into the public sphere or, as Orbach termed it, 'public space' in the mourning on The Mall for Diana. To quote her, 'Diana's death became another moment of participation in which there was a claiming and reshaping of public space, an insistence that public discourse respect the feelings of the people and a moment of potential constitutional change' (Orbach, 1998: 61). Orbach complained bitterly a year later about the betrayal of the promise of that moment, especially the way in which New Labour's subsequent performance had been a return to government as usual, remote and unprincipled, not to mention becoming a defender of the monarchy. How might it have been otherwise?

In the late summer of 1998, floods of books, newspaper pullouts, special magazine editions, television documentaries and videos representing and commenting on Diana came and went, adding to the already gigantic mound of such publications. Contemporary commentary on the meaning of Princess Diana's eventful life and sudden death ran typically from insouciant sentimentality, through popular superstition and conspiracy theory, to earnestly intellectual works of critical analysis and interpretation seeking to read the signs of the time. The common factor linking these discursive poles tended to be hyperbole, though perhaps well-justified hyperbole since few doubt, whatever their particular points of view, that the impact of Diana's death was somewhat out of the ordinary.

This chapter neither endorses the view that the popular response to the death of the celebrity once known as Diana Spencer represented a 'revolutionary moment', albeit one later betrayed by New Labour, nor does it dismiss the events of September 1997 as epiphenomenal and trivial in character. In many respects, I am sympathetic to Nick Couldry's (1999) account of the Diana phenomenon as of palpable significance yet also indicative of a 'politics of lack', pointing up more than anything how 'ordinary people' do not usually have much say in the public sphere of a media-saturated society. My own argument is, however, that the spectacular moment of Diana illustrates the functioning of a particular kind of public sphere, the cultural public sphere, which operates routinely according to affectivity, emotionally and sensuously, alongside the effectivity of the official public sphere of politics where questions of information flow, popular cognition and rational debate are paramount matters of concern.

The cultural public sphere

My interest in the Diana phenomenon is related to a broader preoccupation with the role of popular participation in cultural policy, public debate and politics in general. It is to do with a sentimental modification of the Habermasian problematic of the public sphere that takes due account of its emotional as well as cognitive aspects.

Since the publication of the English translation of Jürgen Habermas's *The Structural Transformation of the Public Sphere* and the breaching of the Berlin Wall in 1989, the concept of the public sphere has met with an extraordinary academic revival, to the extent, according to one theorist (Garnham, 1995), that it has replaced hegemony as the core concept of media studies. Summarily, in Habermas's (1989 [1962]) original formulation, the public sphere refers to the arena of rational-critical debate, which is the culture of a democratic society.

There is an extensive literature on the theory of the public sphere and many different and, indeed, conflicting views have been expressed concerning its historical and philosophical meanings and regarding its applicability to contemporary political cultures (see, for instance, Calhoun, 1992). Two major issues of disputation concerning the present use of the public sphere concept are especially relevant to analysis of the Diana phenomenon and its significance: the tensions between, first, universalism and particularism; and, second, between cognition and emotion (see McGuigan, 1998a).

By definition, it may be argued, the public sphere is a universalising phenomenon. It is associated with the communicative rights of citizenship. The history of Western democracy has – with numerous setbacks and insufficiencies admittedly – been the extension of citizenship. For example, from men exclusively to women inclusively. The 'universe' of the public sphere, however, has been largely delimited by the nation state. The citizen is defined as belonging to the nation state and the rights of political participation for an informed citizenry are thus circumscribed. Transnational bodies, however, such as the European Union, begin to internationalise citizenship and, in principle, create a continental and not just a national public sphere. Moreover, economic and cultural globalisation further erodes the autonomy of the nation state.

Nicholas Garnham (1992) argues that the public sphere needs to be reconceptualised, then, in more international terms. The public sphere, in his view, should remain a unitary and singular ideal, but be global rather than national in scope. Stated so baldly, this universalising perspective can be interpreted as an extreme and unconvincing reiteration of the Kantian wish for world government supported by a global public sphere. It is questionable on two main grounds: first, due to the stubborn persistence of the nation state as the most legitimate and substantive unit of democracy in the world; second, due to the sheer fragmentation of politics and diversity of cultures across the globe.

One of the strongest statements in favour of an alternative, particularistic conception of the public sphere is that of Nancy Fraser (1992), who talks of 'subaltern counter-publics', most notably organised feminism. Fraser's argument is a powerful one since she can point confidently to the actualisation of something like a public sphere in the communicative networks of North American feminism. Furthermore, it is quite evident that the feminist counter-public has impacted consequentially on the official, national public sphere of the United States.

The public sphere is a malleable concept – perhaps too malleable. It is used in a number of different ways, which in itself is not necessarily a problem. As Fraser argues, the public sphere may usefully be pluralised with reference to various networks of communication and political action, but, I would suggest, this particularising move need not lose the older, universalistic sense of the public sphere as a space for national or international debate in general. From such a point of view, we may identify a multiplicity of public spheres – mainly unofficial or semi-official, representing many differences of identity, interest and aspiration yet also, realistically, interacting more or less successfully with official, overarching public spheres that are supposed to be unifying and universalising. Habermas (1996 [1992]) has come to see the public sphere in very much this way himself and in terms of a 'sluice-gate' model of politics, whereby campaigning social movements force issues on to official and mainstream political agendas that would not otherwise be identified and taken up.

There is a second major problem with the concept of the public sphere that bears on the present discussion. Most usage of the concept, including Fraser's feminist usage, tends to assume an excessively cognitive and rationalistic conception of the citizen and public debate. Affect, in the sense of emotionality, is generally seen as a spoiling agent in the public sphere and pleasure is frequently denigrated as 'infotainment' and the like.

While accuracy of information and conditions favourable to the expression of dissent and genuinely dialogic reason are normative requirements of democracy, a solely cognitive definition of the public sphere has serious limitations. If democracy is to be anything more than a legitimising myth in modern, highly mediated societies, then, citizens must be properly informed about serious issues and feel able to participate in rational–critical debate that has consequences for policy.

That, though, is not the whole of life. It is unrealistic to expect people in general to be as engaged with politics on a day-to-day basis and in the official sense of governmental business as they are with their own personal lives and lived or imagined relationships with others. Moreover, it is a mistake to dismiss the possibility that keen popular engagement in the public sphere, when it does actually happen, though perhaps inflected affectively rather than cognitively, may have positive as well as negative features.

A fundamental and, in many cases, quite justifiable critical assumption of much social and cultural analysis is that emotional manipulation is inherently a bad thing, an assumption that has been reiterated in Stjepan Mestrovic's (1997) concept of 'post-emotionalism' where it is not even 'real' emotion, according to him, that is being played around with in news of death and suffering. Yet, as Carol Gilligan (1993 [1982]) has argued convincingly, the suspicion of emotion per se in moral conduct is gendered: it is a widespread masculine prejudice. Furthermore, Arlie Russell Hochschild (2003 [1983]), in criticising some oppressive forms of 'emotion management' at work, notes, however, that the management of emotion in some form is a constitutive feature of social life. Emotion cannot simply be bracketed off. Moreover, the suspicion of emotional response on ethical questions and in public life takes insufficient account of why we might care for others, especially others with whom we are not personally acquainted in our own private lives. As Peter Dahlgren (1995) insists with good reason, the affective and arational aspects of public discourse should not, on explanatory grounds, be sidelined from our thinking about democratic communications and culture.

In his original work on the public sphere, Habermas (1989 [1962]) made a useful but curiously neglected distinction in sociology between the *political* public sphere and *literary* public sphere.

The literary public sphere of the eighteenth century refers to the writings and discussion of the philosophes on how to live and order the conditions of existence. For instance, Voltaire's *Candide* (2006 [1759]), inspired by his dissatisfaction with theological debates concerning the Lisbon tsunami of 1755 in which over 20,000 people died, was an artefact of this emergent public sphere. The literary public sphere was not just about the immediate and transient topics of the day, however – the stuff of journalism, in effect, the normal operations of the political public sphere. Complex reflection on chronic and persistent problems of life, meaning and representation transcends journalism and, arguably, constitutes the stuff of art and literature.

I have found it useful to rework the notion of a literary public sphere in the broader concept of a *cultural* public sphere for a number of analytical purposes (see, for instance, McGuigan, 1998b). The cultural public sphere, in my formulation, is not confined to a republic of letters and fine art but also includes the various circuits and channels of popular culture and entertainment, the routinely mediated emotional and aesthetic reflections on how we live and imagine the good life. This is quite different from an exclusively critical focus on the distortions of the political public sphere, the ideological selection and framing of information, the machinations of spin doctors and so on.

The concept of a *cultural public sphere* – to give the definition once more – refers to:

> the articulation of politics, public and personal, as a contested terrain through affective – aesthetic and emotional – modes of communication.

The cultural public sphere trades in pleasures and pains that are experienced vicariously through willing suspensions of disbelief, for instance in our engagements with soap operas, identifying with characters and their problems, talking and arguing with our friends and relatives about what they should and shouldn't do. Our images of the good life and expectations of what we can get out of this life are thus mediated mundanely through entertainment and popular media discourses. In a revised Habermasian framework, then, affective communication – and specifically entertainment, as Garnham (1992) noted – helps us think reflexively about our own lifeworld situations and how to negotiate our way in and through systems that may seem beyond anyone's control on the terrain on everyday life. The cultural public sphere provides us with vehicles for thought and feeling, for imagining and arguing, such as the saga of Diana and the Royals, which may have no necessary merit or demerit in themselves. It is what we do with them that count.

I want to argue that the articulation of popular sentiment and the debates over the meaning of Princess Diana's life and death are manifestations of a public sphere. They are best understood as representing a diffusely *cultural* aspect of the public sphere with, obviously, a symbolic rather than directly instrumental relation to politics. This particular kind of public sphere is characterised by *affect*. Before proceeding specifically to the topic of Diana, however, another contextualising element must be considered: the role of monarchy in the construction and reproduction of Britishness.

Britishness and the monarchy

Beginning with Walter Bagehot in the middle of the nineteenth century, commentators have stressed the symbolic, psychological and theatrical role of the constitutional monarchy in Britain, how it represents the unity of a multinational State and, in effect, British identity, the 'ceremonial' rather than 'efficient' face of government.

'Britishness' is an extremely 'fuzzy' category (Cohen, 1994). It is not so much a national identity as a transnational one, at one time shared formally by all members of the British Empire and, subsequently, Commonwealth. Now it signifies a shaky yet still, in some sense, shared identity of most English, Scots and Welsh people; and some Irish people as well. For some time now, Britain has been notionally just about to break up into its component parts (see Nairn, 1981 [1977]), but it never quite happens.

In his research concerning popular discourse on the British monarchy, Michael Billig found that it was very difficult for English-born people in particular, irrespective of, say, their party political affiliation, to imagine Britain without the monarchy. He describes the *British* nationalist assumption of English culture in the following way: 'Monarchy adds a unique dimension to the country (England as Britain). Remove monarchy and you remove the very things which distinguish this country from other countries. England/Britain would cease to be like England/Britain' (Billig, 1992: 30). Although judged differently, in effect, Billig has reconfirmed the old Shils and Young thesis on the monarchy and British identity, originally published in *The Sociological Review* in 1953.

Writing on the 1953 Coronation of the present Queen, Elizabeth II, Edward Shils and Michael Young produced a much discussed Durkheimian analysis of the sacred function and morally unifying force of the monarchy. They criticised irreligious intellectuals for failing to appreciate the sociological importance of symbol and ritual in popular culture. Shils and Young also attacked the handful of republican critics of the 1953

Coronation who, in their estimation, simply did not understand how brilliantly it represented British moral unity and one of the most solidly established state systems in the world. Shils and Young did not deny that there was conflict in British society, however. They claimed, instead, that the evident vigour of political debate in Britain was, in fact, safeguarded by the monarchy's uncontroversial symbolisation of social stability. In summary, Shils and Young (1953: 80) argued:

> A society is held together by its internal agreement about the sacredness of certain fundamental moral standards. In an inchoate, dimly perceived, and seldom explicit manner, the central authority of an orderly society, whether it be secular or ecclesiastical, is acknowledged to be the avenue of communication within the realm of sacred values. Within its society, popular constitutional monarchy enjoys almost universal recognition in this capacity, and it is therefore enabled to heighten the moral and civic sensibility of the society and to permeate with symbols of those values to which the sensitivity responds. Intermittent rituals bring the society or varying sectors of it repeatedly into contact with this vessel of the sacred values. The Coronation provided at one time and for practically the entire society such an intensive contact with the sacred that we believe we are justified in interpreting it as ... a great act of national communion.

The Shils–Young thesis was challenged famously by Norman Birnbaum a couple of years later, also in the pages of *The Sociological Review*, in such a way that the dispute over the meaning of the British monarchy became a classic instance of the differences between functionalist and conflict sociology. Birnbaum (1955) attacked the conservatism and complacency of Shils and Young. He made several critical points. For instance, Shils and Young mistakenly attributed a single, shared meaning to the Coronation. They took no account of ambiguity. Also, their claims about society being held together by moral consensus were unsubstantiated in the British case itself or, indeed, comparatively.

Furthermore, Shils and Young treated certain values as universal that are not necessarily so at all. To quote from Shils and Young's (1953: 65) list of such values: 'justice in the distribution of opportunities and rewards, reasonable respect for authority'. Quite apart from whether or not these are universally held values, it is surely debatable that the Coronation symbolised distributive justice. It did, no doubt, symbolise respect for authority. The British may typically adhere to both, but does the monarchy?

Birnbaum stressed how the monarchy was deployed to contain conflict, in effect, *constructing* rather than *reflecting* consensus, according to Stuart Hall's (1982) later formulation on ideological hegemony. Whereas Shils and Young, in 1953, dismissed republicanism as passé, Birnbaum argued, alternatively, that the monarchy had survived in Britain by responding to and incorporating aspects of republicanism. Similar themes of debate were to re-emerge over Diana and the Royals.

The British institution of the monarchy is closely bound up with the fate of a particular dynasty, the Royal Family itself, which has had its own problem of identity, specifically to do with its Germanic name in a century when Britain fought two world wars with Germany. Saxe-Coburg-Gotha was dropped on the occasion of the First World War in favour of Windsor. Similarly, it was wise for Prince Charles's favourite uncle to have called himself Mountbatten instead of Battenberg. When Philip Mountbatten married Elizabeth, he was required to adopt his wife's family name. The most suitable name for this latterly dysfunctional family, however, is the one given by Rosalind Coward (1984) in her essay 'The Royals' on the trials and tribulations of British royalty as an everyday story of titled folk.

It is now very easy to think of the Royals as a living soap opera, a kind of *Truman Show* with, in this case, reality preceding fiction. As Coward (1984: 163) remarked several years ago, 'The fact that "The Royals" is loosely based on reality only adds to its fascination'. This is a family melodrama with controversial marriages, scandal and divorce and tragic death, the primary function of which is, arguably, to entertain the public, mainly the British public who pay for it, but, in the era of global communications, available free of charge to the rest of the world.

A string of questions come to mind. Are the Royals only there to entertain us? What use would they be otherwise? What is their function, constitutionally and symbolically? To hold Britain together, perhaps?

In her original essay on the Royals of the early 1980s, Coward (1984: 166) commented on Diana: 'Lady Di introduced a new element to the story of the Royals.' Other characters had to change position in order to accommodate her – for instance, Princess Ann now had to play the Ugly Sister. More consequentially, as it turned out with the unfolding of the saga over the next several years, Diana represented new dramatic variations on the way: '"The Royals" addresses choices faced by all women' (Coward, 1984: 70). Female autonomy would become an even bigger problem for the Royals than it was in *Dallas*.

This is not the place to try and summarise the plots and subplots of Diana and the Royals, though I will in due course be discussing Beatrix Campbell's feminist version of the story. In passing, however, it is important to stress that story event and moment of disclosure should not be conflated. The publication of Andrew Morton's bestseller in 1992, *Diana: Her True Story*, was both a revelation of what had been concealed or only vaguely rumoured hitherto and itself a factor in the unfolding of the larger narrative. Divorce ensued. There was a battle of the books, with Jonathan Dimbleby's whitewash biography of Charles most notably occupying the blue corner. Both Diana and Charles were interviewed famously on television. The BBC One *Panorama* interview with Diana in 1995 out-sensationalised Dimbleby's marketing of his book by getting Charles to confess to adultery on commercial television. Loyalties towards Diana, on the one hand, and Charles, on the other hand, were fierce and continue to be so. Participants in the debate are many and varied, however, with numerous hybrid positions in addition to purist positions in play. Someone sometime will probably survey the various arguments in detail: that in itself will be at least a book's worth. Here, though, I shall briefly consider just two particular appropriations of Diana – the New Labour and the feminist appropriations.

Death of a princess

Diana had been inscribed into the New Labour project of 'rebranding Britain' (Leonard, 1997) before she died after a late night car crash with Dodi al Fayed in Paris at the end of August 1997. The desired 'Queen of Hearts' role, declared in the *Panorama* interview, which apparently Tony Blair envisaged her realising, was already being performed in Diana's highly publicised adoption of the landmines issue shortly before her death.

This divorced princess, then, who had split from the Royals so unceremoniously, was potentially a parallel monarch – in effect, combining star quality with the magic of royalty, suitably representative of a modernising and caring regime, suggesting the possibility of a spin-off soap capable of eclipsing the original show in the ratings. Diana's glamorous iconography, her showbiz connections and celebrity connotations were in sharp and painful contrast to the mustiness of the older Royals and the apparently well-meaning but decidedly eccentric behaviour of the fading patriarch Charles.

The game being played was a risky one in any event, from the point of view of a government wedded to the myth that the monarchy is the lynchpin of the British State, but especially so once Diana was dead. As it transpired, the New Labour leadership played the game duplicitously and, in terms of the institutional persistence of the British monarchy, successfully so for the time being. Trying to have it both ways, regardless of the contradictions involved, was the strategic character of Blairism. To mix the metaphor, circles always had to be squared in New Labour Britain. Diana was valorised as 'the people's princess' in Blair's morning-after speech. Within days, the Windsors themselves were carefully stage-managed through the distasteful task of satisfying the mass-mediated calls of a grief-stricken populace and hostile 'public opinion' in the immediate period leading up to the funeral. The funeral itself was a pastiche-laden, postmodernist version of something like a Coronation, providing the up-to-date language for what was widely held to be the popular articulation of a moment of 'moral consensus' in the nation. The Queen and Charles had to accept that Diana was more popular than they were, though they had the distinct advantage over that querulous young woman of being alive to fight another day.

Comparisons have been drawn between the death of Diana and the death in childbirth of Princess Charlotte in 1817, which was followed by the Carolinian agitation around George IV's attempted indictment of his estranged wife in 1820. Campbell (1998) sees those early nineteenth-century events as simultaneously inaugurating feminist and socialist politics in Britain. The popular republican opposition to George was enunciated in grief at the death of a young princess and in support for an independent, mature and morally dubious woman.

Whether the parallel between Charlotte and Diana is that close or not is debatable, yet it is reasonable to raise the question of how near the present monarchy was to being called fatally into question in September 1997. The trouble is, that is a 'What if …?' question. What if New Labour had decided to seize the opportunity to ditch the monarchy? Might they have succeeded? At the very least, it can be said that an historic opportunity to really test the institution of monarchy in Britain was missed.

The think tank Demos set itself up in the early 1990s to perform a function for New Labour that right-wing think tanks had performed for Thatcherism from the late 1970s. On a similar model, it was dedicated to thinking the unthinkable. It was no surprise, then, that, in the wake of Diana's death, Demos should consider the arguments for abolishing the monarchy, however cursorily. The young researcher Mark Leonard – who had produced the much debated *BritainTM* pamphlet on rebranding Britain, published quite coincidentally at the time of the death (Leonard, 1997) – issued Demos's *Modernising the Monarchy* pamphlet, in collaboration with Tim Hames, deliberately to coincide with the first anniversary. The ghost of Diana lurks behind Hames and Leonard's deliberations (1998: 18):

There is no doubt that the Princess of Wales had a profound – probably unintentional – effect on public perceptions of the monarchy. She did so not only by effectively providing an alternative court but also by developing a radically different style of monarchy. She made little secret of her distaste for, and alienation from, the formal procedures and ingrained assumptions of the institution. As she developed an increasingly independent approach and became visibly alienated from much of the Royal family, the Princess of Wales broke with tradition in two dramatic ways.

First, she adopted the persona of a celebrity (Hames and Leonard, 1998: 18).

Secondly, and more importantly, were the changes to the symbolic aspects of her position. She realized that her status offered her the opportunity to do things to promote causes, rather than simply open buildings or events and to personify the continuity of royal tradition.

For Hames and Leonard, lessons can be learnt from Diana's performance for the refurbishment of the British monarchy under the Windsors, which, essentially, is what New Labour was putting into practice in the year following Diana's death with the enthusiastic support of a spruced up Prince Charles kissing not just babies but also Spice Girls whenever the opportunity arose.

According to Hames and Leonard, the debate over abolition is 'stale'. The monarchy must be changed, not abolished. The reason for retaining the monarchy, however, is not constitutional. Britain can do without the constitutional device of the Crown in Parliament, but the British cannot do without what Ben Pimlott says is the 'Queen in people's heads' (quoted by Hames and Leonard, 1998: 9).

Hames and Leonard call for a Monarchy Act to set down the terms and conditions for the Royal symbolisation of Britishness under modern conditions. They say (1998: 30–1), 'The primary function of the monarchy should be the promotion of national unity and the cohesion of civil society through charitable endeavours'.

Feminism's Diana

Of perhaps deeper significance than the New Labour appropriation of Diana is the feminist one. From having been viewed as an ideological artefact of conservative femininity in the early 1980s (Simmonds, 1984), Diana would eventually be honoured after her death in, for instance, a series of tearful essays in a radical academic journal such as *Screen* ('Flowers and tears – the death of Diana, Princess of Wales', 39.1, Spring 1998). A number of female journalists, such as Linda Grant in the *Guardian* and Suzanne Moore in the *Independent*, insisted on Diana's positive relationship to feminism and responded angrily to criticisms of the fuss about Diana made by both men and women, accusing such critics of gross insensitivity, cultural elitism and an outmoded socialism. Some of these commentators, both pro and anti, may have later regretted the excesses of what they said in September 1997, but there is no doubting the passion of their words at the time.

The most important feminist text on Diana is Beatrix Campbell's book-length study *Diana, Princess of Wales: How Sexual Politics Shook the Monarchy* (1998). Campbell draws heavily on Andrew Morton's (1997 [1992]) 'data' deriving from James Colthurst's go-between interviews with Diana in 1992. Because of this arrangement, whenever asked, Diana could deny, without a word of a lie, having spoken to Morton himself. Morton republished his book with the interview transcripts in 1997 after Diana's death and confirmed what everyone knew, that he was telling her story as she wanted it told.

The revelation was startling that Diana already had some inkling at the time of the wedding in 1981 that her marriage to Charles was possibly just one of cynical convenience since he could not marry Mrs Camilla Parker-Bowles. She apparently went on, hoping against the evidence of her own experience, that everything would turn out all right on the night.

Depression and bulimia were the result of a disappointing and desperately unhappy marriage, according to the Morton/Diana version. Charles carried on with Camilla just as before and went out fox hunting with her in time-worn aristocratic fashion.

The Diana story, as told by Morton, was a nightmarish rewriting of the paradigmatic plight of the young governess from *Jane Eyre* or young wife from *Rebecca*. Diana actually discovered that the older man's continuing attachment to a predecessor really was as resilient and detrimental to the younger woman in the end as she feared. It was not just a bad dream or explicable in terms of misunderstanding across age, gender and social rank.

Diana's alleged mistreatment at the hands of the Royals, her husband, his mother and so forth, throughout the 1980s – recounted in graphic detail in Morton's book – was so shocking that the veracity of the evidence was bound to be challenged by Charles's camp. A manifestation of the counter-counter-narrative is Penny Junor's *Charles: Victim or Villain?* (1998) book, published to coincide with Charles's fiftieth birthday towards the end of 1998 and contributing to an intense public relations campaign to restore his reputation.

Regardless of contrary and purportedly 'balanced' accounts, however, Campbell does not question the validity of Morton's material at all and she interprets it as compelling evidence of the monarchy's, and specifically Charles's, rearguard action on behalf of patriarchy in a national culture that was, arguably, undergoing a sexual revolution. To quote Campbell (1998: 4):

> The contours of politics had changed. Diana was the first person to enter the royal family from another world that was being transformed – by women. Her revolt against her arranged marriage, the discovery of the deceit and duplicity of her husband, the heir to the throne, and the complicity of his relatives, exposed them as an atavistic family, a family manqué. But there was more – Diana's struggle within the royal family resonated with the stuff that British society was also trying to sort out. Royal manners mattered not because people required of them a Rupert Bear model of respectability, but because the royal family claimed to represent a society struggling with a new settlement between men, women and children; a historic new deal that promised to replace patriarchal power with domestic democracy.

The saga of Diana and the Royals has been, in effect, an artefact of the cultural public sphere, a site of affective communication and popular disputation over the conduct of life, specifically in the struggle to move beyond patriarchal relations between the sexes, as Campbell demonstrates in her book. It dramatised central questions of sexual politics in late modernity. That New Labour sought to put the Windsors back together again, like Humpty Dumpty, at a moment of severe danger for them and the institution of monarchy in Britain must have been a grave disappointment for feminists in the Diana camp who remembered how she complained so bitterly about her relationship with the Royals.

Paradoxically, Prince Charles was said, in some quarters, to have inherited Diana's popularity with the help of New Labour during the year following her death – signified, in particular, by his own public displays of doting fatherhood towards his and Diana's offspring, William and Harry. His relationship with Camilla Parker-Bowles was also brought increasingly into the public eye a year after Diana's death without generating any significant controversy. Much later, they married.

Rosalind Coward was quick to identify what had become the dominant storyline of the Royals on Charles's fiftieth birthday in November 1998. She related it insightfully to the unfolding narrative of (hetero)sexual politics in Western screen culture generally and, specifically, in melodrama. The dilemmas of women were at the heart of the melodrama genre, as it developed in film between the 1950s to the 1980s. In the 1990s, however, the main focus of attention shifted from women to men, as it did in Di and Charles's story (Coward, 1998: 23):

> In the 90s ... films are preoccupied not with the transformations affecting women but those affecting men. What is invariably at stake is men's struggle against the emotional repression of traditional masculinity. Men who start 'inadequate' in some way work through to a more loving, emotional and less repressed relationship with their child. Sometimes these narratives are strongly misogynistic. Mothers get killed off or selfishly abandon their children, while the men make the heroic journey to become better human beings. Often at the end they can do everything and more than mothers could.

Unity and diversity

Recalling the funeral of September 1997 and the amassing of disputants on the streets of London and in the media, Campbell (1998: 250) remarks:

> British society was split not by class or politics, or even gender and generation: it was split into feelings about Diana's death, between those who felt strongly and those who felt little; those who felt that she was a woman wronged who had emerged as a woman with strength; those who felt she was an undeserving 'rich bitch' who didn't merit our time; those who thought she had taken on the Establishment; and those who felt that although Charles had treated her badly he was a victim too. Critics complained that people who didn't even know Diana were crying for her and people who didn't even know her sons were worried about their well-being.

An imagined community, indeed, but a divided one.

In this chapter, the significance of the life and death of Diana has been considered in two main ways: first, as the catalyst for the 'modernisation' of the British monarchy in order to secure its survival into the new millennium; second, as a feminist icon, a Sue Ellen for the 1990s. The fact is, however, that there is no single meaning here; instead, there are different appropriations and inflections. Diana's appeal, very noticeably, was not only to women or ethnically restricted. Men turned out in force at the funeral and, whatever the prevailing mood or range of sentiment represented in the mass-mediated crowd, its social and cultural composition was evidently diverse.

A moment of extraordinary communitas was constructed in September 1997 in the only way that imagined community on such a scale *can* be constructed in modern times, especially at short notice – through the instantaneity of the media, press and, most importantly, television. Some would dismiss it as entirely a mass-mediated construct and, therefore, not 'real'. Such a view provides flimsy grounds for calling the whole Diana phenomenon into question – that the expression of grief and solidarity was merely a matter of media manipulation. Yet, it must be said, the unanimity of the news media in Britain was remarkable and, undoubtedly, accomplished through disciplinary pressure on journalists and the marginalisation of dissenting voices. It is unnecessary, however, to deny the actual mobilisation of popular sentiment, the outpouring of emotion and the sheer spectacle of what happened.

Even a collection of dissenting essays, like the one edited by Mandy Merck, does not deny the 'reality' of the event or its complexity of meaning. In that collection, Sara Maitland (1998) points, for instance, to the curious Catholicity in a Protestant country of symbolisation around Diana's funeral – the profusion of flowers, the flickering candles and the rest. Elizabeth Wilson (1998: 122) is surely right to suggest, moreover, that 'the Diana myth' and the apparent national unity and intensity of feeling around the Princess's funeral were inflected conservatively, exemplifying, in Wilson's words, 'the way in which debate has narrowed as the public sphere has declined'. Still, the moment of Diana did illustrate the possibilities of a genuinely popular, mass-mediated cultural public sphere – however transient, distorted and mystified it may have been.

A couple of exceptional documentaries that were screened on British television to mark the first anniversary of Diana's death aimed to show how it was, at the very least, diverse in its meanings and contested.

The BBC's *The Princess's People* (BBC Two, 6 September 1998) was a vox pop programme of interview material gathered from the crowd that ebbed and flowed around Buckingham Palace, Kensington Palace and Westminister Abbey in the first week of September 1997 but not shown at the time. There was no voiceover narration or explicitly stated argument, yet the selection of interviewees – including black and gay fans of Diana – and the ironic juxtaposition of their words with conventionally royalist voices and familiar footage from the funeral and extracts from the Queen's and Earl Spencer's speeches told a story. There was, more or less openly, according to *The Princess's People*, a debate going on actually within the crowd itself about people's motives, feelings and attachments – particularly concerning whether or not they were genuinely grief-stricken, about what and why or if, opportunistically, they were just there for the fun of a late summer festivity.

The second documentary that sought insightfully to prise open the diverse meanings of the previous year's events was Channel 4's *Diana – The Mourning After* (27 August 1998), made by Films of Fire, which was written and presented by the famously contrarian *Nation* and *Vanity Fair* columnist Christopher Hitchens.

The analytical tone and style of this documentary was very much set by Hitchens himself as onscreen narrator and fierce critic of the media's ideological unification of what was, in reality, a very diverse set of responses to the death of Diana among the British public.

Hitchens's persona is of the kind, colloquially speaking, that you either love or hate. Among his many claims to fame, Hitchens has written in praise of cigarette smoking (Hitchens, 1993), attacked Mother Teresa as a reactionary ideologist (Hitchens, 1995), been the scourge of Bill Clinton's liberal and left-wing apologists (Hitchens, 1999) and, subsequently, turned against the Left itself when he chose to support George W. Bush's invasion and occupation of Iraq.

Back in 1998, however, he still sounded like a tribune of the Left, albeit enunciating with a posh voice his powerfully intellectual argument. Hitchen always displays a certain masculine arrogance that is readily associated in Britain with a public school and Oxbridge education. Still, Hitchens is a characteristically English satirist, although he works mostly in the USA. This satirical approach to journalism is shared particularly with one of the dissenting witnesses interviewed in the programme – the one-time *Guardian* columnist and *Private Eye* stalwart Francis Wheen, who later penned a biography of Karl Marx. There is a scene in which Hitchens and Wheen snigger about the incoherence of the revised lyrics for *Candle in the Wind* ('gibberish', as Wheen observes), which bespeaks a certain kind of left-wing snobbery. Yet, in addition to casually indulging in such educated contempt for the intellectual failings of mass popular culture, Hitchens succeeded in gathering together a much wider selection of witnesses and voices than would typically have been found in a radical gentlemen's club of the old school or were prominently in evidence during the saturation media construction of public response to the death and funeral of Diana in 1997.

The discursive form of Hitchens's documentary, then, was quite different from *The Princess's People* – indeed, it was virtually the opposite in rhetorical style. *The Mourning After* presented an explicit and carefully crafted thesis, using the kind of rigorous argumentation that is required by a much stricter idea of the public sphere than the one I have been discussing in this chapter. The thesis there is another Britain which did not join in the mourning was delivered with panache by the seedy-looking Hitchens himself, on screen at the scene of events and in voiceover for the documentary footage. It was – and remains – a complex thesis. For example, Hitchens identified no less than six different types of mourner for Diana:

> Those who just happened to be there and became part of a shared experience... Those who felt they had been given permission to grieve for an event in their own lives... Those who pegged their own past on her life... Those who lived vicariously through her life... Those who wanted to project their anger and find someone, indeed anyone, to blame... Those who actually worshipped and idolised her and may believe themselves to be actually in contact.

There were also many who dissented. Hitchens quoted disputable evidence to suggest that as much as half of the British population did not actually watch the funeral on television. It is quite likely, in any case, that a significant section of the viewing public watched, as I did, out of a sceptical fascination with the excess of it all rather than obeisance. There was, undoubtedly, widespread passive dissent, the scale of which is immeasurable.

For *The Mourning After*, Hitchens interviewed a number of active dissidents – people who wrote letters to the press complaining of the excessive attention being paid to Diana, people who felt that they were being forced to mourn against their own will, people who could not quite understand why condolences were often addressed to the dead person, Diana herself, instead of the bereaved, and why she was given so many teddy bears and flowers. According to Hitchens, these people represented:

> another Britain, which was there before the Windsors and will be there after they've gone. This Britain is deceptively mild and understated but it refuses to be impressed by mere spectacle or overwhelmed by gusts of fashion. It prides itself on not panicking. It is not cold or inhuman, which is why it is not swept away by demagogues, superstars or messiahs. Travelling up and down this supposedly United Kingdom I found it easy to find and meet examples of this other Britain.

As well as registering the complexity of mass-mediated mourning and public gathering associated with Diana's death and funeral, Hitchens delivered a devastating critique of the imaginary unity that was constructed by the news media. He insisted and brought evidence in support of his claim that 'There is another Britain', a Britain that was *not* distraught at the death of Diana and a Britain sceptical of the need for a monarchy, either established or usurpatory, as in a putative House of Spencer.

Hitchens presented several different voices with their reasoned arguments to this effect that had hardly been heard a year before. Towards the end of *The Mourning After*, with a concluding flourish, Hitchens pointed out that we all know about Diana and the landmines, but probably few of us can actually name the woman who won the Nobel Peace Prize for campaigning against landmines – Jodie Williams.

Conclusion

The main aim of this chapter has been to take the life and death of Diana, Princess of Wales, seriously as the passing vehicle of a cultural public sphere, by which I mean the aesthetic and emotional mediation of questions concerning the politics of everyday life. This should not be denigrated as simply a trivialisation of and distraction from the serious matters of the political public sphere since it is a precious space of heteroglossia – to use Bakhtin's term. Yet, it is not *just* an open and transparent arena for popular disputation. The cultural public sphere suffers similar distortions and suppressions to those of the political public sphere in terms of the selection and framing of issues. Most importantly, however, it is a mistake to simply blame the cultural public sphere for the failings of the political public sphere, as 'entertainment' driving out 'information', in the usual formula. That is to miss the critical purchase and comparative freedom of the cultural public sphere's insulation from 'serious' politics.

The Diana phenomenon is, of course, just one extremely spectacular instance of how mass-mediated celebrity and scandal in high places capture the public imagination in this 'information age' (Castells, 2004a [1997]; Thompson, 1997). Social and cultural analysts need to explore the variable operations of such media phenomena, allowing for the possibility that, in some cases, they may facilitate as well as distort popular deliberation on the conduct of life. Nevertheless, from a critical perspective – and in a concluding observation on this case – it must also be noted how problematic it is that chronic issues of sexual and life politics, which matter to everyone, came so much to the fore with regard to the conduct of a remote and vaguely decadent dynasty – the royal family. Furthermore, expressions of popular feeling for Diana and public debate about the fate of the British monarchy were engendered by the contestable story and pathetic fate of an aristocratic young woman who is said to have done so much for charity yet left none of her own considerable fortune to it. That is exactly the kind of ethical contradiction – falling short of 'scandal' as such, however – that figures routinely as a topic of debate at the everyday conversational level of the cultural public sphere. Mass-mediated idolatory is not only a salient feature of contemporary public culture and an object of disdain for satiric journalists and critical academics but is also challenged, at least occasionally, by popular, subordinate and counter-discourses that typically enunciate mundane scepticism about the powers that be.

THE SOCIAL CONSTRUCTION OF A CULTURAL DISASTER

Introduction

This chapter presents a case study of London's Millennium Dome exposition. It examines the public debate concerning the Dome as constructed in the news media and presents a multidimensional analysis of its cultural, economic and political significance.

From a policy-oriented perspective, it is vital that cultural analysis should engage with current issues of controversy in such a way that contests official discourse and the limitations of journalism. The Millennium Experience – the centrepiece of which was an exposition housed in a dome-like tent – became the biggest news story in Britain during the year 2000. Yet, in spite of the enormous amount of news coverage and comment it attracted, journalists failed to explain satisfactorily how and why the Dome turned out as it did. While many criticisms were made of the exposition, in effect, such criticism proved to be remarkably superficial in light of the in-depth research on its production and reception that is presented here.

Moreover, multidimensional cultural analysis provides a more adequate account of the Dome problem than the kind of managerial explanation (or excuse) that was eventually given by government, as this chapter demonstrates. The problem ran much deeper than a matter of admini-stration, whether in terms of a governmental blame game or the subtle pragmatics of the governmentality perspective in cultural policy studies (see my critique of this perspective, McGuigan, 1996, reprinted in Lewis and Miller, 2003).

The Dome was dubbed a 'disaster' soon after opening by journalist Polly Toynbee in the *Daily Mail* (2000b). Her article was reprinted from the

Guardian (2000a) of the previous day. It had passed, then, from the leading Left–Liberal broadsheet to conservative Middle England's favourite tabloid.

Unlike the journalists who had damned the thing before it opened, Toynbee (2000a and 2000b) claimed to have been favourably disposed towards the Millennium Dome as a site of national celebration – that is, until she actually visited it. She said, 'alas this is not a great exhibition. It is a deep disappointment. It doesn't work on any level, from the most mundane purchase of a cup of coffee to any bit of really good fun' (Toynbee, 2000a: 20).

The 'disaster' for Toynbee was cultural, in the sense that the exposition was unimaginative, tawdry and full of queues on a busy day in the school holidays. That was a personal and educated response but not an explanation.

In what follows, I aim to explain the social construction of this cultural disaster. Nevertheless, it is important to take into account evidence of an 'under-reported success' and the extraordinary gulf between most visitors' responses and the conventional wisdom enunciated at both elite and popular levels that the Dome was a dismal failure.

The case of the Dome is inextricably bound up with the pretensions of the New Labour government that was elected to office in May 1997. The Dome project was begun under the previous Conservative government. The incoming government could have abandoned the project, but, instead, adopted the Dome as a symbol of the new regime. Had the Conservative Party not virtually imploded in the late 1990s, the failure of the Dome might possibly have impacted on New Labour's prospects for re-election in 2001. The Dome turned out not to be disastrous for the government in electoral terms, though it was a huge and continuing embarrassment long after its closure.

While the Dome was the object of incessant dispute in the public sphere, the reasons for its troubles were not delved into very deeply by the news media. The present account offers a multidimensional analysis that seeks to go beyond the usual terms of debate, particularly by focusing on the role of sponsorship in the social production, representation and consumption of the Millennium Dome. Under consideration here is a complex and variously faceted phenomenon. Although it is a particular – and, indeed, peculiar – case, the Millennium Dome also has a general significance symbolically and materially with regard to understanding the intimate relations between government and corporate power today; and, specifically, the coalescence of social democracy with neoliberalism.

New Labour's millennium experience

The publicity slogan for the exposition in a dome-shaped tent at Greenwich during the year 2000 was 'one amazing day'. M. & C. Saatchi's television advertisement for the opening showed a child being amazed by the apparently marvellous spectacle on offer. Responding to critics of the project in his

'People's Palace' speech of February 1998, Prime Minister Tony Blair (1998: 1) had himself already promised amazement:

> Picture the scene. The clock strikes midnight on December 31st, 1999. The eyes of the world turn to the spot where the new millennium begins – the Meridian Line at Greenwich. This is Britain's opportunity to greet the world with a celebration that is so bold, so beautiful, so inspiring that it embodies at once the spirit of confidence and adventure in Britain and the spirit of the future in the world. This is the reason for the Millennium Experience. Not a product of imagination run wild, but a huge opportunity for Britain. It is good for Britain. So let us seize the moment and put on something of which we and the world will be proud.
>
> Then we will say to ourselves with pride: this is our Dome. Britain's Dome. And believe me, it will be the envy of the world.

On adopting the Dome project from the outgoing Conservative government in June 1997, despite the misgivings of senior Labour politicians, including the then culture secretary, Blair (1998: 2) had set down five criteria for it. First, 'the content should inspire people'. Second, 'it should have national reach'. Third, 'the management of the project should be first rate'. Fourth, '[it] should not call on the public purse'. Fifth, 'there should be a lasting legacy'. He went on to say (1998: 3):

> It will bring the nation together in common purpose – to make a difference. It will unite the nation. It will be a meeting point of people from all backgrounds. It will be an event to lift our horizons. It will be a catalyst to imagine our futures.

Blair claimed that the Millennium Experience would be an educative guide to conduct, particularly for children. He said (1998: 4), 'I want today's children to take from it an experience so powerful and memories so strong that it gives them that abiding sense of purpose and unity that stays with them through the rest of their lives'. The demotic and personalising quality of Blair's rhetoric is well known and has been analysed carefully (Fairclough, 2000), yet, the idea that such an exposition might actually influence popular conduct in a fundamental way was well beyond its sell-by-date in the media age. The amazing thing about the Millennium Dome was not so much its would-be Foucauldian impact on the conduct of conduct, but that it was done at all and in the way that it was done.

Although visitors to the Millennium Dome generally approved of it, there was little expression of amazement, except for the building itself, as had been anticipated prophetically in *The New Yorker* (Goldberger, 1998). It was not a dome in the traditional sense but closer to a suspension bridge in engineering terms (Wilhide, 1999), designed by the Richard Rogers Partnership. It was, in fact, a big tent – a *very* big tent, coated with Teflon. Built on the partially reclaimed yet still deeply toxic site of an old coal-fired gasworks at Greenwich Marsh (Irvine, 1999), the Millennium Dome was indeed massive – in the words of the Queen, 'the largest enclosed space on Earth' (NMEC, 2000: 5). It dominates a south-eastern peninsula of the Thames where the Prime Meridian cuts across the tip of the peninsula like a circumcision. The amazing thing did not dominate the cityscape in the way that the Eiffel Tower looms above Paris, however (Barthes, 1979). Tucked far away down the river in East London, the Dome could just about be glimpsed from the top of the London Eye ferris wheel, which was also built to mark the new millennium, on the other side of the Thames from the Palace of Westminster. Unlike British Airway's (BA) London Eye, the Millennium Dome provided no panoramic view of London. The greatest sights on offer were to be inside. As an icon of the new millennium, the Dome was best seen in aerial photography, through mediated rather than direct vision. The world was supposed to be amazed.

More amazing than the thing itself or its image circulating globally was how the project was constructed as a display of Britain's 'greatness' at the turn of the Millennium. It was an artifact of the National Lottery that was introduced by John Major's Conservative government in 1994. A large part of the proceeds from the Lottery were to be spent on celebrating the new millennium.

A Millennium Commission of 'the great and the good' was set up to plan the celebrations (Rocco, 1995). The then deputy prime minister, Michael Heseltine – the politician who had been responsible for bringing about the overthrow of his bitter enemy Margaret Thatcher – was a key figure on the Millennium Commission. He had a ministerial record of promoting urban regeneration schemes. Heseltine (2000) regretted the fact that Greenwich had been neglected in the docklands regeneration of the 1980s, the most prominent aspect of which was the Canary Wharf office complex across the Thames from the Greenwich Peninsula. In choosing Greenwich for the Millennium Dome, Heseltine had sought to make amends for its earlier neglect.

Claims are made, of course, for the local regenerative effect of the project (McGuigan and Gilmore, 2001) but, in 1996, Heseltine (quoted by Nicolson, 1999: 2) enunciated an even grander purpose for putting on a millennium festival with Greenwich at its core:

> I want millions of visitors to visit the country, share in the festival and go away deeply impressed, much excited by British achievements. The excellence of UK companies, the pre-eminence of the City of London as a financial centre, the technological prowess, the innovative genius will leave an indelible impression. We can do that only in partnership with our leading companies. It is not a bureaucratic concept of central government, or a whim of the Millennium Commission. It is about selling ourselves and our country.

Heseltine is especially noted for his patriotic capitalism, which was the cause of his conflict with the Atlanticist Thatcher. For Heseltine, the Millennium Dome was to be a re-run of the Great Exhibition.

Strenuous efforts were made to bring 'British' business on board. No private company, however – not even BA – would agree to run the project. Instead, the New Millennium Experience Company (NMEC) was set up as a curious hybrid of a limited company and a 'non-departmental public body'. The single shareholder in the company was to be the minister charged with overseeing its operations. When the New Labour government was persuaded to adopt the project from the outgoing Conservatives, the minister given responsibility for the new millennium celebrations was not the then Secretary of State for Culture, Media and Sport, Chris Smith, but, instead, the arch spin doctor, Minister without Portfolio, Peter Mandelson. He immediately set about spinning on behalf of the Dome: 'Greenwich is the home of time. The meridian line runs through the exhibition site. It's a chance for Britain to make a big statement about itself and the rest of the world' (quoted by Harding, 1997).

Mandelson was well aware that the Dome was a tricky proposition, already hugely controversial long before opening (Richards, 1997). Its funding was the principal matter of concern. An initial National Lottery grant of £200 million would have to be increased to £450 million, Mandelson realised on entering office. Eventually, £628 million of Lottery money would be spent on the Millennium Experience, in addition to nearly £200 million of 'taxpayers' money', spent by the regeneration agency English Partnerships on buying and reclaiming the site. Another significant source of funding was corporate sponsorship, which was not so readily forthcoming as Heseltine had hoped.

Mandelson – like Heseltine – was one of the leading characters in the Dome drama. Its continuous and interweaving storylines were distinctly soap operatic over the years up to, including and beyond 2000. The Dome's unfolding narrative also had features of situation comedy, with a cast of eccentric characters stuck together for a succession of disasters and temporary resolutions.

Mandelson's maternal grandfather, Herbert Morrison, had overseen the post-Second World War Labour government's Festival of Britain in 1951 (Banham and Hillier, 1976). This, rather more than Heseltine's Great Exhibition, was a constant reference point for Mandelson in promoting the Dome. He was, however, to be accused of wishing to dumb down the exposition on visiting Disney World in Florida for inspiration (Bayley, 1999).

When Mandelson was forced to resign for the first time from the government in December 1998 over a loan scandal, 'Mandy's Place' (Lewis, 1999) became the responsibility of another comic character, Lord Charles Falconer – the old school pal of Tony Blair.

Mandelson was eventually welcomed back into government, but had to resign for a second time when he was accused of selling passports to the Hinduja brothers for their modest and tax-exempting donation to the Dome's Faith Zone. The media had a field day with this 'scandal' and other endlessly entertaining storylines.

The fact of the matter is that the Millennium Dome was the biggest news story in the British media during the year 2000, if only because of the sheer volume of broadcast minutes and column inches devoted to the crisis-ridden exposition (McGuigan, 2002). Journalists at Canary Wharf were constantly reminded of the Dome when they glanced out of their office windows just across the river. It took the lorry drivers' protest at the price of petrol, which threatened to close down the British economy, to topple the Dome from lead news story in September on radio and television and in the press. Yet, even at the height of the fuel crisis, the problems of the Dome's sell-off and its perpetual need for further Lottery subsidy to keep it open occupied second place in the news media.

The cultural disaster

Years of negative comment concerning the good sense of the project seemed to be confirmed on the opening night, 31 December 1999. National newspaper editors, the BBC's Director-General and many other guests for the launch party were detained at Stratford Underground station for a security check that lasted up to three hours before they were bussed to the Dome at North Greenwich. News media immediately dubbed it 'a fiasco'. The Millennium Experience itself was attacked as a cultural 'disaster' by leading commentators in the press. The amazing thing was very soon judged to be distinctly uninspiring by both broadsheet and tabloid journalists.

The Dome itself became the object of incessant popular conversation and, indeed, derision. NMEC's management lost the public relations battle straight away. Then, it transpired that, while the Dome had opened on time, it had not opened on budget. The company's contingency fund had been depleted in order to meet escalating costs as time ran out before opening. Only one-third of the expected number of visitors for January went to the Dome that month. Just over half the predicted 12 million for the whole year actually visited the Dome. On opening, several sponsors had not yet paid up and some of them had not even concluded contracts with NMEC. By the end of the first month, the company was virtually bankrupt.

NMEC asked for and received £60 million of additional Lottery money from the Millennium Commission in February – at the time described as a 'loan' but with no likelihood of its ever being repaid. This was the first of four extra tranches of Lottery funding through the year.

Another £29 million was agreed in May. When the Millennium Commission agreed a deal to sell the Dome to the Japanese investment bank Nomura for £105 million, £43 million was made forthcoming in August as an advance on the sale's proceeds. When Nomura pulled out of the deal in September because of confusion over contractual ownership of properties at the Dome, the Millennium Commission awarded it another £47 million to keep going until the end of the year.

A City 'troubleshooter' was appointed the third chair in succession of NMEC in order to bring about solvent liquidation of the project. This involved breaking up and hastily selling off the contents at knockdown prices in February 2001.

It is not surprising, then, that the key theme of media coverage was the Dome was a waste of public money, which would have been better spent on genuinely good causes. That was particularly embarrassing for the New Labour government since it had prided itself on being more fiscally prudent than Old Labour. Thus, in September, the prime minister issued an 'apology' in a television interview with David Frost in which he blamed the Dome disaster on inadequate management rather than the very concept and social construction of the Millennium Experience as such.

The managerial paradigm

Back in January, a group of sponsors had defined the problem as a managerial one and demanded that something should be done about it. These sponsors commissioned research that purportedly showed association with the Dome was bringing them bad publicity (*The Money Programme*, BBC Two, 6 February 2000), though it did not demonstrate a loss of sales. Long queues at the high street chemist Boots' Body Zone, for instance, had been widely reported as indicative of poor management.

In effect, the sponsors' revolt brought about the sacking of the chief executive officer, Jennie Page – a former civil servant and previously head of the Millennium Commission.

She was replaced as NMEC's CEO by an unemployed thirty-four-year-old former vice president of Disneyland Paris, P.-Y. Gerbeau. He was inaccurately reported as being the man who had been responsible for 'turning around' Disney's French operation. The idea was that Gerbeau would do the same with the Dome. Gerbeau had, in fact, been in charge of ticketing and car parking at Disneyland, Paris. It was his mentor, Phillippe Bourgignon, the CEO, who had presided over the turnaround at the Disney theme park outside Paris.

The replacement of Page with Gerbeau certainly did result in a shift of managerial style. Page was the epitome of the public bureaucrat who had no experience of running a visitor attraction and blamed the problems of the Dome on political interference (Page, 2000). As Blair later argued on television and at the October Labour Party Conference, it was essential to bring in commercial expertise for running a visitor attraction in a business-like manner, which is exactly what Gerbeau represented. He was imbued with the new managerialist 'philosophy' of customer service and flat organisational structure. A stratum of middle management disappeared.

Gerbeau was a showman who became a popular figure in the media and was said to be popular with his employees – the black-and-yellow-clad hosts, the frontline workers suffering from the flak being thrown at the

Dome day by day. Changes were made more or less cosmetically, such as the issuing of time-slot tickets for visiting the Body Zone.

Gerbeau knew whom he had to please first and foremost: the sponsors. He redefined them as 'partners' (interview with the author). Under the Gerbeau regime, large placards were erected in front of sponsored zones, making the corporate benificence quite clear to the visiting public. Access to the Dome's main entrance was cordoned off in order to route visitors through 'the sponsors' village' of shop units and past BSkyB's Skyscape cinema where the *Blackadder Back and Forth* film was screened at regular times during the day.

While Gerbeau ensured that corporate logos were given more prominent display than previously, it would be quite wrong to assume that it was he alone who was responsible for the overweening presence of sponsorship at the Dome. Corporate sponsorship was at the heart of the whole project from its hesitant beginning to its bitter end. Page had said that she would not allow the exposition to become 'Logoland', yet it already was before the advent of Gerbeau. For example, McDonald's sponsored Our Town Stage where children from around the country had their day performing at the Dome. McDonald's had sought copyright on the performances but had to settle for copyright of recordings. Involvement in the Millennium Experience's National Programme, in effect, facilitated McDonald's incursion into schools. Furthermore, McDonald's was a massive presence at the Dome. On the outside, directly across from the main entrance, was the largest McDonald's in Europe. There were two more McDonald's eateries inside. In January, before the regime change, an advertisement appeared on television asking, 'What's in the Dome?' The answer: 'McDonald's.'

Moreover, it is quite inadequate to explain the Millennium Dome's manifest 'failure' – or even its latent 'success' – as simply a matter of management, particularly the lack of private-sector skills for running a public-sector project on opening. That the Dome picked up increasing numbers of visitors towards the end of the year and approval ratings were high are perhaps grounds for the managerial argument. As visitor research shows, however, scepticism of its damnation in the media was a more pronounced motive for visiting the Dome than awareness of improved management. Gerbeau himself admitted in interview that the changes he brought about were not fundamental.

Incidentally, the managerial paradigm framed BBC Television's six-part series *Trouble at the Big Top*. This was a special edition of a long-running programme *Trouble at the Top* that looked at problems of management in various walks of life. The first four episodes were screened at weekly intervals up to and including the opening of the Dome. The fifth episode appeared on the digital channel *BBC Knowledge* (now BBC Four) in June. That particular episode represented sponsors' complaints uncritically and contained interviews with newspaper editors whom had suffered the indignities of the opening night. The final episode summarised the disastrous narrative of the Dome from beginning to end and was screened on its closure at the end of 2000.

Multidimensional analysis

Various different accounts of the Millennium Dome were given before it actually opened, ranging from managerial analysis (Lewis et al., 1998) to belle-lettreiste critique (Sinclair, 1999). While controversy still raged, the Dome was attacked as symptomatic of New Labour's disingenuous populism by a former Conservative politician (Walden, 2000). There are several other insightful and largely journalistic accounts of the Dome's cultural disaster (such as Martin, 2000, and Morrison, 2000). None of them, however, applies a rigorous method of cultural analysis or a critical suspension of partial judgement.

In accounting for such a phenomenon as the Millennium Experience, it is important to look at it in the round – that is, by taking into account the multiple determinations and agencies in its production, representation and consumption.

There are diverse kinds of cultural analysis that focus on particular aspects of production, representation and consumption (for instance, the political economy of cultural production, textual analysis of cultural artifacts and audience research). All of these are valid in their own terms and exemplify a practical division of labour as well as the contest of rival paradigms in cultural and media studies. There is a case for a combined approach, however, for tracing various moments in the circulation of culture and their interconnectedness in order to grasp the ontological complexity of a specific phenomenon (Kellner, 1997). The case of the Open University's study of the Sony Walkman (du Gay et al., 1997) – which adds identity and regulation to the trinity of production, representation and consumption – is a good example of such analysis.

As a comparatively bounded object, the Millennium Dome exposition lent itself to multidimensional analysis, not all aspects of which can be dealt with fully in this chapter. The point is to illustrate the value of multidimensional analysis of a controversial phenomenon to a policy-orientated though critical approach to cultural research. The general framework of the analysis is sketched in here (see McGuigan and Gilmore, 2002, for greater empirical detail, particularly on the data from visitor interviews; and McGuigan, 2004a, for reflections on the Dome in relation to the tradition of expositions universelles, great exhibitions and world fairs; Greenhalgh, 1988).

What, then, are the key features of the Millennium Dome's production, representation and consumption? Here, I shall concentrate on the following aspects. The role of corporate sponsorship in the production of the Millennium Experience is examined. The ideological features of the Dome's representational elements are related to its social-democratic inflection of neoliberalism. A typology of generous and reflexive visiting is presented that aims to explain the paradox of relatively high levels of recorded visitor approval in the face of the mediated construction of the Dome as a disaster. The foregoing discussion of the public debate – political statements and media coverage – is part of this multidimensional analysis since the meaning of the object itself was a highly mediated and contested phenomenon.

The role of sponsorship

Consideration of the role of corporate sponsorship is at the heart of explaining how the Millennium Dome turned out. Sponsorship eventually amounted to less than one fifth (around £150 million) of the amount of public money spent on the Millennium Experience (in excess of £800 million, including £628 million of Lottery money), yet corporate sponsors had a decisive impact on the exposition's focal concerns, design and management. Typically, sponsors were associated with particular thematic zones, so you could see BT's Talk, Ford's Journey, Manpower's Work, Marconi's and BAE Systems's Mind, Marks & Spencer's Self Portrait (the main zones discussed here). Some zones did not attract sponsorship, such as Living Island and Play. Living Island was critical of environmental pollution. Play lost its sponsor, BSkyB, because it was not designed to publicise that company's products.

An obvious motive for sponsorship was commercial promotion of the companies to the public. This was manifestly evident in the cases of BT's Talk Zone and Ford's Journey Zone. Both companies were able to negotiate 'turnkey' contracts with NMEC, which meant that they were allowed to design, build and run their own zones, in effect, with minimal interference from NMEC. The only motor cars in the Journey Zone were Ford. BT and Ford spent a great deal more on their zones than was spent on the zones ostensibly under NMEC's control. On the other hand, several sponsors quite evidently paid less than the official tariff for association and 'value in kind' – equipment and so on – was often supplied instead of money, such as Coca-Cola's ice rink.

NMEC had editors allocated to zones and a Litmus Group of luminaries from the entertainment industry to advise on the representational aspects of the exhibition. There was a great deal of hiring and firing of designers in the production of the Dome's contents, but, even in those cases, it is evident that NMEC relinquished a great deal of control to sponsors. Some sponsors brought in designers that they had worked with before on product launches. In fact, many of the zone designers came from the world of corporate communications rather than museum design. Also, in the Work Zone, for example, its sponsor, the American employment agency Manpower, was permitted to put up a display of jobs on offer through the agency as well as extolling the brave new world of flexible labour.

Left-wing critics of the Millennium Dome attacked its promotional culture. For instance, Jonathan Glancey (2001: 26) noted: 'The Millennium Experience, its entrance flanked by a branch of McDonald's, proved to be an exhibition of corporate sponsorship.' This was an accurate criticism to a certain extent, but not very deep in accounting for the political economy or ideology of sponsorship at the Dome. With a few notable exceptions, such as Greg Palast (2001) in the *Observer*, journalists hardly penetrated the deeper motives of corporations for sponsoring parts of the Dome. It is easy enough to see why Boots took the opportunity to promote pharmaceutical products, but harder to see why BAe Systems put money into the Mind Zone – the most intellectual of zones, designed by deconstructionist architect Zaha Hadid.

One of the largest arms manufacturers in the world, BAe Systems does not sell military hardware directly to the public; nor did the Mind Zone publicise its production of submarines, naval platforms, radar scanners and military aircraft such as the Eurofighter Tycoon, F-22 and Joint Strike Fighter. Thus, unlike the brazenness of several other sponsor–zone relations, Mind did not manifestly promote BAe's core business. Instead, the ostensible purpose of the zone was to represent modern engineering and encourage the education of engineers. Like a number of other sponsors, however, BAe may have had ulterior motives for supporting the Dome.

In 1997, the New Labour government promised to pursue an 'ethical foreign policy', which might have meant not sanctioning the sale of weapons to dictatorships such as the genocidal Suharto regime in Indonesia. Soon, this 'unrealistic' policy was quietly dropped since the production of armaments is one of the few remaining buoyant sectors of British manufacturing and exports in what is said to be a 'weightless' informational economy. The government's U-turn on foreign policy – the unrestrained issuing of export guarantees to armaments manufacturers and the conduct of diplomacy on their behalf – was of more than incidental benefit to BAe Systems. This was of greater significance than the much commented on allegation that the Hinduja brothers' modest donation to the Faith Zone bought them British passports – a story that, incidentally, brought the journalists who broke it the journalist of the year award.

The Hinduja passports-for-sponsorship scandal was only the tip of the iceberg, the greater part of which the news media largely ignored. As the former marketing director of one of the corporate sponsors remarked in interview, everyone had a political deal. This was evidently so for the Work Zone's sponsor, Manpower, aiming to build its business in Britain. Manpower handled human resources for the Millennium Experience, hiring, training and relocating employees on the exposition's closure. Yet more significantly, in association with Ernst & Young, Manpower subsequently won 9 out of 15 contracts for the management of employment zones around the country, a little remarked on feature of the New Labour government's privatisation of public agencies. This may perhaps just be coincidental.

There are several other coincidences to note. The supermarket chain Tesco – sponsor of the Learning Zone and heavily involved in promoting its business through computing in schools – must have been pleased when the government decided to withdraw its proposed legislation for taxing out-of-town car parking at retail estates. BA and BAA (British Airports Authority) – co-sponsors of Home Planet, the closest thing to a ride at the Dome – must have appreciated the government's sanctioning of Terminal 5 at Heathrow in face of popular protest on environmental grounds by locals against its building. It came as something of a surprise when Camelot – sponsor of Shared Ground – had its National Lottery contract renewed by a Labour government that had vowed to replace its profit-making operation with a not-for-profit operator. Rupert Murdoch's BSkyB – sponsor of Skyscape – benefited from the government's light-touch policies on broadcasting regulation, not to mention its relaxed press policy. There are other examples. It may all just be coincidence, but it is reasonable to infer that sponsorship of the Millennium Experience was more than just a publicity exercise.

Ideology and meaning

In carrying out the present multidimensional analysis, it is necessary to demonstrate that the role of corporate sponsorship was not only about behind-the-scenes deals but also had consequences for the construction of meaning at the Dome.

John B. Thompson (1990) identifies a number of different modes of ideological representation (legitimation, dissimulation, unification, fragmentation and reification) each with their typical strategies of symbolic construction (such as displacement and euphemisation for dissimulation). Examples of all these ideological modes and strategies could be found scattered around the Dome, of which only a few brief illustrations can be given here.

Thompson treats ideology as a matter of symbolic domination and subordination, thereby avoiding questions of interest and distortion. This is unfortunate since questions of interest and distortions in ideology critique (Lovell, 1980) are manifestly pertinent to analysing the construction of meaning in representation at the Dome, especially in sponsored thematic zones. It is not necessary, however, to claim that some essential truth was masked over at the Dome or that 'real' reality was simply misrepresented. Instead, it is possible to argue the case from the dialogical perspective of critical theory (Calhoun, 1995) that not only questions the form and content of the Dome's attractions but also imagines what might otherwise have been there. The potential articulation of alternative views in the spirit of rational-critical debate (McGuigan, 1996) could reasonably have been expected from an exposition that was very largely funded by the public in a democratic polity and only marginally by corporate sponsors.

Ideological representation with regard to corporate sponsorship worked differently in different parts of the Dome. Sponsorship was extremely intrusive in some cases, such as in Manpower's Work Zone. In other cases, it was comparatively unobtrusive, as in Marks & Spencer's Self Portrait Zone. The Mind Zone was in between. In yet other cases, it was entirely absent – as in the Millennium Show. Moreover, in the interstices and on the edges, there were signs of something different from 'an exhibition of corporate sponsorship', such as in art works of the likes of Antony Gormley's 'Quantum Cloud' out on the River Approach.

To take the most straightforward example first: Manpower's Work Zone. This was crudely propagandistic for both the agency and government policy on vocational training. Visitors were told didactically to assemble 'new skills' for a flexible labour market in which there are no more 'jobs for life' – communication, literacy and so on – and test them out in the games room at the termination of the zone. 'Old work' was reified as pure drudgery compared to the excitements of 'new work'. Furthermore, there was no mention of past labour struggles to establish worker rights or the extreme exploitation and oppression of sweated labour in the world today.

Quite differently from the crude propaganda of Work, the Mind Zone was very subtle. Its primary ideological mode was dissimulation in that the arms industry was displaced ostensibly from its focal concerns. Instead of representing technologies of warfare, the emphasis was on communications and the networking principle, which has been thoroughly analysed by Manuel Castells (2000 [1996]). Euphemism is commonly used in discourses of war and this was replete within the Mind Zone. With its (post)modern art, Internet and ant colony, the Mind Zone was a curiously dehumanised zone – a celebration of 'the inhuman', in Jean-François Lyotard's (1991 [1988]) words (see Sim, 2001), the coagulation of body and machine alongside the superior yet uncreative powers of artificial intelligence. There was, however, a startlingly humanistic exception plonked into the middle of the zone – Ron Mueck's sculpture, the enigmatic 'Boy'.

In criticising the Mind Zone, it is obligatory to imagine what *might* have been said. It would have been reasonable for the Dome to contain a War Zone that looked critically at the history of military conflict as it has developed into the virtual reality and inhumanity of hi-tech warfare. Instead, there was the intellectual obscurantism of Mind.

The editorial relation between business and design in the Millennium Dome case illustrates an important distinction and a significant transition that was taking place in a cultural project largely funded by the public. It is necessary to distinguish between *associative* sponsorship and *deep* sponsorship.

Associative sponsorship is the standard form of cultural provision in the arts and public sector. Sponsors may accrue kudos through association with artistic culture, particularly prestigious events, but are not supposed to influence their content. As critics have argued (such as Shaw, 1993), this is not what actually happens in practice. Sponsorship exerts all sorts of subtle pressure on editorial decisionmaking, programme selection and so forth. Nevertheless, the norms of associative sponsorship are still claimed and defended officially in order to preserve cultural integrity. For instance, sponsors of Tate Modern are not supposed to select the art works and dictate exhibition policy, though donations of money and work, of course, are gratefully acknowledged.

The purpose of deep sponsorship, however, is, unashamedly, to actually construct culture in the interests of corporate business. This is evidently so in, for instance, product placement in Hollywood films and sponsorship of sporting events, where corporations have even sought to change the rules of the game. The most extreme form of deep sponsorship is autonomously created culture, usually of a popular kind so that the form itself is a vehicle for advertising, merchandising and public relations. Disney was a pioneer in this respect. Corporations' constructions of children's culture, both in entertainment and education, is perhaps the most profound and widespread instance of deep sponsorship.

Several zones at the Dome were instances of deep rather than associative sponsorship – perhaps most notably Tesco's Learning Zone, which connected its display to the supermarket chain's long-standing sponsorship of computer-aided education. Other examples of manifest editorial command by sponsors include zones that were ostensibly under NMEC's control – such as Manpower's Work Zone and, the most patronising of all, the City of London's Money Zone – and the two that were not – BT's Talk Zone and Ford's Journey Zone.

As 'Ford's Dome person' told me, 'We let them [NMEC's editorial staff and advisers] believe they were influencing things but in actual fact we took no notice of them'. The Journey Zone's history of transport included no cars other than Fords. Ironically, however, unlike most of the Dome's contents, it afforded a sense of history.

Mandelson had insisted that the Dome was to be about the future, not the past. The past was to be consigned to the dustbin of history, along with Old Labour. Yet, the Dome generally failed to articulate an exciting new world order. When history is abolished it is difficult to imagine the future. Curiously, though, Ford's autonomous and very expensive Journey Zone was an outstanding exception to the general obliteration rather than representation of time – past, present and future – at the Dome.

The Journey Zone was designed by Imagination – the firm that had for years designed Ford's displays at the annual Motor Show in Birmingham and originally been hired to manage the design of the exposition as a whole. It traced the history of transport technologies, including trains, trainers and planes as well as cars, such as Ford's futuristic gas-powered vehicle, Project FC5. It polled visitors on their attitudes to transport and environmental issues.

Near the end of the Zone, four different future scenarios for travel, devised by the University of Sussex, were presented to view on wide, head-height monitors. On the opposite wall a notice said, 'There is not one future, there are many'. According to the Journey Zone, the future is a matter of choice, not predetermined. Ford, one of the world's greatest manufacturers of mobile pollution, insisted on environmental friendliness.

Journey felt like an exhibit in a trade show. It was also, however, the zone that did most to address the question of time, supposedly the core question of the exposition, with a chronological sense of history and comparatively intelligent speculation about the future. Ford's Journey was, then, a transparent yet somewhat sophisticated example of deep sponsorship in the construction of meaning at the Millennium Dome.

Gerbeau did not initiate deep sponsorship at the Dome; he merely justified it in his fashionable rhetoric of 'public–private partnership' and, specifically, in his argument that you cannot take money from sponsors without allowing them to influence what is on display. Yet, the largest proportion of funding by far did not come from corporate sponsorship but, instead, from 'the public purse'. Lottery money, in this sense, is a kind of public subscription that was disbursed by the Millennium Commission but failed to police editorial integrity at the exposition.

The National Lottery has, to be sure, been criticised as an informal tax on the poor to the benefit of the comparatively well off through the disbursement of funds to 'good causes', especially cultural causes. A visit to the Dome was an expensive day out that attracted visitors mainly from the South East of England – the richest part of the country – though the social demography of visitors was actually quite mixed. Still, the Lottery must be regarded as a means of generating 'public money', even if it is a substitute for tax revenue, in the formal sense, to provide a source of subsidy to culture and other public goods.

Clearly, the Dome was a site of tension over public and corporate control – in effect, regulation. That there were notable instances of associative sponsorship and absence of sponsorship in parts of the Dome also demonstrate the tensions in play. An example of associative sponsorship is Marks & Spencer's Self Portrait Zone, which dealt with British national identity. In this zone contradictions were set up by the juxtaposition of placards extolling the virtues of Britishness – 'creativity', 'fair play' and so on – with Gerald Scarfe's sculptures representing the darker side of Britishness, such as a football hooligan with a boot for a head and a respectable racist. It would have been unlikely for this zone to point out that Marks & Spencer was a 'quality' and hitherto 'patriotic' retail chain that was currently losing custom and turning towards sourcing products from cheap labour around the world as part of the solution to its business problems. Nonetheless, the sponsor did allow a questioning of Britishness and an opening up of debate over national identity to be articulated in its zone. It also did not manifestly promote its own products there, as was the case in several other sponsored zones (see McGuigan, 2004a).

According to visitor research, the most popular feature of the Dome was the Millennium Show in the Central Arena, an aerial ballet choreographed by Mark Fisher with music by Peter Gabriel that told an allegorical love story linked to the emergence, destructiveness and collapse of industrialism. The pivotal motif of a rising and falling gas holder recalled the previous use of the Dome site. There was also a spectacular light show. It is interesting to note that the Millennium Show had no sponsor. Moreover, 'a lasting legacy' from it was intended and perhaps realised. Young people had been selected and trained in the performance skills associated with the Canadian troupe Cirque du Soleil, leaving a greater pool of modern circus talent than had previously existed in Britain.

Generous and reflexive visiting

Analysis of a cultural phenomenon such as the Millennium Dome must take into account its consumption – visitor experience, not just mass mediation – as well as the political economy of production and the ideology of representation. Curiously, even an excellent study of a comparable phenomenon – Susan Davis's (1997) research on Sea World in San Diego – does not seriously engage with visitor research. My research on the Dome's visitors draws on quantitative evidence gathered by MORI (McGuigan and Gilmore, 2001) and qualitative evidence gathered for the Arts and Humanities Research Board (AHRB) project (McGuigan and Gilmore, 2002). The details of that research are not reported here in this chapter. Instead, I shall concentrate on how the paradox of media damnation and visitor approval can be explained in the case of the Millennium Dome.

Although it only attracted 6.5 million – instead of the possibly unrealistic projection of 12 million – those who actually visited the Dome generally said that they liked it. A great many people did choose to find out for themselves whether or not the Dome was any good, in spite of it being damned by the media. NMEC claimed, with some good reason, that it was an under-reported 'success'. MORI polling revealed high approval ratings, stretching into the region of 90 per cent of visitors who had a good day out at the Millennium Dome. The visitor experience at the Dome was not just about numbers and bald approval rating, however. How did visitors experience the Dome?

There are bound to be differences of orientation, interpretation and appreciation. This is worth thinking about in terms of qualitative differentiation rather than just crude percentages for satisfaction and dissatisfaction.

The marketing model of museums, exhibitions and entertainments tends to use customer typologies that stereotype differences of orientation – for instance, 'streakers', 'strollers' and 'readers' (Perin, 1992). NMEC had such a classification of visitors: 'divers', 'swimmers' and 'paddlers'. Divers were the clever ones who could penetrate the deep meanings of the Dome. Paddlers would not really be concentrating, due to their intellectual deficiencies or having to deal with screaming kids. Swimmers were identified as coming between the extremes of 'brainy' and 'thick' (Parton, 1999).

It is necessary for cultural analysis to go beyond such stereotyping in order to explore the actual texture of visitor experience. The following typology, developed for the AHRB project on the Millennium Dome, identifies two major coordinates of visitor orientation – *generosity* and *reflexivity*. These are not mutually exclusive categories or crude stereotypes as you could be generous and reflexive or generous and unreflexive. Equally, you could be reflexively or unreflexively ungenerous. This produces four general modes of visitor orientation. The point of such a typology is to create a general framework for exploring the complex and different ways in

Table 3.1 Typology of visitor orientation

	Generous	Ungenerous
Reflexive	1. Generous reflexive	3. Reflexive ungenerous
Unreflexive	2. Generous unreflexive	4. Ungenerous unreflexive

which attractions like the Dome are negotiated by visitors and, in the case of the ungenerous and unreflexive, perhaps, non-visitors (see Table 3.1).

The typology facilitated the conduct and analysis of conversational interviews with visitors to the Dome. Visitors to the Dome were typically found to be generous in their orientation – willing to give the exposition the benefit of the doubt and keen to make the best of what was on offer. For example, there is the case of a family from Middlesbrough – 300 miles from London – who visited the Dome in March 2000. A grandmother, a mother, a toddler and a boy of about ten had set off by coach from the North East at four in the morning and were going on to the London Eye after the Dome before returning to Middlesbrough at two the following morning. The adults and the boy did not say much except that they were having a great time, which is just as well, considering the sheer expenditure of time, money and effort they had put into their 'one amazing day'. If you went at all, you were likely to make the best of it.

Visitors were well aware of the controversial nature of the Millennium Dome. Typically sceptical of its damnation in the media, they came, in the spirit of practical criticism, to see for themselves. As one visitor summed it up, 'it is nothing like the disaster you read in the newspapers'. Typically, the general experience of the visit exceeded expectations. For some, the Millennium Show was worth the price of the entrance ticket alone. Hosts, however, mentioned a small minority of visitors who had come to confirm their expectation of just how bad it was.

Three general conclusions can be derived from the visitor research for the AHRB project. First, it has to be registered, visitors did not complain much about the role of sponsorship. That does not necessarily mean they approved of it or that it was inconsequential in terms of their experience. Instead, it is reasonable to suggest that many people these days simply take the logoscape for granted, rarely questioning its significance, so normalised has it become under present conditions.

Second, it was not unusual to find visitors expressing approval for the Dome in general – the building and its central attraction of the show – rather more than its particular elements, especially the thematic zones. As a visitor experience, in effect, the Dome amounted typically to more than the sum of its many tainted parts.

Third, the under-reported success that the Dome did, arguably, achieve in terms of visitor response was due more to the generosity of visitors, determined to have a good day out, than of sponsors determined to have their pound of flesh.

Conclusion: a shell for neoliberalism

Among the determining factors of the Dome 'disaster', the role of corporate sponsorship – economically, ideologically and politically – was decisive. It is an extreme case of the impact of corporate sponsorship on public culture, illustrating the inordinate power, symbolically as well as materially, of business in liberal–democratic polities today. For a small fraction of the public money spent on it, sponsoring corporations were allowed to have the loudest say in most of the Dome's thematic zones. The role of corporate sponsorship was actually more important ideologically than financially. The four extra tranches of National Lottery money spent to keep the Dome going throughout 2000 amounted to more than the value of that sponsorship. It might have been possible, albeit ideologically inconceivable, to have put on an exposition without any sponsorship at all. That, though, would have been contrary to the whole point of the project from a governmental perspective, which was to represent Britain as a nation of corporations instead of a democratic people engaged in debate over their time and place in history.

It is a sad coda to the project that the Dome and its site were literally given away to corporate business in the end. A series of failed attempts were made to sell off the place before and after its closure. Had the Dome been demolished, the land would have been more profitable to developers. To let that happen, however, would have been a final admission of failure for the flagship project of the New Labour government. The place was eventually given away to the Meridian Delta consortium in the summer of 2002 in the vague hope that the government might at some time in the future receive a share of the profits. Profit was to be made from use of the Dome as a sports and entertainment venue by the American Anschutz Corporation and property development around it by Quintain Estates and the Australian Lend Lease Real Estate Group. The tent itself is now the O_2 entertainment arena, so it is safely ensconced in the commercial sector of the culture industry.

There is a paradox, however, that needs to be explained – that between the publicly mediated 'failure' of the Millennium Experience – 'the disastrous Dome' – and evidence of an under-reported 'success' according to expressions of visitor approval. Many visitors brought levels of hopeful anticipation and intellectual engagement to the Dome that much of its contents did not actually merit. The Millennium Dome was, to put it mildly, a disappointment despite strenuous efforts on the part of visitors to make it better than it really was. Visitor generosity and reflexivity towards an ideologically distorted exposition in a big tent at Greenwich are symptomatic of the imperiled standing of the public cultural alternative to commercial speech today. In the face of the taken-for-granted dominance of neoliberal values and corporate machinations, there is little mass popular resistance.

The case study of the Millennium Dome further illustrates the operations of cultural policy as display (McGuigan, 2004a; Williams, 1984). It was an extreme instance of both nationalistic hubris – particularly considering its failure to articulate a sufficiently multicultural Britishness – and corporate violation of publicly funded culture. That an exposition on this scale should have been mounted at all in the same year as the official successor to the international tradition – Hanover 2000 – is peculiar to say the least. Interestingly, Hanover 2000 met with a similar fate to that of the Millennium Dome. It attracted only 16 million of a projected 40 million and was an object of persistent criticism and public debate.

The corporate presence was also massive at Hanover and countries such as Nigeria used it as a marketplace to sell off public assets. Unlike the British exposition, however, it played host to countries from around the world, although the USA refused to participate. Hanover 2000 still, however residually, represented a world of nations whereas the Millennium Dome represented a nation of corporations.

The Dome was an incoherent vehicle for old delusions of national grandeur allied to corporate power in a neoliberal world. In toto, though, in complex and variable ways, it represented New Labour's 'Third Way' politics – the reconciliation of 'social-ism' with 'market forces'.

Perry Anderson (2000: 11) has remarked, 'the Third Way is the best ideological shell of neoliberalism today'. The Great Exhibition of 1851 represented the original liberalism of free trade, with imperial Britain in a commanding position. The 1951 Festival of Britain represented a post-imperial, nationalistic social democracy – a vision of the future that was eventually given concrete form in the South Bank arts complex, the pedestrian precinct of Coventry city centre and many other such places around the country. In the 1990s, the British Labour Party, having been out of power for 18 years, relinquished the substance of social democracy while retaining some of its rhetoric in order to subsume Thatcherism in a new governmental project that has reasonably been labelled 'post-Thatcherite' (Driver and Martell, 1998). It not only inherited the neoliberal agenda; it inherited the Dome. New Labour's Millennium Experience, in effect, represented the government's subordination to the imperatives of big business, at great expense to the public.

4 A COMMUNITY OF COMMUNITIES

For the British-born generations, seeking to assert their claim to belong, the concept of Englishness often seems inappropriate, since to be English, as the term in practice is used, is to be white. Britishness is not ideal, but at least it appears acceptable, particularly when suitably qualified – Black British, Indian British, British Muslim, and so on.

However, there is one major and so far insuperable barrier. Britishness, as much as Englishness, has systematic, largely unspoken, racial connotations. Whiteness nowhere features as an explicit condition of being British, but it is widely understood that Englishness, and therefore by extension Britishness, is racially coded. 'There ain't no black in the Union Jack', it has been said. ... Race is deeply entwined with political culture and with the idea of nation, and underpinned by a distinctive kind of British reticence – to take race or racism seriously, or even to talk about them at all, is bad form, something not done in polite company. This disavowal, combined with 'an iron-jawed disinclination to recognise equal human worth and dignity of people who are not white', ... has proved a lethal combination. Unless these deep-rooted antagonisms to racial and cultural difference can be defeated in practice, as well as symbolically written out of the national story, the idea of a multicultural post-nation remains an empty promise. (Runnymede Trust, 2000: 38–39)

Introduction

The Parekh Report, *The Future of Multi-Ethnic Britain* (Runnymede Trust, 2000), quoted from above, was not well received when it was published in October 2000. It was read as an attack on Britishness and as an expression of the New Labour government's political correctness, although the then Home Secretary, Jack Straw, managed simultaneously to launch the report publicly and distance himself from what he mistakenly construed to be its key argument.

In this chapter, I shall consider the reception of the Parekh Report as mediated by the national press in Britain and provide my own exegesis of it. Then, I will compare Labour peer Bhikhu Parekh's thinking on multiculturalism with that of Samuel Huntington – the American policy expert and erstwhile adviser to the Democrats on international relations.

It is important to appreciate that the Parekh Report is not only of national but also of global significance, especially in such a period of martial tension across the world. When considering the politics of national heritage, it is necessary to situate particular issues – to do with, for instance, public symbols and broader negotiations of identity within the nation state formation – in relation to these extended theoretical arguments and cross-national debates concerning past and present-day cultural configurations.

How the Parekh Report was (mis)represented in the press

The Parekh Report was published on 11 October 2000. Its negative reception had already been framed the previous day. A couple of *Daily Telegraph* articles by Philip Johnston, home affairs editor, established the frame.

On the front page, Johnston (2000a) quoted two Conservative politicians – Margaret Thatcher's old war horse Norman Tebbit and Gerald Howarth, who had in his youth been associated with the radical Right. The report was immediately defined as a New Labour document, for which there was some justification. The Runnymede Trust, an independent charity, organised a commission on race relations to inform government policy. Howarth complained about the wish to rewrite British history as multicultural. He said: 'It is an extraordinary affront to the 94 per cent which is not from ethnic minorities. The native British must stand up for ourselves' (quoted by Johnston, 2000a: 1). Thus, the picture was put in people's minds of an overwhelming majority of native Britons being asked to comply with the demands of various minorities that in total only make up 6 per cent of the population.

Inside the *Telegraph* of 10 October, Johnston (2000b) praised Simon Schama's television history of Britain and the episode on the Magna Carta for recording accurately the history of an island race. He acknowledged that King John and the barons at Runnymede in 1215 spoke French. They, however, were white, like 53 million of the current British population of 57 million.

Johnston (2000c) felt justified in taking the credit for alerting Straw to the report's key argument, that Britishness was inherently racist – an insult to the great majority of Britons. At the launch of the report and in a subsequent *Observer* article, Straw (2000: 27) turned on 'the Left' for having let the Right capture 'patriotism' for itself. He went on to say: 'I do not accept the argument that Britain or Britishness is dead. On the contrary, both are now receiving a new lease of life. Enduring British values of fairness, tolerance and decency are at the heart of the government's reforms to build a more inclusive, stronger society.'

It was but a small step then to infer that, in attacking Britishness, the Parekh Report was, in effect, attacking New Labour Britain. Was the Labour home secretary lining up with the right-wing critics of *The Future of Multi-Ethnic Britain*? Not in so many words, yet it was unsurprising that the New Labour government heeded the traditionally Conservative broadsheet, the *Daily Telegraph*, not to mention the populist *Sun* and conservative Middle England's favourite tabloid, the *Daily Mail*. True to form, a *Sun* leader on the 12 October castigated Straw for not distancing himself enough from 'the ludicrous "British is racist" report'.

On 11 October, the *Daily Mail* had a field day. Its banner headline on the front page made all the necessary connections: 'The flashy vacuity of the Dome, the trashy icons of Cool Britannia … and now the idea that to be British is racist. This is a government that knows nothing of our history and cares about it even less.' Inside that issue of the paper, under the heading 'Racism slur on the word "British"', Edward Heathcoat Amory and Gordon Rayner (2000: 6) listed and described the Runnymede Trust's 'panel' members. Included, for instance, were Professor Stuart Hall – 'One of the best-known class warriors of the Sixties and Seventies' – and commission vice-chair Kate Gavron – 'Third wife of millionaire publisher and Labour benefactor Lord "Bob" Gavron'. There was also a piece by a member of the Commission for Racial Equality, Dr Raj Chandran (2000: 7), a Sri Lankan Tamil in origin, who defended Britishness from the slur of racism and extolled Britain's history of tolerance towards others: 'So why rewrite British history in order to junk this proud heritage?'

The point about history was picked up in Paul Johnson's (2000: 12) article 'In Praise of Being British': 'Britain, unlike many European nations, has a long tradition of unbiased, objective and truthful historical writing, avoiding propaganda and hagiography, and not fearing to criticise the ruling elite where necessary.' The *Mail*'s leader on the same page also emphasised the issue of history and, in its headline, accused the Parekh Report of insulting Britain's past and the intelligence of its people.

Insults were a common feature of the Parekh Report's reception in the press, perhaps the worst of which appeared in the 'satirical' *Private Eye* on 20 October. The first of three boxed items here was headed 'Who Are They? The Great and Good Who Make Up the Runnynose Commission, Authors of *Britain Don't You Hate It? The Future of Multiculture*'. It renamed and described the members of the commission, such as: 'CHAIR Lord Hoohi, lecturer in anti-British studies at the University of Humberside (formerly Grimsby Polytechnic); Mrs Pashmina Ali-Baba Brown, Columnist on racial discrimination for the Racial Discrimination Section of The Indescribably Boring [the *Independent*]; and, Professor Adolf Wong, Lecturer in Positive

State Censorship at the Chow Mein Kampf Institute, Sunningdale' (*Private Eye*, 2000: 19). Another box on the same page, entitled 'That Runnymede Trust History of the Country Formerly Known as Britain', began '1948 AD BRITAIN first discovered by Afro-Caribbean explorers on their ship the Empire Windrush'. Ho, ho, very satirical.

You might have expected right-wing newspapers like the *Mail* and *Telegraph* in daily and Sunday editions to be hostile towards the Parekh Report. Less predictable was the critical response it elicited from the Left–Liberal broadsheets, the *Guardian* and the *Observer*. In its front-page headline on 11 October, the *Guardian* followed the *Daily Telegraph*'s lead: 'British tag is "coded racism".' It quoted from the offending passage in the Parekh Report that is quoted at greater length at the beginning of this chapter. This was picked up in the leader column on page 21, where it was said that the Report's 'prescription for harmony ... is spoilt by a bad idea'. On the following Sunday, in the *Observer*, Will Hutton (2000) reiterated this objection at some length. He accused Lord Parekh of being 'silly', which was not the nastiest epithet applied to the Runnymede Commission's chair and principal author of the report on multi-ethnic Britain. To be fair, however, Hutton also complained of the sensational misrepresentation of the Parekh Report in the press. He argued that 'the racial connotations' of Britishness are probably true but do not actually constitute the inflamatory claim that Britishness is necessarily 'racist'. In the same issue of the *Observer*, Stuart Hall (2000) made exactly the same point. Bhikhu Parekh was also permitted to defend the Report in both the *Guardian* (Parekh, 2000a) and the *Telegraph* (Parekh, 2000b), for which latter he received considerable support in letters to the paper. Parekh made it quite clear that rethinking Britain as 'a community of communities' did not mean abolishing the State or outlawing the word 'British'. Nevertheless, the damage had been done swiftly and, yet again, public debate was distorted by perverse misrepresentation in the news media.

The Report itself

A striking feature of the Parekh Report, *The Future of Multi-Ethnic Britain*, is its elegant combination of advanced thinking in the social sciences – including cultural studies, political theory and sociology – with a slate of practical policy proposals.

The Report is divided into three parts. The first part is the most abstractly theoretical, elaborating on a number of linked themes in formulating 'A Vision for Britain'. The second part, 'Issues and Institutions', surveys concrete matters in the areas of policing, criminal justice, education, arts, media and sport, health and welfare, employment, immigration and asylum, politics and representation, and religion and belief. The third part, 'Strategies of Change', makes a series of specific recommendations.

The Report addresses terminological problems in what is undoubtedly a minefield of potentially explosive words, particularly rejecting the use of 'minorities' because it implies marginality and the existence of a homogeneous majority at the centre, which is not historically so. The British Isles have had a long history of conquest, migration and the mixing of peoples and cultures well before the post-Second World War immigration from the former Empire and Commonwealth. This emphasis on heterogeneity in the very make-up of Britain over many centuries is no doubt offensive to those who would like to uphold an essential Britishness. For them, the unity of Britain is not only threatened today by devolution on the Celtic fringe but also undermined by the comparatively recent arrival of alien cultures brought by economic migrants and, yet more worryingly at present, asylum seekers. There has also been a disturbing growth of Islamophobia in response to recent events that are of global but also national significance.

According to Parekh and the Runnymede Trust's Commission on the Future of Multi-Ethnic Britain, the country has reached a 'turning point' in its history. Britain is at a 'crossroads' where choices as to direction have to be made. These alternatives are stated as a set of binary oppositions: 'static/ dynamic; intolerant/cosmopolitan; fearful/generous; insular/internationalist; authoritarian/democratic; introspective/outward-looking; punitive/inclusive; myopic/far-sighted' (Runnymede Trust, 2000: 4). The second terms in these binaries represent the fresh vision for Britain that is proposed by the Parekh Report: dynamism, cosmopolitanism, generosity, internationalism, democracy, looking outwards, inclusive and far-sighted.

The dominant terms still need to be deconstructed. Britain was, in effect, invented in the eighteenth century with the construction of the United Kingdom. Its values were contrasted with the traditional foe, Catholic and then Republican France. That this 'imagined community' was an historical invention makes its reinvention at a later moment in history a serious proposition. Now, it should be possible to reinvent Britain as 'a community of communities' that does not have to depend on older national and imperial myths. These are increasingly irrelevant in any case. Britain is a multicultural society but this does not mean, as Parekh has argued consistently in his many writings (see Parekh, 1999, for instance), that its policies are multiculturalist. It is desirable, then, to go beyond 'multicultural drift' and develop 'conscious policies' of multiculturalism.

In Chapter 2 of the Report, 'Rethinking the National Story', the components of 'the dominant version' of the traditionally 'imagined community' are itemised. The widespread belief that Britain has been unified for a very long time is simply wrong, it states. The idea that Britishness is evenly diffused throughout the United Kingdom is also untrue. English experience has largely stood for Britishness in a way that is unacceptable and no longer credible. Moreover, the British are not best thought of as an island race set apart from the rest of Europe and the world. Anti-Catholic and anti-Irish sentiment and imperial power may have been unifying, though always seriously questionable, forces in the past but they do not refer to a present reality. Furthermore, 'The role-call of traditional British virtues – tolerance, moderation, readiness to compromise, fair play, individualism, love of freedom, eccentricity, ironic detachment, emotional reticence [etc.]' (Runnymede Trust, 2000: 23) is far too complacent.

The legacy of the Empire carries with it the trace of white supremacy. The British Empire has gone and Britain is situated at a much more complicated intersection of global processes. Britain was never so internally unified as the dominant version of the country assumes. In one way or another, too, it has become more open to the rest of the world. There are enormous implications for identity in 'a complex, shifting multicultural reality' (2000: 27). The cultures of host and migrant communities are in reciprocal relation to one another. A great many people feel that they do not have a single and fixed identity. Multiple identities are commonplace. This has implications for how community relations are conceptualised. It is mistaken to regard ethnic communities as entirely separated from one another, as utterly distinct entities. Instead, they interact quite routinely in various ways, setting up channels of mutuality as well as hostility. There is a constant play of similarity and difference.

The key problem is how to achieve satisfactory cohesion, genuine equality and respect for difference. The Parekh Report identifies five models: procedural, nationalist, liberal, plural and separatist. Neither the first nor the fifth of these models are realistic to follow, which does not mean they cannot exist. Proceduralism assumes that the State is a neutral arbiter without cultural preference. No state, however, is actually indifferent to the customs and practices of its society. At the further extreme, complete separation of cultural communities is the end of the State and any sense of shared national belonging. The solution must be somewhere in between. Only nationalism, liberalism and pluralism can be seriously considered for the sake of cohesion, equality and difference.

The nationalist model promotes a single, unified national culture. This has already been deconstructed with regard to the multinational structure of the United Kingdom – encompassing England, Scotland, Wales and Northern Ireland – and the sheer diversity of communities within it. The liberal model partly overcomes this problem by insisting on a single political culture in the public sphere while acknowledging the diversity of cultures in the private sphere. The liberal model is also unsatisfactory, though, because, as the Parekh Report argues, the diversity of cultures should be represented with greater symbolic force in the public sphere. This is the 'community of communities' model of Britishness advocated by the Parekh Report (2000: 56): 'Britain needs to be, certainly, "One Nation" – but understood as a community of communities and a community of citizens, not a place of oppressive uniformity based on a single substantive culture.'

For the Parekh Report, it is vital to be clear about the principles underpinning an actively multiculturalist society in order to combat the various racisms that persist in Britain. The Report makes what has become a conventional distinction between biological racism and cultural racism.

There still are traces of nineteenth-century biological racism across the range of present-day racisms, yet cultural racism is by far the most insidious problem now. Respectable racism is enunciated typically today by cultural arguments that may be relativistic, as we shall see in the discussion of Samuel Huntington's (1996) 'clash of civilizations' thesis later in this chapter.

The Parekh Report distinguishes between 'overt racism' and 'street racism' on the one hand and 'institutional racism' on the other. Overt forms of racism certainly persist, and are stressful and, indeed, dangerous for the victims, especially in conditions of deprivation. Poverty and resentment are often closely associated with racial violence. They occasionally lead to fierce confrontation, even in a relatively harmonious country such as Britain.

Yet more complex and harder to deal with are forms of racism that may be unintentional but are manifestly evident in institutional processes throughout British society. The notion of institutional racism, long known to sociologists, was revived and given much greater public attention by *The Stephen Lawrence Inquiry* (MacPherson, 1999). The Metropolitan Police were found to have been negligent, both on the night when the young black man Stephen Lawrence was attacked and in the subsequent investigation into his murder. The police officers involved had mistakenly assumed that Lawrence was involved in a fight rather than having been set upon out of the blue by a group of racists. The police also failed to put a successful case together against the suspects. Behind the police's action was a set of taken-for-granted assumptions about young black men that amounted to an institutionalised form of racism in policing that is not necessarily intentional but deeply embedded in routine practices.

According to the Parekh Report, 'unwittingness' is not an adequate justification and solutions to the problem of institutional racism must go beyond 'race awareness' training for police officers and other professionals. Moreover, 'colourblindness' in public policy and practice is not good enough. Different groups are treated in different ways, the specificity of which always needs to be understood and acted on. Britain should observe international standards of human rights as a minimum requirement for achieving a more just society and these must be supported by specific policies for eradicating racism.

The theoretical part of the Parekh Report (2000: 105, 107) concludes with the identification of five urgent tasks:

1. 'reimagining Britain's past story and present identity'
2. 'balancing equality and difference, liberty and cohesion'
3. 'confronting and eliminating racisms'
4. 'reducing material inequalities'
5. 'building a human rights culture'.

The second part of the Parekh Report addresses practical matters, from criminal justice to religion and belief. Here, I shall just concentrate on what it has to say about the arts, media and sport as its views on cultural policy might otherwise be neglected for the more urgent issues of, say, policing and asylum.

Evidence is given of what might amount to institutional racism in terms of exclusion in the fields of art, media and sport. For instance, only 0.2 per cent of the first £2 billion of National Lottery funding for the arts was spent on black and Asian artists (2000: 161).

There is still plenty of evidence of misrepresentation or non-representation of African, Asian, Caribbean and Irish communities in the media. Sports participation is also very uneven, with many evident forms of exclusion, such as exclusion of Asian footballers. Policy statements from New Labour's Department for Culture, Media and Sport place very little emphasis on cultural diversity and social inclusion. Furthermore, the higher echelons of public cultural administration and privately owned media and cultural organisations remain almost exclusively white, with a few notable exceptions. No doubt, there have been positive responses to these claims and attempts at a melioration since the Parekh Report was published that are testament to its impact. Nevertheless, such changes even where they are actively sought tend to be painfully slow.

Clearly, the arts, media and sport are key to reworking the national story in terms of representation and participation, raising a great many issues concerning the canon, funding and employment. The success of black footballers should not distract from the many forms of exclusion that still exist. The Parekh Report is replete with practical proposals and recommendations for addressing these and other issues.

The practical recommendations are framed by seven general principles (Runnymede Trust, 2000: 296–7):

1. 'three central concepts: cohesion, equality and difference'
2. 'demonstrable change at all levels'
3. 'addressing racisms'
4. 'tackling disadvantage'
5. 'colourblind approaches do not work'
6. 'empowering and franchising'
7. 'a pluralistic culture of human rights'.

'Clash of civilizations' or 'community of communities'?

The Parekh Report is not just a policy-orientated expression of Bhikhu Parekh's ideas on multiculturalism – other members of the Runnymede Commission on the Future of Multi-Ethnic Britain made important contributions individually and collectively. Any student of cultural studies and sociology, for instance, will no doubt recognise the contribution of Stuart Hall on questions of identity. Nevertheless, the Report is very much consistent with Parekh's own thinking, which has been given its fullest theoretical articulation in his great treatise *Rethinking Multiculturalism* (2000c).

It is instructive to compare the Parekh position with that of Samuel Huntington who has also published a major treatise, *The Clash of Civilizations and the Remaking of World Order* (1996). Huntington's thesis was first announced in the American journal *Foreign Affairs* in 1993. In that article, he put a question mark against the title, 'The Clash of Civilizations?' By the time the book was published three years later, the question mark had been removed. The following year, Huntington published an article summarising his thesis in the British magazine *Prospect* under the title 'The West and the Rest'. This article provides a rather more benign version of the thesis than the book. To find out what Huntington is really saying, it is essential to address the book-length version, especially its concluding chapter, 'The West, Civilizations and Civilization'. The clash of civilisations thesis is the successor to Francis Fukuyama's (1989 and 1992) 'end of history' thesis. It was cited widely after 9/11. Huntington's thesis makes a similar argument to Benjamin Barber's *Jihad vs. McWorld* (1996 [1995]), but rather more comprehensively and, ultimately, yet more scarily.

According to Huntington (1996: 20), 'culture and cultural identities, which at the broadest level are civilizational identities, are shaping the patterns of cohesion, disintegration and conflict in the post-Cold War world'. We now live in a 'multipolar and multicivilizational world'. The main source of international tension after the collapse of communism, in his scheme of things, is culture — that is, civilisational differences — and not economic interest or political ideology.

Huntington argues for the greater explanatory power of his 'civilizational paradigm' over the four extant paradigms of international relations: 'one world', 'us and them', '184 states, more or less' and 'sheer chaos'. Civilisations are made up of a number of elements: religion, 'race', comprehensiveness, longevity and cultural rather than political identity. The most important, Huntington maintains, is religion and this is uppermost, yet not always congruently so, in his identification of seven or eight civilisations in the world.

The first civilisation is Sinic, in which Confucianism is prominent. Although many scholars would include Japanese civilisation in the Sinic category, Huntington does not. In his opinion, it is a distinctive offshoot of Chinese civilisation, so distinctive historically that it must be seen as separate. No mention here that Japan is capitalist and China still nominally communist.

The third civilisation identified by Huntington is Hindu, the fourth, Islamic, the fifth, Western, the sixth, Latin American, the seventh, Orthodox. Finally, eighth, somewhat reluctantly, Huntington sees African as possibly a separate civilisation despite its northern relation to Islam and southern relation to Western Christendom.

I want now to consider three problems with Huntington's clash of civilisations thesis that reveal the questionable nature of his domain assumptions. They are to do with religion, cultural racism and Western identity. Huntington's emphasis on values and their grounding in religion — whether as strength of belief or trace of belief – underplays the role of material interests. It is material interests – diffusely those of the West and, rather more concretely, those related to the particular interests of the United States – that are implicit in his general argument.

For instance, Huntington seeks to resolve the issue of Europeanness by equating it with Christendom, thus demarcating Europe along the fault line with Islam and, more perplexingly, with Eastern Orthodoxy, so that Turkey's claim to European community membership is questioned and even Greece cannot be properly regarded as European. The equation, made by Huntington, of Europe with historical Christendom is consistent with the critique of Europeanness from the point of view of the excluded and marginalised, yet the implication of his argument is to justify exclusion.

Huntington is much concerned with the issue of migration. The influx of Muslims into Europe and – again perplexingly – Hispanics into the USA may give rise to what he calls (1996: 204) 'cleft societies encompassing two distinct and largely separate communities from two different civilizations, which in turn depend on the number of immigrants and the extent to which they are assimilated into Western cultures prevailing in Europe and America'.

That these are already 'cleft societies' which need reconfiguring is not Huntington's view: far from it. The problem, as he sees it, is one of assimilation; and, if not assimilation, then what? Exclusion? This seems to be the deeper implication of Huntington's superficially reasonable argument.

The general position enunciated by Huntington is culturally racist. It is the kind of position that allowed Enoch Powell's apologists to deny that he was a racist. Apparently, Powell did not believe that Asian and Caribbean immigrants to Britain during the 1960s were necessarily inferior beings; he just did not want them diluting Englishness.

Similarly, Huntington makes no claims concerning the superiority of Western civilisation and, like a good postmodernist, he rejects any universalistic pretensions associated with its values, such as democracy and equality, or anything of that sort. In fact, Huntington argues strenuously that the West should not interfere in other civilisations. The Rest should be left to deal with their own problems. The West may have institutionalised modernisation but modernisation and Westernisation are not the same. In the later phases of modernisation among the Rest, Huntington observes, it is common for anti-Westernisation to arise.

At home, of course, it is important to protect the integrity of Western culture and civilisation by, according to Huntington, fighting off the multiculturalists that have done so much to undermine the American way of life. He (1996: 304) is concerned about 'problems of moral decline, cultural suicide, and political disunity in the West'. In fact, Huntington makes his position and concerns abundantly clear in a passage towards the end of *The Clash of Civilizations and the Remaking of World Order* (1996: 305):

Western culture is challenged by groups within Western societies. One such challenge comes from immigrants from other civilizations who reject assimilation and continue to adhere to and propagate the values, customs, and cultures of their home societies. The phenomenon is most notable among Muslims in Europe, who are, however, a small minority. It is also manifest, in lesser degree, among Hispanics in the United States, who are a large minority. If assimilationism fails in this case the United States will become a cleft country, with all the potential for internal strife and disunion that entails. In Europe, Western civilization could also be undermined by the weakening of its central component, Christianity.

Huntington wants to resist what he calls the 'siren calls of multiculturalism', which he sees as particularly characterised by the undermining of a culture of individual rights by the myriad calls for collective rights – not only to do with 'race' and ethnicity but also sex and sexuality.

Huntington's position, despite his arguments concerning non-interference, is not, strictly speaking, confined to splendid isolationism and resistance to multiculturalism in the USA and the defence of apostolic Christianity in Europe. The USA has a much larger geopolitical role than that to perform. In alliance with Europe, he argues, there should be more integration between Western states, the Catholic countries of Eastern Europe should be included in the West, and Latin America should be Westernised. China and Japan should be kept apart. Russia should be recognised as 'the core state of Orthodoxy' and 'Western technological and military superiority over other civilizations' should be maintained while, somehow, the West should avoid destabilisation by refraining from interference in other civilisations. It is a sobering thought that this position was to the Left of the second Bush regime's theory and practice in American foreign policy.

It is also worth noting how the kind of cultural relativism that tends to characterise postmodernism can be given such a conservative inflection by the likes of Samuel Huntington, whose message seems to be, you can hang on to your cultures so long as we can purify ours. The implications for multiculturalism in Western societies are clear: either assimilate Western ways or go away. Such thinking, taken to its logical conclusion, might imagine a gigantic programme of repatriation. Where would it stop? At the New England Puritans, perhaps? To be sure, Huntington is defending the indefensible or even the non-existent – a fixed Western identity when, in fact, identity is in flux and all the better for it.

It has to be said that Huntington's position on cultural identity has a certain resonance in non-Western cultures where the project, for some, is to maintain tradition and restore indigenous identity in the face of the ravages of globalising modernity, driven by neoliberalism and fast communications. The defence of cultural purity is an impossible as well as a perilous project, whether in the West or in the Rest. While globalising modernity is in many ways destructive and on a number of counts needs to be challenged, it may also herald the prospect of greater democratisation of life.

Huntington's canvas is the world; Parekh's is Britain. When looked at closely, however, it is evident that Huntington's reasoning is preoccupied by

Western concerns from a distinctly North American perspective and, specifically, what he considers to be the interests of the USA. Parekh's work is concerned with making multiculturalism in Britain work. It is finely tuned to the specific features of that location, but in an international comparative framework (Parekh, 1997).

An appreciation of local specificity and complexity is necessary wherever you look in the world. The differences, then, between Huntington and Parekh are not reducible to a global framework in one case and a national framework in the other case. The differences are much deeper than that. The nation state still matters despite accelerated globalisation. Citizenship rights remain secured, for the most part, at the national level, qualified to some extent by internationally recognised human rights.

Parekh's position is not faultless. His attempt to reconcile liberal and individualistic rights with collective and communal rights may be queried; and, he may have too sanguine a view of the Canadian resolution where francophone Quebec has become a virtual state within the largely anglophone state of Canada. It is reasonable, however, to expect the future to become increasingly hybrid in political, cultural and personal composition. If there was ever a site of actually existing and potentially greater hybridity, surely it is the State system and network of reciprocal relations that traverse the British Isles, encompassing a diverse range of territories and cultures.

The Parekh Report was criticised for failing to solve the liberalism/collectivism problem, manifest in the fact that its policy recommendations in the main do not transcend the liberal problematic of discrimination (Barry, 2001). It has also been criticised for attending insufficiently to actual communities in Britain and representing predominantly professional, managerial interests (Seaford, 2001). Such criticisms must be taken into account in a continuing dialogue over multiculturalism in Britain. In the particular context of debate, however, these criticisms may perhaps be regarded as carping.

The Parekh Report elicited enormous hostility from the media, thereby poisoning its prospects for widespread public understanding and action. This was especially disturbing at a time when asylum seekers were also being demonised and treated badly by the government.

In a less immediate context, the value of the Report's position is pointed up sharply by comparison with Huntington's position. Is the difference between them just that of woolly-minded idealism versus a grim realism? The truth of the matter is that the thinking behind Huntington's clash of civilizations thesis is deeply unrealistic, though it may provide a spurious 'explanation' for lazy minds of events such as 9/11, though not so easily the USA and Britain's 2003 assault on Iraq. The economic and political tensions in the world today are not reducible to cultural differences, however. In any case, Huntington concocts an extraordinarily schematic and simplistic typology of civilisations. A hundred holes can be picked in it and motives for its blindspots and inconsistencies readily discerned. Where does Judaism fit into this scheme of things? What differentiates Catholic and Hispanic Latin America from Western Christendom other than economics and politics?

The trouble is, this stuff is taken seriously. The defence of an essential Britishness is as lacking in historical foundation and plausibility as the wish to win back an uncontaminated Western civilisation from the incursion of Others. What do we want, a clash of civilisations or a community of communities? This is not only a national question but a global one. German social theorist Jürgen Habermas (1999: [1996]: xxxv–xxxvi) sums up what is at stake rather well:

> Equal respect for everyone is not limited to those who are like us; it extends to the person of the other in his or her otherness. And solidarity with the other as one of us refers to the flexible 'we' of a community that resists all substantive determination and extends its permeable boundaries even further. This moral community constitutes itself solely by way of the negative idea of abolishing discrimination and harm and of extending relations of mutual recognition to include marginalized men and women. The community thus constructively outlined is not a collective that would force its homogenized members to affirm its distinctiveness. Here inclusion does not mean locking members into a community that closes itself off from others. The 'inclusion of the other' means rather that the boundaries of community are open for all, also and most especially for those who are strangers to one another and want to remain strangers.

Relating these broad principles and generalisations to the present discussion, questions of shared identity and multicultural heritage should not be treated in isolation from recognition and respect for difference throughout the world. Across the globe, there are national, local and transnational forces at work in a complex exchange of cultures. The hostile response to the Parekh Report in the media and among politicians gave vent to an outdated isolationism and self-regard in the British imaginary. Multiculturalism needs to transcend such narrowly nationalistic terms of debate in favour of open-minded cosmopolitanism.

5 IDENTITY AND THE CRISIS OF COMMUNITY

Britain, Britain, Britain, land of technological achievement. We have had running water for over ten years, an underground tunnel that links us to Peru and we invented the cat. None of these innovations would have been possible were it not for the people of Britain. And, it is those people we do look at today. Let's do it.

Prologue to the first BBC Television episode of
Little Britain, 2003, BBC DVD 2005

Introduction – *Little Britain*

Little Britain – which is very much an English product – was one of the most successful series on British television in the mid-2000s, as measured by critical acclaim, industry awards and viewing figures of around 11 million at the height of the show's popularity. These are not the highest viewing figures for a British-made and televised programme in this period. The long-running soap operas *Coronation Street* and *EastEnders* – both set nostalgically in 'traditional' working-class areas of England, North and South respectively – battled it out in the recent past for top spot with viewing figures that reached 18 million at their peak. Similarly high viewing figures, with the possible exception of royal weddings and funerals, are now only achieved by football matches featuring the England team in major competitions, especially the World Cup. That, perhaps, is the most significant expression – possibly the sole genuinely significant *mass popular* expression – of English national identity today.

Popular culture is not just a matter of numbers, viewing figures and the like, though. It is also qualitative, articulating a shared sensibility. *Little Britain* has been described as a 'cult' show. The viewing figures suggest, however, that it is more than merely the expression of a cult following. This immensely successful comedy captured a mood that is arguably symptomatic of deep-seated attitudes and feelings that are widespread in the British population.

Little Britain was launched deliberately and, in a sense, artificially by the BBC as a 'cult' show, but a basic definition of 'cult' in the sociology of religion goes as follows: 'a small, flexible group whose religion is characterised by its individualism, syncretism and frequently esoteric belief' (Abercrombie et al., 2000: 81). The audience for *Little Britain* is clearly not a religious cult in that sense; nor is it a cult in the broader sense of belonging to a group with eccentric taste on the margins of society, so why was it described thus?

In the entertainment business today, 'cult' has become little more than a marketing category that is meant to suggest to a mainstream public that they are in on an esoteric culture. The term 'cult' in this context can no longer be taken to refer to an actual culture and principle of identification associated with small minorities of advanced opinion and sensibility on the margins of the mainstream, as it might have done in the fairly recent past with regard to what used to be called 'alternative comedy' (see Hall, 2006, for a useful though uncritical survey of 'cult comedy' in contemporary Britain).

Like many previous and non-cult BBC comedies since the 1950s, *Little Britain* began unremarkably on radio – the 'posh' Radio 4 in this case – and transferred to television on the digital channel, BBC Three which had a relatively small audience reach at the time, then via BBC Two, on to mass popularity on BBC One. The programme's eventual mainstream popularity was built up artfully and patiently as though it was coming from the margins, appearing initially on channels with much lower audience figures than BBC One, its punctual destination on television and window displays for the yet more lucrative live touring show (Barrell, 2006).

The prologue to the first televised episode, quoted at the beginning of this chapter, sets the tone for the show – extremely silly and, therefore, harmless, such as having running water for only ten years and the tunnel to Peru, not to mention inventing the cat. The voiceover narration by Tom Baker, an ex-Doctor Who, parodies BBC English, thereby underlining the populist mode of address that characterises *Little Britain*. This version of the nation, then, is quite definitely neither serious nor intellectual. Some might say it appeals to 'the lowest common denominator', in an old elitist phrase.

Each episode contains as many as 15 sketches of approximately 2 minutes each to fit into the 30-minute programme slot without advertisements on the still publicly funded BBC. These sketches are focused on recurring characters and places, identities and communities: the disabled Andy and Lou, his carer, living on benefits in a dreary townscape; Vicky Pollard, 'a sort of teenage delinquent character' (Matt Lucas) facing up to authority figures in the urban environment (teachers, swimming pool attendants, judges and so on); Dafydd Thomas, ostensibly the only gay in his Welsh village; Marjorie Dawes and her abused Fatfighters class; the inhabitants of old people's homes and hospitals for the physically and mentally ill; and so on. There is a good deal of cross-dressing and play with gender and gendering. The whole show, it has to be acknowledged, is framed by a 'queer' sensibility. From the point of view of identity and community, Dafydd is always protesting that he is 'the only gay in the village', a rural setting that might have been expected to be backwoods homophobic but is actually not at all so: the place is full of gays. Simple catchphrases, often considered one of the lowliest tricks of comedy (satirised possibly in response to *Little Britain* by 'Are you having a laugh?' of the BBC sitcom *Extras*), are a key feature of the programme, such as Vicky's incoherent 'yes but, no but' when she is accused of something that transgresses civilised conduct.

Little Britain is a disconcerting programme in the way that it breaks the taboos of 'political correctness', stereotyping and ridiculing a vast array of people with its scatter-gun approach: the disabled, the elderly, the working-class young, blacks and Asians, the overweight, to list but a few. Even its treatment of homosexuals, transsexuals and cross-dressers might be construed as negative, especially regarding some favourite targets of humorous abuse. Dafydd's complaint is, in effect, against a multinational state ('Britain') – including rural Wales – in which homophobia has been eradicated and where people like him need no longer feel stigmatised and lonely. At the very least, there is a deeply complacent perception of popular attitudes, seen from a 'cool' North London and metropolitan liberal-elitist perspective, behind the repetitive catchphrase, 'I'm the only gay in the village'.

To be sure, it is all meant to be deeply ironic in a postmodern manner, just a flight of grotesque imagination. Different audience members will no doubt read the programme in different ways. In any case, Matt Lucas and David Walliams – the authors, and stars of *Little Britain* – are only having a laugh, displaying a characteristically English insouciance. In spite of the misgivings there must necessarily be about *Little Britain*, the television industry has showered plaudits, including British Academy of Film and Television Awards (BAFTAs), on the programme and even an episode of Melvyn Bragg's prestigious ITV arts programme *The South Bank Show* was devoted to praising its innovative comedy.

There are critics, however, who have gone against the hubbub of praise, most notably the *Independent*'s columnist Johann Hari. To quote from his ironic commentary on *Little Britain* (Hari, 2005: 35):

> Let me tell you a hilarious joke. The other day, I saw an incontinent old woman in a supermarket, and she pissed herself. OK, here's another. I saw a man get up out of his wheelchair, and he was so mentally disabled he just walked into a wall. Wait, I know this might kill you but there's one more. I saw a teenage single mum who was wearing a shell-suit and she was so thick she barely knew her own name. And she had three children. Did I mention she was thick? And fat? And spotty? Did I say she lived on benefits?

It is not insignificant, according to Hari, that Lucas and Walliams both come from well-to-do backgrounds (Lucas went to a famous public – that is, private and fee-paying – school) when noting how they have made ridicule of the poor and disadvantaged respectable once more. Hari also went on the Internet to check out what the most committed fans of *Little Britain* were saying. Many of them were sharing jokes about 'the underclass'. In conclusion, Hari posed a serious question: 'what does it say about us that we are a nation that pines for gags about stupid, poor people and old women pissing themselves in public?'

Interestingly, *Little Britain* has not targeted Muslims, which would, of course, be too controversial and quite possibly inflammatory after 9/11 and 7/7 (the 2005 suicide bombings of the London Underground and a double-decker bus). *Little Britain*, like Islamic 'terror', prefers soft targets.

Following on from the prologue of *Little Britain,* in this chapter, I want to open up questions about identity and what might be considered a 'crisis' of community in present-day Britain by examining the complexity of the nomination, 'the United Kingdom of Great Britain and Northern Ireland', the problem of Englishness, Britain's positioning in relation to the so-called 'clash of civilizations' and policy proposals for an actively *multiculturalist* Britain where different communities might live in peace with one another.

The disunited kingdom

The nationality of British citizens, according to their European Union passports, is 'UK'. Nobody, however, really identifies with the 'Yookay' as a nationality (Williams, 1985 [1983]). Britons may call themselves 'English', 'Scottish', 'Welsh' or, in the six counties of the North of Ireland that are still under British rule, some might actually call themselves 'Irish'; others there will call themselves 'British'. The English, the Scots and the Welsh are also British. The United Kingdom, then, is a multinational state that functions in terms of identity merely as an official label, not as an identification. It is now commonplace to say that identities are multiple and in process, not singular and essential. This is fundamental to any sense of national identity in the 'British Isles', with the possible exception of the Southern Irish.

As Benedict Anderson (2006 [1983]) pointed out so acutely, a nation is an 'imagined community'. You will never meet most of your co-nationals, so you have to imagine something that you have in common with all these strangers. The media, then, are vital in the task of establishing the sense of an imagined community among a population in a nationally defined space.

According to Anderson, the print media were crucial to establishing a modern sense of national identity all around the world. The national press is more important in Britain than the local and regional press. Since the 1920s, in addition to the press, broadcasting has been crucial to framing national identity for the British.

Until the 1950s, broadcasting in Britain was largely confined to BBC radio and then television. Commercial broadcasting, satellite communications, transnational media and so on have since opened nations up to a much wider range of representations and possible identifications (including 'American') on a scale only ever previously approached by religions.

Christianity and Islam have and do both transcend nations and offer another compelling point of identification in addition to national self-identity. Still, however, national broadcasting matters and it remains an arena of collective imagining. Hence, the significance of the BBC's *Little Britain*, which may be just as important as the news in addressing the nation and featuring in something like a cultural public sphere (see Chapter 1).

Historians have researched the complexities of national identity in the British Isles in recent years, paying special attention to the problem of Englishness (for instance, Colley, 1992; Colls, 2002; Kumar, 2003; Samuel, 1998). Britain has been the site of multiple migrations since the Roman conquest 2000 years ago. The Celts moved West, the Angles, Saxons, Normans and others moved in. Wars were waged between the Anglo-Saxons and what we would now call the Irish, Scots and Welsh. The Norman Conquest of 1066 was the last successful invasion; for hundreds of years the ruling class spoke French while the populace's language was more Germanic (see Crystal, 2004). The languages fused together to give us something like modern English, which is, for the great majority, the language of the Irish, Scottish and Welsh.

There have been various attempts at a Gaelic revival and resistance to English. Since De Valera's government of the 1930s, the Republic of Ireland has had Irish as well as English placenames on its signposts. More recently, in Wales, the Welsh language has similarly doubled up with English. These language revivals have had some success but they have failed to overturn the hegemony of English in the British Isles.

While there are longstanding ethnic differences in Britain, 'ethnic minority' today usually refers to immigrant communities from the Commonwealth, the former Empire, which included the Indian subcontinent, much of Africa and the Caribbean, as well as countries like Australia, Canada and New Zealand, whose indigenous peoples have not tended to migrate to Britain (interestingly, migrants from Eastern Europe, like 'white' Commonwealth migrants, are defined typically as 'nationalities' instead of 'ethnicities'). Now, in mainland Britain, it is routine for public communications (from, say, schools to parents) with Asian Britons to be in their own native languages as well as English. There is no real debate over whether Britain is a *multicultural* society or not: it is and has been for quite sometime, going back into the mists of history well beyond post-Second World War migration. Whether or not it is a harmonious *multiculturalist* society is another issue.

Britain has adopted American hyphenation, so we have Asian-British, Black-British and so forth. Seldom have the hyphenated nominations included English, though this seems to be changing.

As we shall see, Englishness is the most problematic identity, so hollowed is it in the wake of the Empire and its declining dominance in the British Isles. Historically, it dominated the British Isles and commanded the union of 1707 that came up with the designation the 'United Kingdom of Great Britain' and later included 'Ireland'.

During the eighteenth century, as Linda Colley (1992) has documented, a sense of Britishness was constructed against the Other of Frenchness. According to this binary opposition, the British had men with 'hearts of oak' and were plain-speaking Protestants. French men were effete, weak and obfuscating Catholics or downright irreligious. National stereotypes are constructed thus, particularly when there has been a history of warring enmity, exacerbated by the contest for colonies in the eighteenth century. The French were the traditional foe, only to be displaced by the Germans in the twentieth century and, after the Second World War, the Russians.

The enemy now seems to be Islam – a religion not a country. When the Bush regime yoked together al Qaida and the irreligious Saddam Hussein in its 'war on terror', the British government followed suit. Tony Blair, prime minister at the time of the second Gulf war, the 2003 invasion and subsequent occupation of Iraq, was widely derided as George Bush's poodle. Of course, the British had been there before and had actually created Iraq as a 'protectorate' back in the 1920s.

It is important to appreciate that Britain hangs between America and Europe, the USA and the EU – not quite a full member of either. The market reforms initiated by Margaret Thatcher in the 1980s and carried forward with enthusiasm by the New Labour government from 1997 into the 2000s became known on the European Continent, particularly among social democrats, as 'the Anglo-Saxon model'. More broadly speaking, the whole world is subjected to the sway of the US national imaginary through its entertainment industry, including Britain. At times it does not seem to be an exaggeration for critics of American hegemony to call Britain 'the fifty-first state'. In world affairs, Britain's standing is really rather low – 'Little Britain' – but not so low as it would be without 'the special relationship' afforded by the USA. This is a deep and abiding problem for a country that once commanded the most extensive empire in the world.

To be fair, though, the British are capable of laughing at themselves, cherishing the harmlessly popular and, on occasion, even probing their doubts and uncertainties. At London's Millennium Dome exposition in the year 2000, situated on the Thames and dominated by the Anglo-Saxon model of commercial speech and economic machination, one of the most interesting zones was Self Portrait, sponsored by Marks & Spencer. The zone did not, of course, enquire into its sponsor's financial crisis that was being relieved by turning to outsourced product from cheap labour markets around the world. As an associative sponsor of the old school, however, Marks & Spencer permitted a certain creative freedom within its zone. Self Portrait was not an especially popular zone but visitors, like good Brits, as is their wont, did queue on the way in. This was in order to read cards extolling the best of British – from *Sergeant Pepper's Lonely Hearts Club Band* to the Imam Khoesi Islamic Centre – sent in by members of the public from around the country. Inside Self Portrait there were placards, largely inspired by Mark Leonard's (1997) *BritainTM* pamphlet, boasting about Britain's great attributes: 'creativity', 'diversity', 'fair play', 'humour', 'inventiveness' and so forth. The placards were juxtaposed with Gerald Scarfe's caricature statues, such as 'Bootman', a football hooligan with a boot for a head and the apparently respectable 'Racist'. There was also a 'couch potato', about to be engulfed by vomit from his television set, beside the notice 'British culture – how many of us sit lazily in front of our televisions, letting them spew substandard culture all over us?' The couch potato was next to the placard on British Creativity. The interior of Self Portrait set up a series of contradictions in the British 'character' that may well have made visitors think hard about the strengths and weaknesses of their national identity (see McGuigan, 2004a, for further details and Chapter 3).

The problem of Englishness

At base, the problem with the English is that England used to be top dog, not only in the British Isles but throughout the world, with the largest colonial possessions overseas of any nation ever. That it is no more hardly requires stating. England's hegemony around the globe was never as great as the USA's today, but the USA is not, strictly speaking, an 'empire', in the sense of having formal command over other countries. Its command is informal – economic and cultural – except for when it is military.

The British Empire made England rich in the eighteenth and nineteenth centuries, though it became a burden financially in the twentieth century. Decolonisation not only resulted from independence struggles but also Britain's own relinquishing of the 'burden' of responsibility. It was supposed to be replaced by the economic and cultural alliance of the Commonwealth, but that turned out to be a pious failure. Until the 1960s, former colonial subjects in the Commonwealth had British citizenship rights. These were abolished in order to stem the tide of immigration to the once great Motherland.

In the heydays of the Empire, 'Englishness' had connotations of sup-remacy and an insufferable sense of superiority at home and abroad. It was also characterised by belligerence, especially on the high seas. Of the subordinate British nations, Scotland was the most enthusiastic partner in the imperial crime, secured by military prowess and solidified by migration.

Despite their prominent role in colonising and managing the British Empire, there is no love lost for the English among the Scots. Today, Scottish national identity is very much associated with difference from the English. It is almost defined by antagonism towards the English, to the banal extent that Scots are even reluctant to support England teams when they play against foreign football teams at, say, football when their own team is out of the competition. Scottish antagonism to England and the English remains a striking cultural phenomenon, albeit with questionable historical justification (Davidson, 2000) and despite the fact that Scotland has benefited disproportionately from the United Kingdom budget, has the most significant measure of devolved government in the UK and a great many leading politicians at Westminster are Scots.

Similarly, the Welsh are no great fans of England and the English, with antagonism played out, for instance, around language questions and rugby. The Welsh/English tension is less marked than the Scottish/English tension with regard to government and self-government, though. Wales also has a measure of parliamentary devolution, but it is relatively insignificant.

It is understandable that subordinate nations should be resentful towards the dominant nation historically – none more so than the Irish. Curiously enough, they do not tend to be quite so antagonistic towards England and the English as the Scots and, to a lesser extent, the Welsh. The Southern Irish and Catholics in the North have well-founded historical reasons for being deeply indignant, not just resentful, about English hegemony. The avuncular Irish, however, have benefited greatly in recent decades from European Union relief for what was once, but is no more, a 'backward' region.

Scottish Nationalists advocate independence from the UK, to become a full member of the EU, thereby breaking the historical bond with England, but the canny Scottish electorate hitherto has not been so sure about going that far. The long-forecast 'break-up of Britain' (Nairn, 1981 [1977]) is still delayed, perhaps by lingering emotional bonds that constantly put off the divorce proceedings.

Intranational antagonism within the UK is hardly severe, especially when compared with international situations, so should not be exaggerated. It is manifestly evident, however, that 'subordinate' nations in the British Isles have a much stronger sense of national identity than do the English. English nationalism is a feeble phenomenon indeed, usually associated with conservative nostalgia for the imperial past and a lost 'golden age' that never existed. Sometimes British/English national fervour is conjured up magically around events such as the Falklands/Malvinas conflict and, with calendrical regularity, by the pomp and ceremony of a beleaguered monarchy – the Queen's various anniversaries and so forth – supported as late as the mid-2000s by two of the three leading men in succession to the throne – Diana's sons, William and Harry – becoming Army officers, thereby, echoing the old role of Barbarian princes. As far as real war is concerned, like the one in Iraq, imperial nostalgia is a sick joke, better satirised – indeed, only satirised – by Channel 4's *Bremner, Bird and Fortune* on television rather than a trivialising *Little Britain*.

The truth of the matter is that the English have a problem regarding identity, which is particularly evident in hysterical expressions of Englishness. Instances of these are the celebration of the Falklands victory when the fleet returned to Portsmouth from the South Atlantic in 1982 and football hooliganism abroad, most especially, on periodic occasions when England play Germany.

In order to signify Englishness, the red cross on a white ground of the St George's flag, instead of the Union Jack of Great Britain, has become ubiquitous since the 1990s. Jim Pines (2001: 57), commenting on the meaning of the St George's flag at the 1998 World Cup, remarked somewhat debatably, 'The English flag invoked a sense of multicultural inclusiveness which had not been seen before, and certainly not seen in relation to the Union Jack' (also, see Gilroy, 1987; and Perryman, 2005). At that time, the St George's flag had strong associations with English fascism and still does to some extent. The claimed seizure of the St George's flag by progressive forces, it may be surmised, has left the extreme right British National Party holding the Union Jack forlornly when it might prefer to be waving the St George's flag itself. After all, the heartlands of working-class fascism in Britain tend to be in England. For instance, the BNP has had its greatest success so far (at the time of writing) in winning 12 seats on Barking Council to the East of London (Bragg, 2006).

In his book on English football fandom, *Ingerland*, Mark Perryman (2006) stresses how the meaning of the St George's flag has been recuperated for a less retrogressive sense of Englishness than in the past since its adoption at Euro '96, the European Championships held in England. English fans stopped waving the Union Jack and decided to raise the flag of their own country instead. During the 2006 World Cup, the St George's flag was everywhere in England, hanging on houses and out of car windows. Perhaps this was merely the expression of a 'banal nationalism', neither left- nor right-wing (Billig, 1995). Asian football fans adopted it too, suggesting a stronger identification with England and Englishness – in place of Britain and Britishness – than had been evident in the past amongst ethnic minorities.

Perryman considers the adoption of the St George's flag and its spreading popularity to be wholly benign and quite possibly a 'progressive' articulation of English national identity that is shorn of any fascistic connotations, which, albeit with some justification, is a rosy assessment – perhaps too rosy.

There is, however, a tradition of English identity to be noted that is not necessarily associated with imperial power and the more sinister branches of right-wing politics. It is the tradition of 'the free-born Englishman', imagined since the indigenous population's suffering under 'the Norman yoke', invoked by the Robin Hood myth and recalled, for instance, by Tom Paine in the eighteenth century. It is a constituent feature of English radicalism, 'related to popular notions of "independence", patriotism, and the Englishman's "birth right"' (Thompson, 1968 [1963]: 85).

Such sentiments, as E.P. Thompson recognised, can just as well be recruited to an atavistic 'Little Englandism' as they can to the expression of national pride on cosmopolitan sites, such as the cultural interchange and mutuality of fans from different countries at an international football competition. At present, however, the full expression of that residual sensibility is confined to a kind of marginal eccentricity, such as the organisation founded in the East Midlands in 1988, the Movement for Middle England, which has issued pamphlets against racism (MFME, 1992). More recently, the musician and folk intellectual Billy Bragg (2006), has written a book calling for a 'progressive patriotism', which is very much framed within a working-class tradition of dissent that is not xenophobic, while recognising and welcoming the mixing of different peoples in the past and in the present.

Clash of civilizations? (spelt with an American z)

Today, talk of a 'crisis of community' within a country like Britain usually means ethnic tension between 'indigenous' people and incomers from somewhere else. Over the years, Britain has experienced considerable tension in this respect. For instance, in the East End of London, the local working-class community was depleted and disordered as a result of the decline of work in the docks and flight to the outer-suburbs during the second half of the twentieth century and this coincided with an influx of migrants from the Commonwealth, particularly from Bangladesh, India, Kenya, Nigeria, Pakistan and Uganda, as well as the Caribbean, who were often cast as scapegoats for local woes. These communities followed, in a long line of immigrant succession, the Huguenots running away from Catholic oppression in France, destitute Irish peasants seeking work and Jews escaping the pogroms of Central and Eastern Europe, all of whom had fetched up there at one time or another in the past. Brick Lane is now an enclave of Asian restaurants servicing members of the professional and managerial class who have moved eastwards in search of affordable housing to gentrify in a very expensive city. The Hong Kong Chinese are most in evidence on the other side of Central London, in the restaurant district of Soho. In fact, the East End, Greater London and most parts of Britain are more akin to the cosmopolitan 'melting pot' – not only in terms of cuisine – long espoused by American 'liberals' than representing a 'clash of civilizations' – a phrase coined by American political scientist and former hawkish adviser to the US government in the prosecution of the Vietnam War, Samuel Huntington.

After 9/11, the phrase 'clash of civilizations' also became widely used in Britain. As elsewhere, it was especially frequently used on television, nearly always signifying tension between 'the West' and Islam. Its users, in the main, are most likely unaware of what it really means or, to be more precise, what Huntington meant by it. They have probably not read Huntington's *The Clash of Civilizations and the Remaking of World Order* (1996) from its cheerful beginning to its bitter end.

Post-communism, the idea that the great world religions mark out the major divisions in the world – an excessively culturalist view of actual and potential conflict – was latched on to rather too casually in order to explain the resurgence of political Islam, frequently, though to an extent erroneously, called, 'Islamic fundamentalism'. The great majority of those who might be considered fundamentalist in their Islamic beliefs and practices do *not* support al Qaida's terrorist strategy and tactics. If they live in Britain, they would rather integrate into British society and culture than blow people up. Support for al Qaida, particularly among young men, however, was hugely boosted by the 'War on Terror' and the invasions of Afghanistan and Iraq. George Bush has been the greatest recruiting agent for Osama bin Laden. The reasonably well-founded assumption that 'the West' has it in for Islamic countries, with the notable exception of Saudi Arabia, is widely held across the Muslim world, especially by its poor members, not just Muslims in Britain.

Huntington was – as Enoch Powell was – a cultural racist, which is the late-modern form of racism. This form is not based on fallacious biology but on the defence and preservation of cultural 'purity', which is an utter nonsense in an increasingly hybrid world. Huntington's sequel to *The Clash of Civilizations – Who Are We?: America's great debate* (2004) – makes this very clear indeed. There he is defending the 'American Creed', derived from 'the distinct Anglo-Protestant culture of the founding settlers of America in the seventeenth and eighteenth centuries' (2004: xv), and involving the English language, Christian religiosity, the rule of law, responsible rulers, individual rights, duty and so on. He is especially perturbed by all the Catholic Hispanics in the USA talking Spanish at school and in the community and would like to stop them doing so.

Huntington's xenophobia may be about to achieve concrete expression in the US Congress' proposed fence along the Mexican border, stretching for 700 miles and costing $6 billion. The aim is to stem illegal migration into the USA from Central and South America. That the US is massively dependent on cheap Latino labour to do 'Jobs that US citizens don't want to do' (Vargas Llosa, 2006: 36) – cleaning, looking after old folk, labouring in the fields and the factories – sets up something of a tricky problem for such an exclusionary strategy. Moreover, Huntington himself does not complain about Mexican workers *in Mexico* making US automobiles and TVs at a fraction of US labour costs, so long as they stay there (see McGuigan, 2006, [1999] and Chapter 4 earlier for detailed criticism of Huntington's 'clash of civilizations' thesis).

Back in Europe, over recent years there has been a series of flashpoints around ethnic-religious tensions that have occasionally had violent consequences. Examples include the murder of the director of the Dutch film *Submission*, which attacked Muslim oppression of women, and the anti-Islamic Danish cartoons controversy, as well as, in Britain, for instance, Sikh protest that closed down the *Behzti* play at Birmingham Repertory Theatre and the furore that erupted when government politician Jack Straw complained about Islamic women wearing the veil at his constituency surgery in Blackburn as he could not see their faces.

These and many other such incidents are condensations of tension between communities – symptomatic, no doubt, of a 'crisis of community', in Britain and elsewhere. They are all grist to the mill for the sensationalism of tabloid journalism and, more generally, a pervasive demonisation of vulnerable communities by respectable as well as disreputable racists.

Far-right racial politics have never really taken off in Britain, however. This is quite possibly because mainstream politicians – Conservative, Labour and Liberal Democrat – have been so responsive to its illiberal concerns in successive panics about immigration, such as, latterly, of migrants from EU-member countries in Eastern Europe as well as 'illegals' from outside Europe. The irony is that many such migrants are highly educated and hard-working yet poorly paid contributors to 'the British economy'. They typically make up for labour shortages that are unfulfilled by native workers for one reason or another.

Debate in the public sphere usually turns on questions of freedom of expression and censorship when it comes to a 'clash of civilizations'. Muslim spokespeople – who may or may not represent the feelings of their communities accurately – have called for censorship of offensive material and generally complained about misrepresentation of 'the Islamic community'. On these occasions of public dispute, Enlightenment secularists typically defend absolute freedom of speech.

Attending to such debates, I often find myself agreeing with both sides, which probably makes me a wishy-washy liberal and/or indicates that I have finally succumbed to the 'undecideability' of poststructuralism and postmodernism. Personally, I prefer Habermasian dialogic democracy instead, which recognises that the positions in the debate may be falsely polarised and assumes that absolute freedom of speech is a myth and censorship, in some respect, is always with us but should be argued over and democratically accountable (McGuigan, 1996). The value is in the debate itself and the struggle for mutual understanding, not necessarily in obtaining agreement, whereby differences are erased.

Conclusion – community of communities?

We no longer tend to think of 'community' exclusively as a place inhabited by a homogeneous set of people in Britain: the Northern working-class in Hunslet; the London working-class in Bethnal Green; fishing and shipbuilding communities on the coast, as well as other traditional emplace-ments for sociological community studies. Place still matters but nowadays 'community' is most typically connected to 'identity' – 'Muslim', 'English' and so on. To belong to a community is to identify with others who are significant though not necessarily met. Community identification may be global, transcending the nation state, and not only local in the sense of co-presence in an actual place.

As we saw in the previous chapter, in the year 2000, the Runnymede Commission's Parekh Report *The Future of Multi-Ethnic Britain* came up with a nice idea: 'a community of communities'. This is not an either/or proposal but, instead, a both/and idea. It involves respect for cultural diversity across different communities and a democratic framework for cohesion between communities, obviously at the national level, as Parekh argued, but also (I would add) at international levels.

On its publication, the Parekh Report was roundly denounced in the news media and across the press, from the *Daily Mail* to the *Guardian*. There was a particular passage in the Report that made critics take umbrage. It included the following sentence (Runnymede Trust, 2000: 38): 'Whiteness nowhere features as an explicit condition of being British, but it is widely understood that Englishness, and therefore by extension Britishness, is racially coded.'

The Labour Home Secretary at the time, Jack Straw, simultaneously launched the Report at a press conference on 11 October and rejected it for this very reason, having been alerted to the problem by the *Daily Telegraph* the previous day, thereby undermining its potential impact.

The Report did not, in fact, denounce Britishness – or, for that matter, Englishness – as inevitably racist. That would have been absurd since race relations in Britain are, arguably, among the least bad in the world. This is partly due to the positive influence of American civil liberties discourse since the 1960s. It cannot be denied, however, that Britishness and Englishness *have* been inherently racist, which is a legacy of the Empire, when colonial subjects were heavily racialised by their 'civilising' colonists – considered inferior and childish people – with explicitly racial ideology to back up the denigration. There is also the legacy of the Crusades, when European Christianity attacked Muslims in their homelands – (lately recalled by the Pope himself), and have gone on doing so ever since, not only with words but also with bombs. This is a burden of history that cannot be erased. At first, George Bush wanted to call his 'War on Terror' a 'Crusade'. His advisers pointed out that this was unwise. Still, however, the 'rough music' (Ali, 2005) plays on in Britain, as elsewhere.

6 SOCIOLOGY OF THE MOBILE PHONE

Introduction

The rapid take-up and increase in the use of the mobile phone has proved an immensely significant social and cultural phenomenon. Market hyperbole and utopian dreams have greatly exaggerated its importance, however. The fundamental issue for sociology is the process of change and, since the mobile phone is so much bound up with contemporary issues of change, it constitutes a prime object for sociological attention, at both the macro and micro levels of analysis.

This chapter considers the strengths and weaknesses of four clusters of method for studying the sociality of the mobile phone – (social demography; political economy; conversation, discourse and text analysis; and ethnography) and the different kinds of knowledge they produce and the interests they represent. Recent ethnographic research on the mobile phone, particularly motivated by issues around the uncertain transition from second (2G) to third generation (3G) technology and beyond, has examined the actual experience of routine use. The advent of the all-purpose mobile communication device further complicates matters. Interpretative research is now supplementing purely instrumental research, thereby giving a more nuanced understanding of mobile communications in mass popular use. Going further, however, critical research that asks questions about the quality of communication in an age of increased mobility whilst also exploring the connections between exploitative conditions in the manufacture of mobile technology and the cool seduction of consumer culture, of which there is little as yet, should be developed in order to produce a fuller sociological account of mobile communications.

To begin, let us consider the following quotation from Howard Rheingold's celebration of the cooperative properties of peer-to-peer wireless communications, *Smart Mobs* (2002: 157):

On January 20, 2001, President Joseph Estrada of the Philippines became the first head of state in history to lose power to a smart mob. More than 1 million Manila residents, mobilized and coordinated by waves of text messages, assembled at the site of the 1986 'People Power' peaceful demonstrations that had toppled the Marcos regime.

Do you notice anything odd about that statement? Rheingold is illustrating the value of mobile telephony in organising popular protest with reference to the overthrow of Estrada in 2001. Yet he underlines this point by reference to a much earlier and comparable event in 1986 when, presumably, mobile phones had not played a significant role in mobilising the masses.

That's one example; here's another. My daughter and my son, both in their early twenties, find social life virtually inconceivable without a mobile phone. Maintaining a friendship network and arranging meetings would be just too much hassle without the mobile, supplemented by Facebook. Yet, when I was 20, I had friends, too, and somehow I managed to meet up with them and maintain an active social life without a mobile.

I make these observations merely to reflect on how a recent luxury has become a current necessity and register a note of scepticism concerning the allegedly transformational capacities of newer information and communication technologies. Commercial hype and utopian anarchism, to my mind, mystify rather than illuminate the significance of the mobile phone. That is not to say it is insignificant. The mobile phone is indeed significant, in all sorts of ways.

At the beginning of his book *Constant Touch: A global history of the mobile phone*, Jon Agar (2003) smashes up his mobile phone to scrutinise what it contains. The raw materials in its many components are culled from around the world, such as nickel for the battery from Chile, microprocessors and circuitry from the USA. Petroleum for the plastic casing, moulded, say, in Taiwan, and for the liquid crystal display (LCD) comes from somewhere like the Persian Gulf, the North Sea, Russia or Texas. The rare metal tantalum – essential for capacitors, which store electrical charges – comes, most likely, from the aboriginal lands of Western Australia or the Democratic Republic of Congo. During the 1990s, the price of tantalum per pound shot up from US$30 to $300. Columbite-tantalite (coltan), mined in the North East of Congo, is a source of civil war over mineral rights and the revenue from its mining continues to fund hostilities there. That's one way of defamilarising what has become a very familiar object over the past few years.

The mobile phone is not reducible to a simple material object, a commodity circulating in the global economy of transnational operations, however. It is also a means of communication with considerable social and cultural significance. For some users, the sign value of this object might actually exceed its use value, functioning as a magical fetish, which is certainly the message of much advertising. The mobile is a symbol in itself, an obscure object of desire and a sign of the times. Early efforts have been made to map out a general sociology of the mobile phone (Katz and Aakhus,

2002; Geser, 2003). This chapter has no such comprehensive ambition. The following notes towards a possible sociology of the mobile phone aim to identify key issues in theory and methodology. It is important to situate the mobile phone in relation to the sociology of change – the macro level – and everyday sociality – the micro level.

Social change and new communications technology

The core subject matter of sociology is change. To put it very simply, historically, as a discipline, sociology emerged in order to make sense of modernisation. Classical sociology was preoccupied with analysing the differences between tradition and modernity. Social life was changing dramatically and sociology sought to understand and explain the emerging modern condition.

Towards the end of the twentieth century, sociology returned to its focus on the dynamics of macro-change to make sense of the emergence of what had been called 'the postmodern condition' (Lyotard, 1984 [1979]). Many commentators discerned a transition occurring between epochs, comparable to the shift from tradition to modernity, and named the new condition in various ways – 'post-industrialism', 'reflexive modernity', 'global neoliberalism' and 'the information age', as well as 'postmodernity'.

One of the most compelling accounts of epochal change at the turn of the millennium was given by Manuel Castells (2000 [1996], 2004a [1997], 2004b [1998]) in his three-volume magnum opus *The Information Age*. The first volume is entitled *The Rise of the Network Society*. Castells places great emphasis on the role of information and communication technology (ICT) in contemporary change, though it has to be said that modes of communication are integrally related to any social formation. The general argument is transhistorical. If you want to understand any kind of society, you should look at how its members communicate with one another.

According to Castells, it is the complex, proliferating network principle that characterises computer-mediated communications. Complex net-working also characterises social relations in the information age. This seems to imply that changing social relations are an effect of technological change. In consequence, Castells's thesis is vulnerable to the critique of technological determinism (Williams, 1974; Winston, 1996).

On the topic of technological innovation in communications and its social impact, there are two general questions to ask. First, how do new communication technologies come about? Second, what is the relation of new technology to social and cultural change?

The ideology of technological determinism awards absolute primacy to technology. It assumes a linear process of autonomous scientific discovery that is more or less swiftly applied to technical invention, resulting in smooth diffusion and eventual social transformation. When the history of any such technology is looked at closely, however, it becomes evident that a combination of cultural, economic and political determinations is involved in putting the accelerator or brake on technological innovation. Against sheer determinism, intention comes into the process, involving decisions, wise and unwise, along the way, that have unintended as well as intended consequences. Always, alternative decisions could have been made that would have resulted in different outcomes and might yet still do so. It is in the interests of corporations in the business of developing and marketing new technologies, however, to make extravagant claims about inevitable and beneficial effects on society and social relations.

Castells is careful to defend himself against the criticism of technological determinism. He argues that there are two other major dynamics, in addition to the information technology revolution, shaping network society. These are the three interrelated processes identified by Castells (1997):

1. *the information technology revolution* since the 1970s – the microchip, desktop computers, telematics, exploitation of the Internet and so on
2. *the restructuring of capitalism and statism* in the 1980s – shift from Fordism to post-Fordism, globalisation, collapse of communism, undermining of the welfare state and trade unionism and so on
3. *The cultural social movements* that emerged from the 1960s – peace, feminism, ecology and so on.

John Urry (2000) has explored the implications of such change for sociology itself in his book *Sociology Beyond Societies*, which is subtitled *Mobilities for the twenty-first century*. Urry places less emphasis on technological development than does Castells. His view is closer to Zygmunt Bauman's (2000) notion of 'liquid modernity'. In the late-modern world, change is about increasingly rapid movement. According to Urry:

1. sociology has neglected mobility, particularly of people, as a cardinal feature of sociality.
2. mobility not only refers to the movement of people but also to that 'of other entities, of ideas, images, technologies, monies, flowing across various scapes' (2000: 188).
3. The object of social analysis can no longer be conceived of as 'society' in the static form of a nation state but, instead, sociology should study global flows.

Curiously, in his treatise on mobile sociology, published in the year 2000, Urry barely registered the mobile phone. There are a few passing mentions, however, such as his noting of ringtones in the social landscape (2000: 102): 'The 1990s sound icon is the mobile phone.'

Around the turn of the millennium, then, neither Castells nor Urry saw much social significance in the mobile phone itself, except as one feature of ICT development and of a pervasive mobility in the late-modern world.

This may just indicate how even the most up-to-date and far-sighted sociologists can be taken somewhat by surprise, just like everyone else.

The shift from first generation (1G) to second generation (2G) during the 1990s, from be-suited business users with their bricks on display to mass popular use of much more discrete versions, particularly as a leisure medium for the young, was astonishing. Nobody genuinely believes that the same kind of sudden 'tipping point' is occurring in the transition from 2G to 3G and 4G, although Nokia, Apple and other companies talk it up incessantly. In the business, there was great uncertainty over the launch and viability of 3G mobile telephony in the opening years of the twenty-first century.

In 1997, the British government commissioned a games strategy unit at University College London, led by Ken Binmore, to design an auction for the sale of 3G frequencies. This succeeded spectacularly. At the height of the dot.coms boom in 2000, five 20-year licences were sold at a combined total of £22.5 billion to Orange, BT, One to One, Vodaphone and Hutchison. Very soon this 'licence to print money' looked far from guaranteed with the collapse of financial confidence in dot.coms. Similar lucrative auctions took place in other countries, most notably Germany, with similarly shaky results. Perhaps the Finnish government was wise to give its licences away for nothing. Initially, the small percentage of expected take-up in Japan of the I-mode system (between 2001 and 2003, 10 per cent of mobile users) was also hugely disconcerting, although it was later to grow quickly.

Around the time of the British auction, there was a health scare concerning mobile phones. Might the radiation emitted from them cause brain cancer, especially in the vulnerable young? A public inquiry in Britain was recommending caution in the use of mobiles, while the government, before publication of the Stewart report (IEGMP, 2000), leaked its findings inaccurately as providing a clean bill of health for mobile telephony.

Adam Burgess (2004) has surveyed the health issues concerning the effects of radiation in heavy use of mobile phones and proximity to the communication towers that have sprung up all over the place. Stories regularly appear in the media about the effects, especially on children living close to towers, stories that are not dissimilar to those about ill health in the locality of nuclear power stations. Public protests against the emplacement of towers have brought the issue to widespread attention. Burgess, however, is sceptical of the evidence of adverse effects on health and comes to the conclusion that anxiety in this respect is unfounded because mobile telephony is not a proven health hazard.

Use of wireless technology is a classic risk issue as nobody really knows the long-term effects, for good or ill, of this massive real-life experiment on the public, the results of which may not be known for several years, by which time it will be too late for the sufferers (Beck, 1992 [1986]). The phone companies are acutely aware of the possible risks and have patented protective shields for mobiles but are reluctant to market them because it might cause a panic detrimental to profits. Despite occasional media panics and much less well-publicised concern within the industry, the public are not well informed of the potential health hazards of mobile telephony (BBC Four, 13 January 2003).

Anxiety over health is not what held up a swift transition to widespread use of 3G – in effect, Internet interconnectedness and a whole array of add-on services. This had more to do with business finance, building infrastructure, spiralling consumer costs and the stuttering search for a 'killer application' – to use the industry's unfortunate 'technical' term.

The long sought after 'killer application', it was believed, would persuade everyone to switch from comparatively inexpensive 2G to the inevitably more expensive, yet more expansive in application, 3G multipurpose mobile device. We had the fad of picture messaging a few years ago, but the real 'killer application' came with the combination of telephony and music downloading – that is, combining the mobile phone with an MP3 player, as exemplified by Apple's own touchscreen iPhone. Again, the take-up in the late noughties was not as great as expected because, quite apart from technical hitches, at first the handsets were expensive and, yet more importantly, contracts were too expensive for many users to afford.

Questions of method

The theories of Castells and Urry may set the general framework for a sociology of the mobile phone but they do not prescribe how to study it. Here, it is necessary to say something about knowledge and interest. Jürgen Habermas (1972 [1968]) once distinguished between three kinds of knowledge interest, each in turn defined by their different research orientations, as follows:

1. *Instrumental* research, orientated towards utility, similar to Jean-François Lyotard's (1984 [1979]) performativity principle. Lyotard argued that postmodern knowledge is not about the search for truth but, instead, for pragmatic results. This is undoubtedly the main knowledge interest and orientation of scientific research now and, most consequentially, funding and investment.
2. *Interpretative* research, orientated towards understanding, framed by the values of mutuality irrespective of cultural differences.
3. *Critical* research, orientated towards emancipation – that is, political amelioration of injustice.

Lyotard was dismissive of both interpretative and critical research as passé, yet both can be seen in play, as well as prevalent forms of instrumental research, in sociological study of the mobile phone.

The orientations themselves do not necessarily specify methodological principles and research techniques. There are many potential ways of framing research problems and strategies regarding the mobile phone. Here, I shall identify four broad and appropriate methodological clusters in relation to knowledge interests:

- social demography
- political economy
- conversation, discourse and text analysis
- ethnography.

Social demography

This is where most effort is put into data gathering, identifying the scale and range of usage in different segments of the population. It is useful to business and government. Phone companies want to know about the market, to open up new markets and develop products that are marketable. From a policy point of view, governments require facts and figures, too.

We know, for instance, that Finland has the highest number of mobile phones per head of population in the world (Puro, 2002) and, perhaps surprisingly, mobile use has been comparatively low in the USA. That does, indeed, tell us something about culture and society in Finland – a large mass of land on the northern edge of Europe with a relatively small and dispersed population – and in the USA – where local landline telephone calls have usually been free. The mobile phone and related industry is the leading element of the Finnish economy and a matter of national pride.

Generally speaking, however, social demography is not so much sociology in the explanatory sense but a means of description, providing evidence that may be interpreted and used according to various interests – and not necessarily the interests that were present in its construction.

Political economy

The term 'political economy' is used to distinguish a particular kind of research from positivistic economics. Politics and economics cannot be divorced from one another. The political economy of communications is usually critical. It looks at how corporations command the field and increasingly usurp the role of government. Typical issues, from this perspective, are media imperialism, neoliberal communications policy, deregulation, privatisation and 'the digital divide' (see, for instance, Schiller, 1999).

Business structures and processes of mediated communication amplify economic inequality and political power relations. Even Castells in his earlier work said that this was so of ICT development, with sub-Saharan Africa, in particular, hugely disadvantaged. The Internet, however, was also seen as a new means of communicative access.

Recently, attention has shifted to the mobile phone as *the* means of emancipation. It is relatively cheap to access and, for regions with poor landline telephony and digital connectedness, the mobile phone and the all-purpose communicational device are said to leap a stage of technological development. Indeed, Castells and his collaborators (Castells et al., 2007) argue that mobile technology is leaping a stage of technological development in Africa, where landline infrastructure has lagged behind the rest of the world. Also, because of the saturation of markets in richer parts of the world, the telecoms companies have seen a business opportunity in producing cheaper equipment for sale in poorer parts of the world.

Then, of course, there are serious problems concerning the manufacturing industry in low-wage economies where conditions of work are harsh and unhealthy, hours long and wage levels deeply exploitative. Joseph Wilde and Esther de Haan (2006), for SOMO, the Centre for Research on Multinational Corporations in the Netherlands, have documented such conditions around the world, especially in Shenzen, China. Most of the mobile technology used by consumers in the affluent world has been made by poorly paid and mistreated workers, predominantly women and often under age, in newly developing countries (NDCs), which puts the commodity fetishism of such gadgetry among the comfortably off into a grim perspective. See McGuigan (2010) for a fuller discussion of these issues.

Conversation, discourse and t ext analysis

Social demography is useful and political economy essential. Neither of them, however, have much to say about meaning. For this, we turn to various techniques of linguistic analysis.

Obviously, conversation analysis is relevant. Language, however, is more than the minutae of conversational turntaking and so on (see Emanuel Schegloff's 2002 contribution to the collection of papers edited by James E. Katz and Mark Aakhus).

Mobile communications have discursive properties linked to social behaviour in different contexts. The very design and representation of the object itself and its diverse social uses are meaningful.

Then, of course, there is the surprising phenomenon of text messaging, which caught on – especially among young people – to an extent that nobody predicted. The abbreviated language of text messaging is a new kind of shorthand, which may or may not have an impact on language generally (see Crystal, 2008 on language and text messaging). It is also a medium of subcultural identification. Many older people, even now, just can't get the hang of it.

Ethnography

This takes us into the territory of ethnography, which derives from the anthropological practice of immersion in other cultures in order to grasp and convey social reality from the point of view of 'the native'.

This qualitative approach to studying everyday life has become popular in sociology and cultural studies where the researcher may be studying his or her own culture and society. Seldom is research of this kind conducted with the depth of classical anthropology. There usually is not enough time and insufficient resources for such detailed research. Often the work is small-scale and brief, deploying unstructured and semi-structured interviewing and focus group techniques, as well as, normally to a lesser extent, observation.

In practice, the selection of interviewees and groups aims to be representative, but not in the statistical sense, so the concept of typicality is crucial. Ethnographic data is representative if in some sense it is justifiably deemed to be revealing typicality.

Ethnography is subject to criticism for being slight and unrepresentative by those who prefer large-scale sample surveys. Qualitative research in an ethnographic mode, however, has its own criteria of validity that are not quantitative. It is concerned with typicality, the rich texture of everyday life and fine differences of culture.

When done well, this may work better in practice than attitudinal surveying and opinion polling, though qualitative and quantitative methods can complement one another and be combined together in a project. Facts and figures give a broad picture of what is going on whereas ethnography is better at representing the nuances and complexities of everyday life. Incidentally, the use of focus groups has become increasingly common in market and political research as well as in 'disinterested' research.

Ethnographic studies

Three British studies of the mobile phone's social use are worthy of consideration here:

- James Crabtree, Max Nathan and Simon Roberts (2003), *Mobile UK: Mobile phones and everyday life*
- James Harkin (2003), *Mobilisation: The growing public interest in mobile technology*
- Sadie Plant (2002), *On the Mobile*.

All three studies use ethnographic methods. None of them, however, can, strictly speaking, be regarded as 'disinterested'. *Mobile UK* was funded and conducted by the charity the Work Foundation, which is dedicated to conducting research in the interests of British business. *Mobilisation* was commissioned by the British-based firm O_2 and conducted by the New Labour think tank Demos. *On the Mobile*, which can only be accessed digitally, was carried out for Motorola, an American-based phone company.

Mobile UK

The *Mobile UK* report must be seen within the business context and anxieties around the launch and viability of 3G mobile telephony in the opening years of the twenty-first century. In effect, *Mobile UK* sought to bring a bit of realism to the telecommunications industry. It criticises research that gives disproportionate attention to certain groups of mobile users – 'young urban professionals, mobile business people, and teenagers' (2003: 6) – who are generally said to be the early adopters of newer communication technologies. *Mobile UK* is therefore concerned instead with the more mundane and widespread use of these technologies.

In an earlier piece of research *(Reality IT)*, the same researchers distinguished between 'enthusiasts', 'quiet pragmatists' and 'aversives', but, in this later research, they found these categories to be less fixed and more overlapping. It is advisable, then, to explore how the mobile phone is embedded in the most typical routines of indivisible everyday life. To this end, ethnographic research is appropriate.

It must be said, however, that the ethnographies conducted for *Mobile UK* were very limited in scope. In the report, there are just four case studies of individuals and their social interactions through mobile telephony. They are, nevertheless, insightful. The case studies are focused on Denise, a hairdresser who is married with children; Jack, a plumber; Louise, an unemployed single mother; and Darius, an IT worker. The case study of Denise, for instance, illuminates how family relations are managed with the aid of the mobile phone, especially childcare. The case of the plumber, Jack, is also very interesting. If you have ever tried to get hold of a plumber in an emergency, knowing his or her mobile number is handy. Jack, however, often has his phone turned off because he isn't short of work and doesn't want to be disturbed on the job. He is also reluctant to move on to using a comparatively expensive 3G handset because it might suggest to his customers that he is inordinately well off as a result of charging them too much.

These examples may be considered merely anecdotal, but they do illustrate the mundane character of mobile use and redress the balance of attention, moving it away from more extreme and less routinely practical uses and extravagant predictions concerning future use.

Mobile UK stresses the practicalities of everyday life, the embeddedness of 2G in routine habits, and advises caution about the take-up of 3G. It also points to the financial realities of mobile use. With the explosion of mobile use in the late 1990s, it was possible to sell phones very cheaply or even give them away. Pay-as-you-go deals were popular as they enabled people to control their expenditure on mobile telephony. It is very difficult to wean people off such deals and sensible habits, encourage them to spend much more casually and access expensive new services.

The recommendations to the industry made by *Mobile UK* are less than amazing. It suggests that upgraded devices should facilitate specific tasks, exploit networking, be priced reasonably, target users' mobility and be simple to use. That is the wisdom revealed by instrumental, market-orientated research concerning the advent of 3G mobile communications.

Mobilisation

The Demos report for O$_2$, *Mobilisation* (Harkin, 2003), was also anxious about take-up for 3G, but its message is aimed more directly at government than business. It displays the typical features and, indeed, contradictions of New Labour/Third Way politics. If *Mobile UK* is instrumentally market-orientated, *Mobilisation* is instrumentally government-orientated. It is more socially concerned but in what may be regarded as a patronising and, indeed, unrealistic manner.

Mobilisation registered a certain social hostility in some quarters to the mobile phone but argues that this is largely mistaken. The full potential of mobile telephony is yet to be realised and, in this, government has a role to play. The report says that 'government bodies will need to open up their intestines to mobile users' and mobilisation offers 'more flexible models for public service delivery' (2003: 10). The aim of the report is to issue 'a wake-up call for Britain'.

The research conducted by Demos was rather more extensive than the Work Foundation's *Mobile UK* project. Four focus groups were studied and ten individual users and nine experts interviewed. One of the focus groups was on the Isle of Man where O$_2$ conducted a pilot study of 3G with 200 participants. Another group – in Bromley, Kent – consisted of 16–18-year-olds.

For regular users, the mobile phone has become a prosthetic, an extension of the body. It has several different functions already. The industry has mistakenly promoted it as a toy, thereby trivialising its actual and potential uses. Particularly important, according to *Mobilisation*, is 'declining reserves of trust in modern society' (2003: 18). The mobile is a means of protection and a bonding device for friends and family. This is particularly so for young people: it overcomes shyness and facilitates subcultural formation through SMS (text messaging) and shared use. Still, however, the mobile is a 'locus of social anxiety' (2003: 26), particularly regarding health and crime.

Perhaps the most interesting observation made by the *Mobilisation* report is that, if the Internet is about globalisation, then, the mobile is about localisation. It tends to cement local social bonds and, with further technical development, it can easily be a usable location device, a means of orientation in place. This illustrates its capacity to do things that other technologies cannot do.

Typical of Third Way thinking, *Mobilisation* recommends the mobile's potential for marketing and customer relations while simultaneously calling for tough 'anti-spam laws' that even though, it admits, these are hard to enforce.

The author of *Mobilisation*, James Harkin, is also struck by the fact that, in just one hour in November 2002, 200,000 votes were cast by text message for contestants in the television programme *Popstars*. While some might see this as an instance of a pop culture trivialisation of democracy and distraction from it, not he. He advocates that government should learn from the public's enthusiasm for mobile voting. Perhaps, in future, party political manifestos could be downloaded and clips from political speeches viewed in this way, as well as remote voting in elections, not only in game shows.

Other political suggestions flowing from *Mobilisation* include restricting police access to mobile location data to cases of serious crime and terrorism, as well as government information online accessible by mobile and setting up a mobile government forum for 'stakeholders'. Also, there has been considerable public disquiet about the location of masts and base stations. Harkin argues, however, that local authorities should not be allowed to restrict such development. So much for democracy.

On the Mobile

Sadie Plant's (2002) research for Motorola, *On the Mobile*, is the most interesting of the three studies under consideration here and it is more properly sociological in a theoretical sense than the others. Formerly of Birmingham and Warwick universities, now freelance and an author of well-regarded books on French situationism, women and computing and drugs and writing, Sadie Plant was once described in a broadsheet newspaper as 'the cleverest woman in Britain'.

Her research for Motorola was of the international comparative kind, with data from Tokyo, Beijing, Hong Kong, Bangkok, Peshawar, Dubai, London, Birmingham and Chicago. Plant conducted face-to-face interviews with individuals and groups. She also interviewed people by e-mail. Like a good social anthropologist, Plant observed behaviour with the mobile phone in public places, too. In order to explicate her data, Plant draws on ideas from sociologists Erving Goffman (1971 [1959]) and David Riesman et al. (1989 [1961]). In effect, she produces a fairly rich cultural analysis of mobile phone use.

The most conspicuous use of the mobile phone is in Tokyo, whereas its use is largely confined to the elite in Peshawar. Mobiles are used most in Nordic countries and there is a very high rate of use among the young in Britain. Otherwise, however, according to Plant, mobile use does not differ as much as you might expect from country to country.

Plant is observant of the rituals of use in public places. Being 'on the mobile' in public is itself a ritual act. There are, however, different types of responses to a call. Some take flight on receiving a call, removing themselves from the immediate social situation, stepping outside or whatever. Others put the people they are with in suspension while they take the call. Another typical kind of response – that of persistence – occurs as well, whereby communicative interaction is maintained in co-presence, the person simultaneously taking the call and being present with the people he or she is with.

Plant distinguishes between what she names as 'innie' and 'outie' behaviour by mobile users. Innies use their phones as unobtrusively as possible whereas outies integrate phone conversation into the situation of co-presence.

These different kinds of responses and habitual behaviour are associated with complex rules of etiquette that have developed around mobile phone use. For instance, Plant compares formal restaurant and informal café situations in England. Mobile phone use is often banned in formal situations and, in any case, people tend to keep their phones turned off or use them very unobtrusively in smart restaurants. The hubbub of an informal café, however, includes the placing of phones on tables and a great deal of mobile chatter.

Differences between masculine and feminine behaviour are also noticeable, though they are not always as sharply different as might be expected. There is a tendency for men to show off more with their phones – stage phoning – and competitiveness between men, particularly with alpha males displaying their newer models. The young in general – both male and female – also tend to be concerned with the fashionable value of the phone. Women tend to be more discrete, usually with their phones tucked away in bags – except, that is, for single women in public places, who are apt to display and use their mobiles as a kind of protective device.

There are sets of stances, gestures and body movements associated with the phone. Plant distinguishes between 'speakeasy' and 'spacemaker' stances. The speakeasies are extravagant with their gestures, throwing their heads back, bouncing around and so forth. The spacemakers are more introverted and make cocooning gestures in public when on their mobiles. There are also different styles of grip and touch.

As Plant notes, the advent of the mobile was bad news for philanderers as there are more clues to illicit behaviour, such as the phone being turned off unaccountably in the middle of the day and messages that a suspicious partner can find.

The mobile has all sorts of other emotional functions, too, of course. Texting may be used more readily than speech by the shy and reserved. Generally, the mobile helps to maintain established relationships. This is particularly noticeable in girls' friendship groups – boys tending to use the mobile more as a toy.

Plant sees the mobile as a feature of fragmented identity, as a kind of prop for the self, and she gives animal and bird analogies to identify typical modes of use, such as 'the hedgehog way' of managing privacy. Her bird analogies are the Swift Talker, Solitary Owl, Calm Dove, Chattering Sparrow, Noisy Starling and Flashy Peacock.

As a less amusing but more sociologically grounded typology, Plant draws on Riesman et al.'s (1989 [1961]) distinctions between 'tradition-direction', 'inner-direction' and 'outer-direction'. Tradition-directed people are still likely to be scandalised by the use of mobiles in public places, in that they cross the boundaries between public and private. The inner-directed person, however, may use the mobile but be concerned about not breaking the traditional conventions of appropriate conduct in public, while the outer-directed person will embrace the boundary-breaking nature of mobile telephony as part of a looser and more flexible lifestyle.

These three types are associated with specific fears: for the tradition-directed, fear of dependence; for the inner-directed, fear of guilt; for the outer-directed, fear of isolation.

Plant is obviously on the side of the mobile phone, viewing it as a tool of emancipation for not only the relatively well-off but also the poor of the world – a stimulus to growth and modernisation in developing countries. For her, the critics are just fuddy-duddy old traditionalists. That conclusion may have been consoling to Motorola, though I am not sure quite how useful such research turned out to be with regard to stimulating the sale of state-of-the-art devices.

Critical research

You will look in vain to find genuinely critical research on the mobile phone that opens up debate on its cultural value and social purpose, especially any such research commissioned by the likes of Motorola. The mobile has, however, been studied and extolled as a valuable tool for organising public protest (Rheingold, 2002).

There is, of course, still a good deal of carping about the mobile in public life, usually by what are loosely called 'grumpy old men and women', now the title of two series of television programmes. I suppose these are Plant's tradition-directed types. This is unfortunate as there is a critical question to be asked of the mobile phone, the answer to which perhaps anyone might be interested in. While the mobile phone extends and increases the sheer volume of communications, does it actually improve the quality of communication?

Some would say that this is not a legitimate question for social science, not least because it is methodologically impossible to answer. All the same, we can think and argue about it. To this end, I would recommend a little book by the literary academic George Myerson (2001) entitled *Heidegger, Habermas and the Mobile Phone*.

Myerson compares the theorising in social philosophy on the constitution of and blockages to satisfactory communication between people with the promotional discourse of the mobile phone industry, which seems to promise imminent realisation of the philosophers' dream. The industry's claims are shallow market speak, however, not serious grounds for a communicative Utopia. To quote Myerson (2001: 27): 'In the mobile version, we have millions of goal-seeking atoms, making basic contacts through the power of the network. In the philosopher's version, you have the slow, distinct "conversation" through which parties seek a deeper contact'. In Myerson's (2001: 65) estimation, the mobile functions to systematise the lifeworld, 'replacing meanings with messages, consensus with instructions and insight with information'.

Myerson's philosophical critique is challenging and should be taken seriously. The problem with such a critique, however, is that it tends to be idealist rather than materialist. It may even inspire those who believe that the clock should be turned back to some bygone age, as did Martin Heidegger but not Jürgen Habermas; that the Apparatgeist – in Katz and

Aakhus's (2002) neologism for the mobile phone – could somehow be disinvented.

This is hardly likely, nor desirable. It bespeaks a hopelessly romantic technophobia. The spirit of the machine in our mobile age of neoliberal globalisation is not a phantasm to be wished away, but something deeply embedded already in routine social practices and relationships. That is not to say it is beyond criticism.

The mobile phone is most popular with youth and designed and marketed to be so, catching them young before maturity sets in. It is a 'cool', miniature and mystified gadget, no longer considered a luxury but felt to be a necessity by many. The mass-market potential of mobile telephony has been exploited to a remarkable degree in a very short period of time.

Current and future developments in the industry are about further market expansion without limit, keeping the commodity process turning over relentlessly. The all-purpose mobile communication device is now linked to the Internet and providing a plethora of newer and ever-updated services does not come cheap. The industry is forever desperate to persuade people to move on to the next generation, throw their old mobiles away and pay for new and much more expensive models and services.

It is yet to be seen if that will happen to the extent sought by the telecoms companies, which are, in any case, not so sure about it as they were a few years ago when they shelled out huge sums for the franchises in Britain and Germany. Whether or not the latest thing is all that it is cracked up to be and catches on widely is always questionable and not only a matter of intellectual scepticism but also of popular judgement and consumer reluctance as well as enthusiasm.

From a sociological point of view, actual and potential social uses across the generations and in different circumstances of life are more important topics for discussion than sheer technological capability and overly hyped marketing gimmicks. Still, behind it all, there exists a murky industry in which labour is exploited and wasted ruthlessly and customers are targeted persistently with the fetishisms of cool seduction, not unlike cigarette smoking 50 years ago.

7 RISKY CULTURE

Introduction

In its basic dictionary definition, 'risk' means 'exposure to danger' (*Oxford English Dictionary*). The forms and extent of 'danger', however, are not specified exactly. So, it is possible that danger might be experienced in the imagination as much as in reality. You may *feel* endangered but not actually be so.

Other words are sometimes used instead of 'risk', such as 'uncertainty', the dictionary definitions of which include 'not certainly knowing', 'not to be depended on' and 'changeable' (*Oxford English Dictionary*). These definitions of uncertainty may invoke what it feels like to be in a risky situation.

There is also 'the uncertainty principle' of physics – that the momentum and positioning of a particle cannot be measured precisely at a given moment in time, which is often generalised from in order to provide a metaphor for modern life, signifying that it is difficult to be sure of anything these days.

Then there is 'chance' – 'the way things happen without known cause or agency' – with its associations of 'luck' and 'fate', all of which suggest a sense of riskiness, rewards for success and penalties for failure. Positive connotations are associated with 'chance', such as 'to take one's chance, to risk' (*Oxford English Dictionary*). You might be lucky. The ordinary experience of 'taking a risk', however, is both frightening and exhilarating. That is the way it is in a risky culture.

This chapter is about risk and culture. Mainstream perspectives on risk see it as a matter of the scientific calculation of probabilities, not a cultural thing. While this may seem like a neutral, technical exercise, it is, in fact, bound up with insurance and public policy where values inevitably play their part.

In contrast, some social scientists, such as Mary Douglas and Aaaron Wildavsky (1982), see the question of risk as being almost entirely a matter of culture – how the world is framed, understood and acted on. There are problems here of philosophical idealism that underplay the sheer materiality of risk, especially from an ecological perspective. Also, Douglas and Wildavsky are very much concerned with combating the claims of environmental campaigners and, in effect, give succour to corporations and governments looking to overcome criticism.

A much more critical approach to risk is provided by Ulrich Beck and Elisabeth Beck-Gernsheim, whose work is considered at some length in the present chapter. For them, risk is grounded in environmental concerns, though it has much more general significance for everyday life and culture in the broadest and, indeed, narrowest senses.

There are strong and weak senses of 'risk'. 'The risk society thesis', in its original formulation, represents the strongest sense of risk – that human beings are putting their very existence on planet Earth in danger for short-term gain, risking long-term extinction. The risk society thesis warns us of imminent ecological catastrophe resulting from pollution, global warming, unsustainable and reckless use of resources and the rest of it.

Nobody may feel personally responsible for any of this: the decisions are made elsewhere. Are there identifiable perpetrators who can be called to account or is it 'the system' that is to blame? Who commands 'the system' anyway and why do we consent to it? Is the convenience of cheap air travel, for instance, really worth the risk of destroying the environment?

According to Ulrich Beck (1992 [1986]), 'risk' must be distinguished from 'hazard'. Human beings have always had to live with hazardous nature, the vagaries of the weather, extremes of heat and cold, mysterious diseases and the possibility of being eaten alive by wild animals, to name but a few. Now, these hazards are under greater control, if not complete control, than they have ever been. Of cource, disastrous eruptions such as the South Asian tsunami at the end of 2004 and earthquakes generally are still always likely to happen, however much we know about or seek to deal with them. Interestingly, that tsunami was largely addressed as a matter of scientific knowledge (the movement of tectonic plates), relief (charitable aid) and the political economy of recovery and future protection – not as an act of God or something equally irrational, which was the case with past responses to such catastrophes (Voltaire, 2006 [1759]). Although there was some discussion about whether or not 'we' were to blame, rationality, in this case, discounted strictly human culpability as well as the work of supernatural forces. In the cases of the devastation of New Orleans as a result of being hit by Hurricane Katrina (September 2005) and the earthquake in the Hindu Kush mountain range of Pakistan (October 2005), however, although they were 'natural' disasters, certainly each had at least an element of human culpability in the form of the inadequately built environments there that offered little protection.

Modern risks are quite different from natural hazards old and new. They arise as a consequence of human actions, mainly resulting from industrialisation and capitalist accumulative rationality: modern risks are manufactured. As Beck (1992: 98) himself puts it:

> Human dramas – plagues, famines and natural disasters, the looming power of gods and demons – may or may not quantifiably equal the destructive potential of modern mega-technologies of hazardousness. They differ essentially from 'risks' in my sense since they are not based on decisions, or more specifically, decisions that focus on techno-economic advantages and opportunities and accept hazards as simply the dark side of progress.

This argument makes a 'realist' claim – that the risks of industrial modernity do actually exist and are not just a matter of perception or the irresolvable contest between catastrophic and complacent discourses (Lupton, 1999); that some people see (hu)man-made hazards and impending disasters all around them and others do not.

Beck argues that the unintended consequences of using nuclear power, depleting natural resources, polluting the atmosphere, eroding the ozone layer and so forth really are building up big trouble, the evidence for which exists manifestly – not only latently, which is more usual – in disasters that have already happened. The explosion at the Chernobyl nuclear plant and its aftermath in the 1980s is emblematic for Beck (1995 [1988]). If you do not think that bad things are likely to happen with the environment, then, look at the bad things that have happened already. They are harbingers for a doom-laden future.

There are many criticisms of Beck, not least of which concerns the excessively totalising character of his risk society thesis. It seeks to explain a great deal and, in effect, too much. The implausibility of such an all-encompassing analytical framework is at risk, it can be said, of undermining Beck's many particular arguments, which are exceptionally insightful. That is the basis for a *theoretical* critique of the risk society thesis. The *empirical* criticisms are rather more obvious and straight-forward. For instance, Beck's writings on risk are criticised for placing too much emphasis on anecdotal evidence, such as the Chernobyl disaster (Mythen, 2004).

Bjørn Lomborg (2001 [1998]), the self-styled 'skeptical environmentalist', does not cite Beck in his extensive treatment of the statistical evidence for environmental degradation. Yet, Lomborg's arguments can be taken as the exemplary empiricist critique of widespread alarm at the extent to which we are said to be putting our natural environment at risk.

Lomborg was himself once a member of Greenpeace, the environmentalist NGO, and admits to possessing stock left-wing views on the state of the world in general. His is not the work of some American think tank dedicated to defending the system against its lifeworld opponents. Lomborg's book *The Skeptical Environmentalist* should be required reading for ecological activists who are sympathetic to Beck's risk society thesis so that they can test out their arguments and strengthen them against reasonable scepticism or – if convinced by Lomborg – perhaps relinquish them tout de suite.

Lomborg (2001 [1998]: 3) questions what he calls 'the Litany of our ever deteriorating environment'. This includes natural resources running out, insufficient food to feed a growing world population, air and water pollution, the extinction of species, deforestation, depleted fish stocks and dying coral reef. Lomborg (2001 [1998]: 4) responds to this familiar litany of assumptions by arguing, for instance:

> We are not running out of energy or natural resources. There will be more and more food per head of the world's population. Fewer and fewer people are starving. In 1900 we lived for an average of 30 years; today we live for 67. According to the UN we have reduced poverty more in the last 50 years than we did in the preceding 500, and it has been reduced in practically every country.

Lomborg backs up his claims with exhaustively researched statistics. He is not arguing a complacent case, however. The evidence suggests that 'things are *better* – but not necessarily *good*'. For example, the effects of global warming are exaggerated, in his opinion, but it is happening and may indeed have worrying consequences. Another example: 'The food situation has vastly improved, but in 2010 there will be 680 million people starving, which is obviously not good *enough*' (Lomborg, 2001 [1998]: 5).

Lomborg argues that policies for improvement are not helped by blanket condemnation of everything that is occurring on the environmental front. It is necessary to identify the worst problems and do something about them, such as the persistence of mass starvation in an unequally rich world where the material conditions of life are generally improving rather than worsening.

He recommends cost–benefit analysis to establish priorities in dealing with problems. From such a point of view, he argues, the eradication of AIDS is a more urgent and tractable problem than containing or reducing global warming. Despite, or perhaps because of, its dull economism, this line of reasoning amounts to a defence of modernity against myths of a better past and advocacy of returning to traditional ways, exemplified by deep-green politics, while retaining the Enlightenment impulse of fearless criticism in favour of human betterment founded on reliable evidence and emancipatory reason.

The toing and froing of claim and counterclaim is characteristic of public debate on chronic issues such as risk and environmental degradation. Empirical counter-evidence is also used by those on the other side of the environmental debate from that occupied by Lomborg. For instance, George Monbiot (2005: 23) has challenged David Bellamy's claim that the world's glaciers 'are not shrinking but in fact are growing' according to the Glacier Monitoring Service in Zurich. Monbiot checked with the Glacier Monitoring Service and was informed, without reservation, that Bellamy was wrong and the evidence he quoted for his erroneous claim was not furnished by the Zurich-based monitoring unit at all. On further investigation, Monbiot found that Bellamy's figures – used to back up his claim that, since 1980, glaciers have been growing not melting – were derived from a well-organised American lobby, supported by dubious science, against the mounting evidence of perilous climate change and campaigns to halt it. So, in this case and many others, Beck's theoretical analysis is by no means lacking in empirical substantiation.

I do not wish to adjudicate between Beck's thesis and Lomborg's counter-evidence in this chapter – after all, ambivalence is a pronounced feature of late-modern consciousness and sensibility (Bauman, 1991). Instead of trying to resolve the contrary views argumentatively, the intention here is to illustrate uncertainty about the present condition and the difficulties of knowing quite what to think and do, which is typical of the current conjuncture, and, moreover, why we should take the risk society thesis seriously.

Beck (2000: xii) himself stresses the ambivalence of risk. It is not exclusively about impending global catastrophe, though that may be so. It is also about a pervasive sense of risk, uncertainty and chance in a plethora of weaker senses than the catastrophic and maximalist version of the extent of environmental risk. Actually, when we talk of a culture of risk, this is what is probably meant most commonly in the lifeworld when we are confronted by an uncertain future dictated not only at the outer reaches of the system but also in mundane activity. The palpability of the lifeworld always outstrips that of a remote and apparently unfathomable system over which people ordinarily feel they have little if any control (Habermas, 1987 [1981]). That is not to deny the operations of the system have determinate consequences for everyday life, sometimes fatally so. For many, however, impending global catastrophe is too awesome to contemplate, whereas there is a sense that the travails of daily and knowable existence can at least be addressed and something done about them by us and significant others in our lifeworld.

In what follows, the proposition is explored that a sense of risk has pervasive and acutely cultural manifestations today, ranging from the routinely agonistic experiences of everyday life and the course of life to the specialised practices of cultural production and circulation, the dynamics of which are accentuated by neoliberal globalisation.

To my knowledge, the risks of creative work and their severe manifestations under conditions of neoliberal globalisation have never properly been considered from the risk society perspective. First, however, and since this is a general chapter on risk and culture, it is necessary to consider the mediation of risk, how risks are represented in contemporary communications media and how popular understanding of societal and global risk is thereby framed.

Mediating risk – culture, media and risk

Ulrich Beck appreciates that public understanding and political struggles over risk are hugely dependent on how they are articulated by modern media of communication. According to Beck, risk issues are defined in the public sphere by the contest of contending forces – most especially between environmental campaigns and corporate public relations – in relation to the processes of mass mediation. As Beck (1998: 18) puts it, however, a 'mismatch exists in risk society between the character of hazards, or manufactured uncertainties, and the prevalent *relations of definition*'. The cardinal implication here is that, for whatever reason, the media are not up to the job of representing risks adequately and in such a way that public support for policies to eradicate them is mobilised effectively.

Media researchers have complained that Beck's account of mediated risk is too vague and imprecise (Cottle, 1998). This opens up a busily worked seam of empirical research, closely examining various cases of risk and their mass mediation (for instance, Allan et al., 2000).

It is an elementary truism of media research that news does not simply reflect reality but instead constructs versions of reality that usually legitimise what is going on politically. In any event, in terms of public understanding, reality is always a mediated affair. Moreover, the political culture in general sets limits on the reportable and so do corporate interests linked to media organisations. Famously, the Soviet news media covered up the Chernobyl disaster as best it could. Such a deliberate omission is less likely in the news media of liberal-democratic countries. Important issues, such as famine, disappear from view for long stretches of time, however, and reappear intermittently. Furthermore, the news is necessarily selective so all sorts of matters are hardly reported at all.

There is a cycle of news reporting whereby an issue remains current only for a comparatively brief period, until it goes stale, and then another issue crops up to take its place. The time of news is incommensurate with the time of 'real' reality – that is, in the realm of prediscursive occurrence from the point of view of the media. News is event-driven and, especially in television, impelled by the visualisation of dramatic incidents. So-called 'real-world' problems, however, remain acute even when news coverage has moved on to something else. Critics complain about the neglect and sidelining of deep and long-term issues in favour of topical events. Additionally, they question the slant news coverage puts on its reporting of selected topics and the particular ways in which different voices are admitted to the news and given greater or lesser credence according to hierarchies of power and authority. Such complaints are routine features of critical media research.

More generally, there is a complex exchange and, indeed, frequent confusion between ontology – what exists – and epistemology – what is known. It does not follow that, if we do not know about something, then it does not exist.

Beck has argued persistently that the discourse of proof in environmental debates restricts understanding of subterranean processes that are not immediately observable and measurable. Barbara Adam (1998) notes how radiation is imperceptible in everyday life. It only becomes manifest to public understanding when it has demonstrable effects, which are typically much delayed, as in the case of leukaemia, for example.

Proof of harm normally has to be adduced for the risk to be taken seriously enough in mainstream media and public policy, as in claims concerning the effects of radiation from mobile phones and the emplacement of towers (Burgess, 2004). Occasionally, alarmist reporting and flare-ups of public concern are refuted rapidly when there is no hard and fast evidence of harmful effects from such radiation, although they may actually exist.

In this respect, the use of mobile phones remains a classic risk society issue, in Beck's terms, and a massive real-life experiment on the public, the results of which may not be known for quite a while. The telecoms companies themselves, however, have taken the putative risks seriously, patenting protective shields, but, at the same time, they are reluctant to put them on sale since it would incite widespread alarm and, hence, reduce custom and use, which for them has priority over public health.

In this kind of instance, where dire warnings have been issued and largely ignored, the precautionary principle – that potentially harmful action, which as yet remains unproven, should not be taken – hardly applies at all. So, one of the most mundane features of everyday life now – the heavy use of mobile phones – goes on uninterrupted, oblivious to genuine medical concern about its possible longer-term effects. It is strangely reminiscent of what used to be thought, said and done about the risks of smoking.

Critical research on news media and risk does not complain so much about lack of coverage as risk issues, in fact, constitute a staple feature of the news. If anything, it might be argued that there is too much news of risk, though it is inadequate in its representation. In practice, critical research questions the *kind* of coverage given to such issues – its sensationalism, fragmentation and atomisation, bias towards official witness (positivistic science, politicians and accredited spokespeople generally), short span of attention, apparently random selectivity and so on.

Lomborg's take on news coverage of environmental problems concurs with that of critical media research. He says (2001 [1998]: 39), 'The basic job of news is to report individual, unrelated events from many different parts of the world'. He (2001 [1998]: 39) is fully aware of the scale of news values in the Western media: 'Hunger in Africa is nowhere near as good news as a plane crash.' Thus, Lomborg notes, coverage of the Ethiopian famine of 1984 was almost accidental. The BBC journalists who picked up on it and broke the story were actually in Addis Ababa on their way to report a completely different story. Their reports alerted the global media to a humanitarian crisis that might otherwise have been missed. It generated international concern with enduring ramifications in global politics and was followed at the time by popular charitable activities such as the Band Aid record, the Live Aid concert and the still running biennial Comic Relief Red Nose Day. By the time of Live 8, however – a global network of rock concerts timed to coincide with and put pressure on the G8 summit at Gleneagles in July 2005, yet actually serving to distract attention from genuine protest – serious questions had to be asked about the value of such events. The role of the former pop star Bob Geldof and another ageing rocker Bono had transmogrified into that of providing band aids for the leaders of rich countries to cover up their use of hypocritical ploys when ostensibly addressing poverty in the world, especially Africa.

No discussion of media representation, misrepresentation or sheer lack of representation is entirely satisfactory without some consideration of how all of this plays with audiences. Audience research, however, is fraught with difficulties and has been dominated by artificially created data of psychological 'effects' on behaviour.

Somewhat neglected with regard to risk is George Gerbner's (1995) longitudinal research on the American media's cultivation of a 'mean world syndrome', which eschews crude demonstrations of effects. His argument is that, over time, the day-to-day violence presented on US television and, most notably, the enormous body count on crime shows, particularly in fiction programming, is not only frightening but encourages a stay-at-home culture since the city streets are widely understood – most acutely so by older people – to be the sites of continuous mayhem. The everyday lifeworld is thus rendered even scarier than it actually is, though functioning as a self-fulfilling prophecy when the streets are deserted after dark.

The public's fear of danger in the USA, not only on its city streets but also from external enemies of the American way of life, especially since 9/11, is deeply felt. A recent BBC and much-acclaimed documentary series *The Power of Nightmares* argued that contemporary politics is all about instilling fearfulness into people (McGuigan, 2005a).

Frank Furedi (2002 [1997]) has written of 'the culture of fear', which penetrates deeply into everyday life so that everything becomes potentially very scary. In his opinion, demotic talk of risk has moved inexorably from the positive connotations of 'taking a risk' to anxieties over being 'at risk'. Now, as a result, everyone is at risk of becoming the victim of counselling. Furedi's work is an important counterpoint to what might be deemed a neurotic obsession with risk in contemporary culture. Yet, it probably goes too far in casting doubt on the palpability of intense problems of insecurity today – and not only psychological insecurity.

Such arguments concerning a 'mean world syndrome' and a 'culture of fear' are general propositions that go beyond audience research as such and for which the causal connections that are made between media and effect need to be treated circumspectly and located within a much broader cultural context than mediacentric research tends to do. Nevertheless, risk-consciousness is undoubtedly a discernible phenomenon.

There is further confirmation of this phenomenon from empirical research. In their focus group research on attitudes to environmental sustainability, Phil McNaghten and John Urry (1998: 221) found that 'Nearly all groups remarked on an emerging climate of uncertainty and the sense that life has become increasingly unpredictable'. Their respondents felt powerless to do anything about the problems that concerned them since these were considered so deeply entrenched yet of long-term consequence. The typical attitude was that of resignation in the face of terrifyingly uncontrollable forces.

Living with uncertainty – on your own in the face of risk

A corollary of the risk society thesis is the thesis of individualisation. The prospects of ecological catastrophe may seem remote, but the dilemmas and uncertainties of everyday life are much closer to home.

The individualisation thesis was announced in *Risk Society* (Beck, 1992 [1986]: 135):

Individualization of life situations and processes ... means that biographies become self-reflexive; socially prescribed biography is transformed into biography that is self-produced and continues to be produced. Decisions on education, profession, job, place of residence, spouse, number of children and so forth, with all the secondary decisions implied, no longer can be, they must be made. Even where the word 'decision' is too grandiose, because neither consciousness nor alternatives are present, the individuals will have to 'pay for' the consequences of decisions not taken.

This is reiterated with Elisabeth Beck-Gernsheim in *The Normal Chaos of Love* (Beck and Beck-Gernsheim, 1995 [1990]: 6):

Individualization means that men and women are released from the gender roles prescribed by industrial society for life in the nuclear family. At the same time, and this aggravates the situation, they find themselves forced under pain of material disadvantage, to build up a life of their own by way of the labour market, training and mobility, and if need be to pursue this life at the cost of their commitments to family, relations and friends.

The human-made hazards brought on ourselves by a global risk society are complemented at the everyday level by individualisation, which is both liberating and disconcerting, combining personal freedom and high anxiety. Older ties of tradition and collective identification are loosened and individuals are increasingly responsible for themselves and the consequences of their actions. In that sense, there is a correspondence between societal risk and personal risk. In the risk society, individuals expect to control their fates – to spend their money and time as they so wish, be in command of their bodies and living spaces. These expectations are increasingly commonplace, though with the highly educated and comparatively well-off leading the way in authoring their own biographies, determining career paths, accepting and rejecting social obligations. Older fixities of class and status are less acceptable. The ideals of bourgeois individualist ideology, the dreams of romanticism and the grim vision of existentialism are realised for potentially everyone. Are we all existentialists now, condemned to freedom, alone in the world? More likely, individualisation is experienced in a common rather than philosophical sense as a kind of Americanisation of the self.

Individualisation might mean the dissolution of class identity and, hence, class struggle. It has implications for ethnic, gender and sexual identity. Most immediately, it signifies a crisis for familial relations – not the end of the family but a renegotiated contract governing intimate conduct, outlawing masculine dominance and liberating hitherto subordinate members. The 'nuclear family' was a cornerstone of industrial capitalism and simple modernity, reproducing labour power, sustaining patriarchy and serving, ideally, as a safe haven for the individual. Feminism, the rising divorce rate and the virtual emancipation of the child from parental authority have undermined that institution's stability for many members of a reflexively modern society.

Typically, 'personalised contradictions' are experienced in individual conduct and primary relationships. No role is rigidly prescribed by tradition any longer. Women, in particular, struggle with contradictory aspirations in work, partnerships and childcare. Singlehood, serial monogamy, multiplex families, arising from divorce and remarriage – in none of these arrangements are rules and conventions reliably established.

In personal life – and not only in wealth creation, science, technology and official politics – risky decisions have to be made with no guarantee as to outcome or, normally, sufficient insurance cover. That is not to say there is no guidance or assurance on offer, just that they are unreliable in a chancy social world.

In global terms, these features of individualisation are most pronounced in problems experienced by the comparatively wealthy, yet they are spreading down and further around. Divorce, for instance, used to be too expensive for the poor as well as stigmatising for both parties, but this is not so now in affluent parts of the world. Inevitably, such developments provoke ever-hardening resistance, such as the Islamic fundamentalist reaction to these modern ways.

There are also Christian forms of religious revivalism, such as papal edicts confirming the official prohibition on contraception despite the spread of AIDS, at its chronic worst in Africa, and the disqualification of women from the priesthood and priests from marriage, as well as the extraordinary political clout of Protestant fundamentalism in the USA and its dissemination to South America.

Beck and Beck-Gernsheim (2002 [2001]: 22–29) have distilled the individualisation thesis into a set of basic propositions that are interlinked with one another in their essay 'A life of one's own in a runaway world' (see Beck and Beck-Gernsheim, 2002 [2001], Chapter 2) that can only be touched on briefly here (see McGuigan, 2006 [1999] and 2010 for more extended discussion). There is a 'compulsion', in Beck and Beck-Gernsheim's words, 'to lead a life of one's own' in a highly differentiated risk society (2002 [2001]: 23). That is, individualisation is more pronounced where a modern complex division of labour and separation of spheres of activity exists.

Individualisation is not an individual matter. Certain kinds of institutional arrangements foster individualisation among the many, not just the few. This may be experienced as surviving 'the rat race' by being proactive, inventive and successful in achieving one's goals. Quite possibly, everybody is trying to do the same. Individualised activity, it has to be stressed, does not run counter to social institutions; it is embedded within them and required by them. There is nothing necessarily rebellious about institutionalised individuality – it is a kind of conformity.

In the risk society, life is no longer scripted in advance for the individual. The individual is 'free', so to speak, to author the narrative biography of his or her life course. There is always the possibility, however, that one's own life story will go disastrously wrong, for which the individual will be held to account. There is no point in trying to blame, say, your poverty and debasement on 'society'. There is no let up. Not being vigilant about one's own health, for instance, is a personal failing. Illness, addiction, unemployment and the like are no longer seen as blows of fate or societal effect but deemed to be matters of individual responsibility.

In a globally networked world, the person's position is displaced – that is, it is affected by forces operating in other places. Moreover, migration is an ever more pronounced feature of life under conditions of increased mobility. Traditions do not exactly disappear in these circumstances but are constantly reinvented. Old classifications have to be discarded and new ones formulated. There are no set rules for conduct; new ones are persistently tried out to see if they will work.

Successful self-realisation requires the weighing up of contradictory evidence, negotiating one's way in uncertain conditions where older arrangements, such as established family and work relations, are dissolving in a situation of flux. Flexibility in negotiating the uncertain conditions of modern life, being a survivor, becomes the standard of socially approved success. Life is lived in a culture of process rather than in compliance with static tradition.

Living with uncertain prospects and no traditional authority to rely on results in fresh political possibilities. Democratic negotiation and renegotiation of everything is always on the cards. For example, there is a hidden green message in the thesis of individualisation. The autonomy and defence of the personal life may connect to protecting the environment as such. Beck and Beck-Gernsheim (2002 [2001]: 28) claim that 'The dominance of the life of one's own thus leads to an opening and a sub-politicization of society, but also to a depoliticization of national politics'. The old collective identifications of party politics – the 'party of the working class' and so forth – are becoming unhinged. Here, Beck and Beck-Gernsheim refer explicitly to the New Labour project in Britain – a pragmatic politics under the cover of a long-standing front (the representation of labour) that has little substance these days. Subpolitics has a more radical aspect, however, in the shift from party politics to 'single-issue' campaigns. This is most obvious in environmental politics but also relevant to such matters as the mobilization of an anti-war constituency in 2003 against the Anglo-American assault on Iraq. These issues resonate with individualisation in the sense that one-off campaigns do not necessarily require any permanent sense of collective identity.

Individualisation looks very much like the kind of subjectivity and approved way of carrying on called into being by neoliberal globalisation, constructing a type of individual attuned to living in such a harshly modern civilisation. Neoliberalism, first and foremost, is a reaction to post-Second World War Keynesian command management of the national economy and the social wage guaranteed by the welfare state, public protection of the individual from the travails of poverty and unemployment, ill health and old age, from 'cradle to grave'.

The shift from Fordist organisation and job security to the flexible networking of post-Fordism in a 'global world' is a feature of the neoliberal political economy that has had a dramatic impact since the 1970s. It is a reversion to nineteenth-century principles of free trade in an international economic order, minimal State intervention, except for coercion (police and military), and competitive individualism, entailing precious little help for the weak who fall by the wayside and exorbitant rewards for those who bully it out at the top. As Margaret Thatcher noted, the reason the Good Samaritan could be charitable was that he was rich.

Beck and Beck-Gernsheim deny the link between individualisation and neoliberalism. They put it down to a misunderstanding or mistranslation into English of a German meaning (Beck and Beck-Gernsheim, 2002 [2001]: xxi):

One can hardly think of a word heavier with misunderstanding than 'individualization' has proved to have been in English-speaking countries. To prevent the discussion of this book [Individualization – their collection of essays on the concept] from running aground on these misunderstandings, it is necessary to establish and keep in view the distinction between the neoliberal idea of the free-market individual (inseparable from the concept of 'individualization' as used in the English-speaking countries) and the concept of Individualizierung in the sense of instituionalized individualism, as it will be developed in this book.

This is a curious disclaimer since the appropriate neoliberal subject has two not unrelated roles – the sovereign consumer and the entrepreneurial self – neither of which would seem contrary to the notion of individualisation. Admittedly, for the Becks, individualisation does mean more than that. It involves liberation as well as subjugation to prevailing imperatives. The popular appeal of neoliberalism, however, is similarly experienced as liberating, albeit that this is somewhat illusory: for everyone, freedom of choice and opportunity to make it on your own. Surely, that particular imaginary is deeply institutionalised now.

Taking a chance – culture and capitalism

Capitalism has always been a risky business, investing now for later profit – a gamble, in fact. The safer the investment, the more modest the likely profit. High-risk investment may yield greater profits or, indeed, greater losses.

Historically, capitalism has gone through periods of boom and bust, once regarded as the inevitable fluctuations of the trade cycle. Thus, capitalism, however successful, is always vulnerable to crisis. Speculation has often been associated with periodic destabilsation and dramatic collapse, such as the Wall Street crash of 1929. The 1930s was a decade of severe disorder, economic recession, mass unemployment and the ascendancy of radical politics: communism, fascism and national socialism. Nazism rose and fell but communism endured much longer, sweeping up Eastern Europe, gaining power in China and spreading its promise to poorer parts of the world generally.

The historical insecurities of capitalism and the challenge of an alternative economic system prompted liberal-democratic states to organise society in more stabilising and socially equitable ways, heralding the period of 'the welfare state' and 'the mixed economy'; and 'the golden age' of 'full employment' and 'the consumer society'. Social-democratic principles were, in effect, hegemonic for a while at the nation-state level in 'the West' and even, to an extent, in the bastion of capitalism, the USA. That set of arrangements faltered in the 1970s and the popular gains of the previous 30 years came under siege.

In the past 30 years, neoliberal globalisation triumphed as communism collapsed and social democracy went into retreat. The effects have been manifold, including the restructuring of industries and labour relations along more capitalistic lines. These and other features of the present condition have impacted upon cultural industries and cultural work generally.

If capitalism in general is inherently risky, then capitalist cultural or creative industries and work within them are doubly risky and, therefore, exemplary – not least because they are considered to be at a cutting edge of economic development (Rifkin 2000; Florida, 2003 [2002]). Bernard Miège (1989) argues that cultural industries are confronted with the problem of regularising and marketing output, which is difficult to achieve, especially for autonomous works of art that are not easy to pigeonhole.

Nicholas Garnham (1990) points to the contradiction at the heart of the industrially produced cultural commodity: it is not typically used up in the act of consumption. The consumer can view a DVD over and over again whereas a loaf of bread cannot be eaten twice. Cultural industries, therefore, adopt strategies of artificial scarcity and perpetual novelty in order to encourage consumers to seek new products. In fact, most cultural commodities fail in the marketplace. Taste is very difficult to predict, so hits have to pay for misses.

For Dag Björkegren (1996), cultural business is characterically 'postmodern', *avant la lettre*, since it is multirational. Most businesses only pursue a single, commercial rationale. Cultural businesses, however, are obliged to combine a cultural with a commercial rationale. The actual mix of commerce and culture varies from sector to sector, with some still putting culture before commerce, which is much harder to do in increasingly fierce market conditions. Yet, it still remains the case that (Björkegren, 1996: 43):

> A prominent feature of arts-related businesses is ... a high level of uncertainty in the market response to individual products. Because of this uncertainty, the business strategies of arts-producing organizations tend to be 'emergent' rather than deliberate, an outcome of interaction with the environment rather than the result of internally generated business plans.

While that may be so, it does not stop cultural businesses from seeking to perform like any other cost-conscious business. Certain strategies are peculiar to cultural business, however. Rather like Nike products (which might be regarded as quasi-cultural commodities), more money is usually put into marketing would-be Hollywood blockbusters than making them. If there is not a quick return from the initial sales push on release, however, the product (the movie) is quickly abandoned as yet another turkey. Also, a past history of spectacular failure, such as the way Michael Cimino's *Heaven's Gate* brought down United Artists (Bach, 1985), has resulted in huge and routine efforts being put into budgetary control, micro-management and product testing. This is done in order to reduce uncertainty and tame wild creative types, such as the ill-fated Cimino, whose great success with *The Deer Hunter* prompted him to overspend extravagantly on his next production.

The example of cultural business casts some doubt on the sheer novelty of riskiness in the risk society, at least in this area of human endeavour. Nonetheless, it is true that cultural businesses have become more risk-conscious and, indeed, risk averse, which has prompted them, in addition to synergistic multiple exploitation of successful properties, to devolve risk further in two especially salient ways. First, in post-Fordist structures of outsourcing by the major corporations so that they continue to command distribution, the locus of power in the cultural industries, as noted by Garnham (1990), while saving their businesses from other risks. Production is done 'independently' and so is research and development by 'indies' of one kind or another. The second way of devolving risk, closely related to the first, is to lay it on the workers. Here, we return to the theme of individualisation, linked in this particular instance to the uncertainties, anxieties and downright riskiness of cultural work.

Interestingly, the French word risqué has often been used in English language discussions of creativity, signifying artistic daring with an erotic charge. While 'creativity' is still worth thinking about (Negus and Pickering, 2004), it takes a back seat to the neoliberal relations of production and economic imperatives now in charge of the fashionably yet ironically named 'creative industries'.

Creative work has never been easy or secure. Many feel the calling, as they do in sport as well, but few enter the elect, leaving large numbers of talented and dedicated people, mostly young, not quite making it and having to find alternative occupations from which to earn a living. In this respect, near success should be distinguished from abject failure. The difference between the successful and those who nearly succeeded may often be just a matter of chance. Despite the poor odds, a great many ambitious young people are prepared to take a chance on making a creative career for themselves. In her research on young creative workers in London, Angela McRobbie (2002: 516) observes, 'Creative work increasingly follows the neoliberal model, governed by the values of entrepreneurialism, individualization and reliance on commercial sponsorship'.

Young creative workers these days are object lessons in the more general process of individualisation in response to social and economic change, which is only partly grasped by the risk society thesis since it places too little emphasis on how capitalism has been restructured over the past 30 years. Crucial here is the isolation of the individual worker from collective representation and the relative absence of solidarity with those in a similar plight. If you do not make it, it is your own fault.

During the 1980s in Britain, for instance, Thatcherism attacked 'restrictive practices' in broadcasting, where strong unions had in the old days protected their members and bargained for comparatively high wages for permanent staff. Union power was much weakened, as it was also in other industrial sectors. The 'job for life' was to become something of an anachronism.

With the exception of core administrative functions, 'flexible' labour and contractual insecurity became commonplace for most new entrants to the broadcasting industry. For some older broadcasting workers it became harder to sustain their careers, though some of them benefited from new business opportunities that were opening up for those with established reputations and contacts. It became more difficult to build a career for each successive age cohort of broadcasting personnel in this period (Patterson, 2002).

A sharp division occurred between the securities of higher management – accountants and the like – and the insecurities of 'creatives', who had to manage themselves from project to project. Many are now obliged to move perpetually between temporary jobs, reliant on whatever reputations they have built up, or be prepared to work for very little, sometimes both.

Among other institutional reforms that particularly affected commercial television (Ursell, 1998), both the BBC and ITV were required from the 1990s to obtain 25 per cent of their programming from independents – that is, the kinds of companies that had sprung up in the heady days of the1980s to supply the 'publishing' broadcaster Channel 4 with innovative programmes. Broadcasting in Britain was thus transformed from bureaucratic and cumbersome Fordism to the looser structures of post-Fordism (Arthurs, 1994).

Costs were driven down in this highly competitive independent sector – now supplying proliferating cable and satellite channels as well – so wages shrank and working conditions became intolerably stressful. Poor pay and overwork all grew apace (Sparks, 1994). It is thus exceptionally difficult for women to sustain a broadcasting career when they have children (Jones, 1998) and for women generally in creative and information industries, not only in Britain (Beale, 1999). Unpropitious conditions are typical of work generally in the creative industries, from the arts world to the fashion industry, despite the glamorous image of such work. Still, 'more and more young people opt for the insecurity of jobs in the media, culture or art in the hope of success' (McRobbie, 2002: 521).

Below the level of the very successful, many are complicit in their own exploitation, imbued, as they are, with success stories of making it on your own. Club culture, 'cool' yet non-disruptive attitudes and frantic networking to make the big breakthrough deflect attention from the dire circumstances of work for these young people in a neoliberal cultural economy until they are worn out by it all and go off to do something less risky. In news coverage of the media, there is a steady flow of celebrity stories, rarely relieved by stories of how tough it can be in cultural work, such as union disputes in job-shedding Hollywood and occasional reports of young people literally working for nothing in order to get a foothold in media and cultural occupations. Modern media are self-obsessed but they display remarkably little reflexivity in this sense. Cultural policy today tends to promote rather than resist this state of affairs, so driven is it by the economic imperatives of 'the creative industries' (McGuigan, 2004b; Chapter 8 in this book).

For Romanticism, the ideal form of work was art. It was creative and made personal expression concrete in the work itself. For the lucky few, fame and fortune were the rewards. For most, however, rewards were meagre and the struggle was hard. Posterity might revalue the work but by then the artist would be dead. The worst kind of work was constant toil and lack of control, which has always been the commoner state of affairs, much more so than self-realisation in the creative activity.

Which of these kinds of labour approximates closest to cultural work today? Many are still motivated by its productive pleasures and perhaps also by the prospects of fame and fortune. The risk is high and the wages are low. Creative work under neoliberal conditions thus embodies the ubiquitous process of individualisation in a risky culture.

Conclusion – risk society and the neoliberal way of life

In this chapter I have sought to demonstrate the applicability of the risky society thesis and its corollary, the individualisation thesis, to understanding contemporary cultural processes in general and in particular – from how problems in the world are framed in the media to the struggle to make a creative career for oneself.

The risk society thesis is extremely fruitful in generating questions of social and cultural analysis. The risk society and individualisation theses, however, are not faultless. Several faults have been itemised in the foregoing account or, at least, contrary views have been tabled that call its cardinal propositions into question. Perhaps the natural environment is not at great risk after all and maybe we are too anxious about the supposed risks of everyday life.

The risk society thesis does not explain everything. Its greatest fault is the implied suggestion that it does. Other perspectives, combined with aspects of the risk society thesis, however, offer rich prospects for making sense of what is going on. When Ulrich Beck's *Risk Society* was published in English in the early 1990s, Mike Rustin (1994) complained that it had an insufficient account of the role of capitalism in contemporary social transformation. In this chapter, following that criticism, I have combined an analysis of neoliberal globalisation with insights derived from the risk society thesis, especially concerning how risks inculcated by an increasingly fierce mode of capitalism are lived on a daily basis in terms of individualisation.

On the surface, particularly in wealthy countries, capitalism today does not look so bad, except for the occasional scare threatening to bring the whole edifice tumbling down, such as the financial crisis of 2008. Still, on the surface, the capitalist way of life is 'cool' (McGuigan, 2010). We live in a cornucopia of consumption, drowning deliriously in a sea of branded goods. This is nothing like the miseries of nineteenth-century capitalism in Europe that Karl Marx wrote about so scathingly (1976 [1867]).

That is because the miseries have been devolved to cheap labour markets and sweatshops in poorer parts of the world – to newly developing countries (NDCs), where conditions of work are every bit as bad, if not worse, than in Victorian times (Klein, 2000). This is storing up big trouble for the future in terms of social injustice, realising popular aspirations for overconsumption, depletion of resources and all the horrors warned of by the risk society thesis.

Back in the already rich countries, work is not so much fun either. Even in the glamorous cultural and media industries, the so-called 'creative industries', it can be seriously stressful, too.

8 NEOLIBERALISM, URBAN REGENERATION AND CULTURAL POLICY

Introduction

Neoliberalism is a global phenomenon – not only in the sense that it operates geographically on a worldwide basis, which it does, but also it is pervasive across an extensive range of practices and policies. It is a truly hegemonic phenomenon of our time, concerning both political economy and ideological process in the broadest sense. Neoliberalism has an overwhelming discursive and cultural presence that is crucial to securing legitimacy for current stratagems. Its thought and practice are deeply embedded now in intellectual frameworks, popular culture and everyday life generally. This is evident in the way people talk these days and dream their dreams.

In the wake of the economic and political crisis of the 1970s in advanced capitalist states, neoliberalism arose to prominence as both cause and solution to any number of problems, such as deindustrialisation and strategies for revitalising urban life. Of special interest from the point of view of cultural policy, neoliberalism sets the regeneration agenda in once great cities that have fallen on hard times. A key policy device in this respect is culture. Somehow creative industries and public cultural activity, it is claimed, will save these places from their woes, heralding a vibrant future, however implausible that may be. The word 'vibrant', incidentally, is obligatory in such rhetoric, especially when applied to the urban environment. This and other claims associated with the neoliberal imaginary should, at the very least, be treated with scepticism.

Neoliberalism

It is vital to grasp the historicity of neoliberalism. Briefly defined as the 'revival of doctrines of the free market' (Gamble, 2001: 27), neoliberalism is both new and old, with chilling resonances from the past.

We should remember that only 30 or 40 years ago, the very idea that market forces should operate unrestrained on efficiency grounds and in the public interest was regarded as seriously deficient. Alternative ways of thinking and acting prevailed during the middle decades of the twentieth century. Liberal economics had been discredited in the 1930s. Moreover, there was already a retreat under way from pre-First World War globalisation. These developments were partly due to the impact of socialist and communist politics but not wholly so. Fascists had also advocated and sought to put into practice a greatly expanded State apparatus and command economy.

From the Depression of the early 1930s onwards, liberal democrats in capitalist societies shared a similar view, best exemplified by Franklin D. Roosevelt's New Deal programme in the USA to put the unemployed back to work and stimulate economic growth. That predilection was further enhanced by the Second World War and the immediate aftermath, hugely to the advantage of US capital.

The mid-twentieth-century consensus – which can roughly be called a 'social-democratic' consensus – became hegemonic. It defined the reality of nation states in terms of advanced capitalism and international relations, including the establishment of a model, sometimes with a communist inflection, for developing and post-colonial countries to emulate.

As early as the 1940s, critics argued that all this was leading inexorably to 'the road to serfdom' (Hayek, 1944). It was not until the 1970s, however, that neoliberalism really took hold beyond a cabal of right-wing critics of State intervention and Keynesian economics (Yergen and Stanislaw, 2002 [1998]). This coincided with a crisis of capitalism and, then, the decline and eventual collapse of soviet communism. The OPEC hike in oil prices of 1973 hastened the shift from a Fordist to a post-Fordist – and, arguably, neo-Fordist – regime of accumulation and mode of regulation. This meant, among other things, an attack on organised labour in older capitalist states and the devolution of much manufacturing to the much cheaper labour markets and poor working conditions of newly industrialising countries (NICs). This global transformation was facilitated and speeded up by developments in information and communication technologies (Castells, 2000 [1996]).

It is important not to underestimate the role played by the collapse of communism and the retreat of social democracy in the transition from the social-democratic consensus to neoliberal globalisation. To put it summarily, resistance backed up by the threat of something potentially more transformative was broken and accommodation to the demands of labour movements gradually eroded and, to an extent, actually withdrawn.

Transferring manufacture from richer to poorer countries, reducing the social wage, labour movement decline, expanding global business and speeding up communications, each contributed to the victory of market ideology and practice during the recent period. The International Monetary Fund (IMF), World Bank and World Trade Organisation (WTO) all subscribe to neoliberal doctrines of free trade (as opposed to fair trade), as well as privatisation and deregulation. The extension of free trade policies to services and cultural goods – allowing transnational corporations to infiltrate or circumvent, in principle if not necessarily in practice, say, national health services and cultural agencies – has raised many contentious issues. The audio-visual sector is a major focus of debate around WTO deliberations (Pauwels and Loisen, 2003). With regard to cultural policy, the operations of the General Agreement on Trade in Services (GATS) and Trade-Related Intellectual Property Rights (TRIPS) are of immense significance.

Although there are dangers in exaggerating the impact of neoliberalism and treating it as if it were manifest 'everywhere and in everything' (Gamble, 2001), it is, nevertheless, astonishingly pervasive – for instance, in the global production and circulation of audio-visual commodities and the burgeoning tourist industries of poorer countries.

Hollywood doubled its share of the world film market in the 1990s. Just as consequential, the new international division of cultural labour (NICL; see Miller et al., 2005 [2001]) exploits cheap labour and resources around the world, often supported by governmental inducements and tax breaks to attract Hollywood production companies.

Take Mexico, for example. It is not only an especially convenient location for making movies but also for making viewing equipment for customers in the USA (Paredes, 2003).

Mexico and other Central American countries are, furthermore, sites of comparatively inexpensive tourism for the affluent of the world. Governments in poorer countries see tourism as a means of economic development after the failures of State-led modernisation, yet workers in tourism are paid very little and profits are siphoned off by global players. In the West, we tend to distinguish between 'good' and 'bad' tourism. Bad tourism is seen as vulgar mass behaviour and damaging to the host environment. It is debateable to what extent good tourism, such as eco-tourism, is any better, according to research in places like Belize (Duffy, 2002).

Global and continental agencies, such as UNESCO (for instance, WCCD, 1996 [1995]) and the Council of Europe (for instance, EFTDC, 1997), have issued dire warnings concerning the cultural and ecological costs of tourism, yet there is not much they can do about it. Such agencies have, in any case, largely succumbed to 'the reality' of neoliberal globalisation and its ineluctable force. The widespread belief, even among those who would wish to resist and oppose it, that 'there is no alternative' is a defining feature of neoliberal hegemony. Doubting Thomases are deemed to be simply 'unrealistic'.

Yet, contradictions abound, not least of which is that between global communications and the astounding rate of exploitation on a global scale today that would make Karl Marx blink incredulously were he still around. Critics and campaigners (such as Klein, 2000) constantly point out just how fierce global exploitation is these days, with large segments of the world's population living on less than, say, a dollar a day, earned either by working long hours under appalling conditions in sweatshops or in barely subsistent economic activity outside the loop of globalisation. The worst abuses, exploitative circumstances and dire poverty persist. Compassion fatigue is endemic, however, when nothing seems to change for the better (Cohen, 2001).

We are all, whether we like it or not, caught up in this system of intense exploitation and extreme inequality, however distantly located the sweatshops that manufacture the logo-laden goods for those who brand themselves at 'affordable prices'. Sweatshop workers also watch television, though, and see images of the good life that are constantly held up for them to admire and desire. The glittering consumer culture of latter-day capitalism has seduced everyone, including those who have precious little access to it (Sklair, 2002).

A political economist (such as Harvey, 2005) would no doubt innumerate various other and multiple contradictions that suggest the neoliberal order is unstable and, ultimately, unsustainable. It follows from a critical account that this is only a moment in history, not the end of history by any means, and perhaps as transient as the nostalgic 'golden age' (Hobsbawm, 1994) of the mid-to-late twentieth century, which had its own dirty secrets and is never to return. That is because history does not work like that. The future is hard to foretell, but it is unlikely to be a simple reversal of fortune and reprise of an earlier condition.

There is something more to add to such a sketch of the present condition in terms of cultural analysis that might help to explain the strength, resilience and undoubted popular appeal of neoliberalism.

Ideology and everyday life

Neoliberalism is an ideological formation, not the absolute truth of economic law. It operates on several levels — from high theory through various kinds of expertise down to the most banal level of common sense. While this ideological formation may be contested at the higher level of theory, shown to be wanting conceptually and evidentially, it is also important to appreciate how deeply ingrained certain dispositions are in the everyday life of neoliberalism.

For our present purposes, ideology has two general features: *distortion* and *justification*. It is axiomatic that ideological distortion of reality is motivated by unequal power relations. Distortion, however, is not enough of an explanation as either cause or effect. Ideology also operates to justify a given condition and win popular consent. It has to be plausible and so must address actual problems and offer credible solutions.

Language is ideologically loaded and, in this case, the loading is especially manifest in what we might call, after Bourdieu, 'NewLiberalSpeak' (Bourdieu and Wacquant, 2001). In public discourse, certain words become unspeakable whereas other words are repeated endlessly. For instance, words such as 'class', 'exploitation', 'domination' and 'inequality' are hardly ever spoken these days, but we hear a great deal about 'globalisation', 'flexibility', 'governance', 'employability', 'underclass' and 'exclusion'. It is particularly striking how policy-orientated social scientists now talk about 'exclusion' instead of 'exploitation' (most notably, Manuel Castells). Understood literally, this might imply that the 'excluded' should be admitted to the ranks of the properly exploited rather than left out in the cold to fend for themselves, neglected by the system.

Expert language works, typically, with a set of binary oppositions whereby, in general terms, 'the State' is, by definition, negative and 'the market' is positive. Negatives include 'constraint', 'rigid', 'closed', 'immobile', 'outdated', 'stasis' and so on. Positives include 'freedom', 'flexible', 'open', 'novelty', 'dynamic' and so forth. These linked binary oppositions conjure up the ideological universal of neoliberalism in public and expert discourses (Bourdieu and Wacquant, 2001: 5).

More broadly, at work and in leisure, neoliberalism promotes the language of branding, consumer sovereignty, market reasoning and management (Cameron, 2000) and, it can be argued, the language of individualisation as well (McGuigan, 2010; Chapter 7 in this book). It works its way down the generations to the young – for instance, in 'the buying and selling of teenagers' of viral marketing (Quart, 2003). Neoliberal discourse offers solutions to all of life's problems. For example, Harvard Business School professor Rachel Greenwald wrote an advice book for young women entitled *The Programme: Fifteen Steps to Finding a Husband after Thirty*, written in the language of management and marketing. Female singletons are exhorted to adopt 'a strategic plan' and cultivate 'a personal brand' in order to situate themselves advantageously in the marketplace of coupling and improve their terms of trade in close relationships (Walter, 2004: 25). This is merely one symptom of a more ubiquitous process that has been described as 'the commercialization of intimate life' (Hochschild, 2003).

Various attempts have been made to describe the distinctive culture of capitalism in its neoliberal phase. One commentator names it 'the culture of the new capitalism' (Sennett, 2006), while other nominations include 'the new spirit of capitalism' (Boltanski and Chiapello, 2005 [1999]), 'cultural capitalism' (Rifkin, 2000) and 'cool capitalism' (McGuigan, 2010). Clearly, the newer spirit of capitalism is nothing like the older one. It is no longer puritanical but hedonistic, having incorporated 'the artistic critique' of deferred gratification, conformism and so on in its self-image and, to a significant extent, its lifestyle practices as well.

Because cultural production and circulation has become such a massive feature of the global economy, it is tempting to assume that capitalism has superseded the old smoke-stack world of material production and we now live in an 'experience economy', where it is meanings that are produced and consumed instead of things. That, however, is a skewed view of what is actually going on. It is a view of the world seen from the perspective of Western 'knowledge' workers and the privileged consuming subjects of cultural capitalism. Somebody somewhere is making the things that bear those meanings.

Still, the global appeal of capitalist culture at present cannot be denied. There is no more profound site of it than China (Gittings, 2005). China is not simply being absorbed wholesale into Western consumerism and the global economy, however. China combines the most excessive features of not only capitalism but also communism and feudalism in a combustible mix.

The preferable term for naming the present cultural condition, in my opinion, is 'cool capitalism' in so far as this invokes the seductive and apparently rebellious features of capitalism today, especially for the young.

Creative industries

Turning to questions of cultural policy, there has been a marked shift from aesthetics to economics. The twentieth-century tradition of public arts patronage was concerned with funding culture that was not considered economically viable, including heritage and experimentation. Cultural policy constructed in this way differed from communications policy, in which economic considerations were always of greater concern.

Communications policies typically regulated access to and use of the airwaves, for instance, and sought to frame industrial conditions, sometimes by funding public organisations that represented an alternative to those in the marketplace. Although differently focused, both communications and cultural policy offered 'protection' of some kind or another. The boundaries between these two spheres of action have been gradually erased and now cultural policy, like communications policy, is mainly driven by economic considerations.

There is a genealogy to be traced in the rhetorical shift from 'culture industry' to 'cultural industries', then 'creative industries'. This has brought about a remarkable convergence of theories and practices. Since the 1940s, the term 'culture industry' was used negatively to designate what had already been called 'mass culture' – in effect, the object of criticism enunciated on behalf of 'authentic' cultural practices in the fine and avant-garde arts (Adorno and Horkheimer, 1979 [1944]). Although formulated from a left-wing position, 'the culture industry' critique was backward-looking and, in certain respects, reactionary.

By the 1980s, the term 'cultural industries' – significantly, plural – was at least neutral in its usage and, indeed, becoming distinctly positive in its connotations. It was argued that the publicly subsidised arts were marginal to cultural life in general and governmental policy should turn its attention to the real action in 'the cultural industries' instead (Garnham and Epstein, 1985). This term entered policy discourse and, in some cities especially, cultural industries were developed in order to replace declining industries of a more material kind.

Later in Britain, the shift from 'cultural industries' to 'creative industries' rhetoric was signalled by the New Labour government's Department for Culture, Media and Sport's publication of *The Creative Industries: Mapping document* (CITF, 1998). This reported the findings of a task force made up of politicians and officials from various ministries, including Trade and Industry, and business leaders such as Richard Branson (music, retail and transport entrepreneur), Alan McGee (record producer), Gail Reebuck (publisher), Paul Smith (fashion designer) and David Puttnam (film producer).

The mapping document listed the following as creative industries: advertising, architecture, arts and antique markets, crafts, design, fashion, film, interactive software, music, performing arts, publishing, software of any kind, television and radio. Emphasis was placed on the sheer scale of the UK's creative industries, generating revenues of £60 billion a year at that time and employing 1.5 million people. To quote from the document (CITF, 1998: 8): 'The value of the creative industries to UK gross domestic product is ... greater than the contribution of any of the UK's manufacturing industry.'

'Creative industries' rhetoric is articulated in relation to the generic forms of 'information' and 'knowledge society' rhetoric, blurring and, indeed, effectively obliterating the border between, on the one hand, arts and culture and, on the other, the informational mode of development (Castells, 2000 [1996]). A creative industries 'paradigm' has even been announced in cultural studies, aimed at reorientating research and pedagogy in the field (Hartley, 2003; Hartley, 2005) and heralding a bright, new tomorrow for 'the creative class' (Florida, 2003 [2002]).

The new creative industries paradigm promotes several themes that bring together culture and economy. Integral to the paradigm is the very idea of a creative class. There are said to be 38 million members of this rising class in the USA alone, calculated questionably by Richard Florida (2003 [2002]) to be 30 per cent of all people in employment. The creative class, to quote from its most influential author, includes 'people in science and engineering, architecture, and design, education, arts, music and enter-tainment, whose economic function is to create new ideas, new technology and/or new creative content'. It 'also includes a broader group of *creative professionals* in business and finance, law, health care and related fields' (Florida, 2003 [2002]: 8). These people deal with complex problems and 'share a common creative ethos that values creativity, individuality, difference and merit', according to the managerial expert on the creative class and its fun culture. Apparently, such people can regenerate run-down places.

They are also, it must be said, the people most likely to benefit from neoliberal urban regeneration.

Urban regeneration

Although the question of urban regeneration is of major concern, in the wake of deindustrialisation in Europe and North America, the city as such is not in decline, seen from a global perspective.

Between 1950 and now, the number of cities with populations of over a million has shot up from 86 to 400 and is forecast to rise to 550 by 2015. Two-thirds of the global population growth occurred in cities during the second half of the twentieth century, creating a huge urban population that is increasing currently at the rate of a million a week. There are more people living in towns and cities today than there were on the whole of planet Earth in 1950. Growth of the total world population in the foreseeable future – expected to reach a peak of 10 billion by 2050 – will be in urban areas, 95 per cent in developing countries (Davis, 2004; Davis, 2006).

As well as the urban birth rate, enormous migration from the country to the city is another and more important factor. There are also significant cultural changes associated with urban concentration and migration – such as the Spanish counter-colonisation of Los Angeles – and, more generally, the increased complexity of cultural mixing, which has always been a feature of urban expansion. That is all before even mentioning badly rewarded and insecure employment, overcrowding and sheer misery. What is happening in a city like Liverpool in the North West of England, with a plummeting population over the second half of the twentieth century, and similar cities in the rich countries of Western Europe and North America, may quite reasonably be considered trivial in comparison.

The growth and decline of cities represent two sides of a general phenomenon that connects richer and poorer parts of the world: neoliberal globalisation. This is an economic phenomenon that is driven politically and has significant cultural aspects. It is a mistake, however, to reduce cities to signs and symbols. That is a cultural reductionism at least as problematic, if not more so, as economic reductionism.

Critical geographers interested in the impact of neoliberalism on urban change in North America and Western Europe recommend a case studies approach to the path-dependent and contested character of neoliberal regeneration within the general context of uneven economic development (Brenner and Theodor, 2002). The connections between 'market-orientated economic growth' and developments favourable to 'elite consumption practices' in deindustrialised cities are especially salient features of what are described as 'culture-led' regeneration strategies in a great many places. Civic boosterism and 'postmodern' festival and spectacle generally are especially congenial to the professional managerial class, renamed recently 'the creative class'.

In the 1980s, an astute commentator on the American scene asked, 'how many successful convention centers, sports stadia, disney-worlds, and harbor places can there be?' (Harvey, 1989: 273). In the 1990s, serious doubt was cast on the actual economic benefits to local people derived from such schemes in Western Europe (Bianchini and Parkinson, 1993). Still, they go on being built relentlessly and great claims are made for them.

To illustrate the issues at stake, let us look next at the European Capital of Culture programme and the experience of Liverpool 2008, which are revealing.

European Capital of Culture

The annual European City of Culture (now renamed Capital of Culture) festival, inaugurated in the 1980s, was a means of celebrating universally acknowledged great cities. In 1985, it was Athens, in 1986 Florence, in 1987 Amsterdam, in 1988 Berlin, in 1989 Paris. Then, in 1990 it was Glasgow in the West of Scotland. Glasgow? If it had been Edinburgh or London, nobody would have been surprised, but Glasgow?

The selection of Glasgow signalled a turning point in the competition (Richards, 2000). No longer was it merely about honouring what already existed; it had become about something new, about regeneration.

Glasgow had been famed in the past for its shipbuilding and, indeed, radical politics – it was the infamous 'Red Clyde'. By the 1980s, however, it was in a terrible state – a decrepit place of deindustrialisation and mass unemployment. It was also notorious for street violence and religious bigotry, manifest in the rivalry between its great football clubs – the Catholic Celtic and Protestant Rangers. There was also a particularly negative stereotype of working-class masculinity associated with the city. The Glaswegian working-class man was routinely depicted as drunk and dangerous with a guttural accent that was particularly offensive to the Standard English-speaking Southern middle class and also, indeed, to refined Edinburgh folk, among others.

Debate over Glasgow's year as European City of Culture still goes on. The rebranded Glasgow is now said to be second only to London in the British Isles for shopping and 58,000 of its inhabitants are employed in what is loosely categorised as tourism whereas the shipbuilding industry, even at its height, employed only 38,000. Yet Glasgow still contains the three poorest constituencies in Britain, where life expectancy is more than ten years below the national average. It might be concluded, from such contrasting evidence, that *cultural* policy is no substitute for *social* policy.

A distinctive yet seldom mentioned feature of neoliberal development is to translate issues of social policy into questions of cultural policy. In its turn, cultural policy ceases to be specifically about culture at all. The predominant rationale for cultural policy today is economic – in terms of competitiveness and regeneration – and, to a lesser extent and as an after-thought, social, as an implausible palliative to exclusion and poverty.

A similar process to the paradigmatic case of Glasgow occurred in the case of Britain's subsequently designated European Capital of Culture, Liverpool, in 2008.

Liverpool, capital of culture 2008

Rather like Glasgow, the port of Liverpool on the Mersey Estuary in the North West of England experienced a precipitate decline in the post-Second World War period. It had been one of the greatest international trading ports in the world around 1900. Since 1945, however, the population has fallen by over half – from a peak of 850,000 to 415,000.

When Liverpool FC won the European Champions League in 2005, it was reported that over half a million people gathered on the streets of the city to greet the team on its return home from the final in Istanbul. That was more than the whole of the official population of Liverpool. Busloads of well-wishers must have been coming in from all over.

So, Liverpool was not just a place for the Beatles to leave. It has long been run down. In the 1980s, Liverpool was widely considered something of a political as well as an economic basket case, particularly when a Trotskyist faction within the Labour Party, the Militant Tendency, briefly captured control of the city council.

Significantly, as with Glasgow, Liverpool also had a negative working-class and masculine stereotype heavily associated with it. The stereotypical Liverpudlian, the Scouser, was widely constructed and perceived as a whinger, bemoaning his current lot and nostalgic for a past when Liverpool ruled the waves – not only the sea waves but also the airwaves with the Merseybeat, wacky comedy and gritty drama.

Like other deindustrialised cities, Liverpool has a complex and multilayered history. It was a bastion of labour as well as a place of significantly mixed in migration. The largest numbers were Irish, but Liverpool has one of the oldest black communities in the UK, dating from the slave trade. It also has bourgeois splendour. Liverpool was once considered a gentlemanly city, more sophisticated than Manchester. The buildings on the Mersey waterfront – the Port of Liverpool Authority Building, Cunard Building and Liver Building, known as 'the three Graces' – are symbols of past mercantile grandeur and Liverpool's Georgian terraces are reminders of gracious living in a once great trading city. Institutions such as the Walker Gallery also signify Liverpool's moneyed heritage.

With imperial expansion and industrialisation, migrants poured into the city and its past role in transatlantic slavery and trade was marked by the unusual presence, for Britain at the time, of people of African descent. Liverpool was thus a pre-eminent site of not only the international flow of commodities and peoples but also of cultures. Indeed, Liverpool's advanced position in Europe with regard to American black music – brought over by sailors – is one of the historical preconditions that led to the formation, emergence and global popularity of the Beatles from the 1960s.

Liverpool has a genuinely outstanding heritage of popular culture, best known of which is its music but also its comedy and drama (Du Noyer, 2004 [2002]). Paul McCartney was involved in setting up a fame school in the city. The airport has been renamed after another of its most famous sons, John Lennon. Liverpool is not starting from scratch. It has had a culture-led regeneration strategy for some time, exemplified by the cultural transformation of its disused Albert Dock, including a branch of the Tate Gallery, a museum of Transatlantic Slavery, stylish cafés and restaurants. Enterprise culture and vicarious heritage were already established at the Albert Dock in the early 1990s (Mellor, 1991).

It is not at all surprising, then, that Liverpool won the UK competition for designation as European Capital of Culture 2008. It is a perfect test case for the efficacy of culture-led regeneration. All the necessary ingredients are there.

Liverpool's bid and supporting documentation answered the questions convincingly (ERM Economics, 2003; LECC, 2002; Liverpool Vision, 2003). Its theme was 'The World in One City'. There is a timeline of themed years leading up to and following 2008: Celebrating Learning 2003, Faiths and Community Service 2004, Celebrating the Arts 2005, Year of Sport 2006, Celebrating Heritage 2007, The World in One City 2008, Celebrating the Environment 2009 and Celebrating Innovation 2010. Major flagship developments were announced in Liverpool's bid document, such as the 'Fourth Grace' – a futuristic centre for art and culture on the waterfront.

Soon after Liverpool's victory in the competition for Capital of Culture 2008, it was decided that this last ambitious project would not actually go ahead for financial reasons (Wilks-Heeg, 2004: 346). At the same time, it was rumoured that local government money was being diverted from neighbourhood projects to city centre projects. Plans that went ahead included a new tram system, though even that was cut back, and the Duke of Westminster's Paradise Street retail development, which had been touted as largest shopping centre in Europe, but was still a building site in 2008 and had displaced the Quiggins alternative retail centre – the focus of much popular protest in the city (see Connolly, 2008). Quite where the shoppers are to come from for the new Paradise Street development is not clear. Euphoria at Liverpool's 2004 victory in the European Capital of Culture competition for 2008 soon tailed off and a great deal of scepticism and suspicion have surrounded the whole project within the city (Ward, 2006). At the time of writing it is too soon to evaluate the part played by culture and the Capital of Culture designation in Liverpool's regeneration, which will take years to unfold in any case, but the early signs are not good in spite of the evidence of spectacular building projects, making the city attractive to 'the creative class'.

Winning the Capital of Culture title has multiple purposes, of which the Liverpool Culture Company was very well aware, so, in its bid, urban development for economic growth was combined with strategies for social inclusion. This is said to have swung the judges in Liverpool's favour and away from the bookies' favourite, Newcastle–Gateshead.

Where did the money for all of this come from? Mainly, from public purses: local, regional, national and international (European Union funds), with a comparatively small amount of corporate sponsorship. It is therefore reasonable to ask where will the balance of benefits rest between corporate business and the public? Neoliberals would say, of course, that these two kinds of benefit are not really distinguishable from one another as what's good for business is good for the public.

Conclusion

When I spoke of these matters at a seminar in Liverpool between the designation and the year itself, my sceptical perspective was met with considerable levels of agreement. A couple of audience members, however, made contrary responses that made me think. The first asked, 'What else is there to do?' Good question. The second remarked that the European Capital of Culture designation had made the people of Liverpool feel better about themselves and their city. I am sure that is true. In the longer run, however, the upbeat mood is unlikely to last and the good question remains on the table still to be answered.

The most general conclusion regarding the issues at stake emerges with a deep sense of irony. There is an ironic contradiction between neoliberal rhetoric – trust business rather than government – and the governmental processes through which the aims of corporate business are realised. In effect, it is the case that governments sponsor neoliberalisation rather than businesses sponsor progressive change in the delivery of public goods, cultural or otherwise. I came to much the same conclusion in my research on London's Millennium Dome exposition (see Chapter 3). There, nearly a billion pounds of public money (from both the Lottery and taxation) was spent to promote corporate business, much of it actually American (such as Ford and Manpower), matched by only an estimated £150 million of corporate sponsorship, a significant proportion of which was 'in kind' rather than cash. I concluded by describing New Labour's Millennium Dome as a social-democratic shell for neoliberalism. This observation would seem to apply as well and more generally to culture-led urban regeneration projects such as the European Capital of Culture programme.

9 APPRENTICES TO COOL CAPITALISM

Introduction

The Apprentice – an American series with versions elsewhere, including a British franchise and a Chinese copy, *Winner* – is an emblematic television programme of the 2000s. This chapter aims to produce a critical analysis of the discourse of the third series of the American *Apprentice*, shown on US television in 2005 and in Britain in 2006. Reference will also be made to the 2007 British series and points of comparison drawn between the two versions, particularly concerning how class is signified in both countries but differently.

The case study presented in this chapter is part of a larger project on 'cool capitalism' (McGuigan, 2010). At a time when the power of capitalism globally has never been so great and so extensive, its hegemony is little challenged. The public face of capitalism, however, has changed from its earlier and, some might argue, its original form in Protestant asceticism (Baehr and Wells, 2002) to a much more hedonistic and 'cool' appearance.

Cool capitalism is largely defined by the incorporation of signs of disaffection and resistance into capitalism itself, thereby contributing to the reproduction of the system and reducing opposition to it. This is a vital feature of capitalism's hegemonic dominance now. It is a truism to say that hegemony has always to be won against counter-forces, its ideological principles constantly affirmed in the face of opposition, however weak. A programme such as *The Apprentice*, then, performs an ideological role in projecting the values of free market business in a seductive manner that disarms criticism.

A fully satisfactory analysis of media products should be multidimensional, taking account of various moments of production and consumption in the circulation of texts (Kellner, 1997). It has become an established assumption that texts are consumed actively and, therefore, audience agency has a privileged position in media analysis. This may result in a virtual dissolution of the text, however – in effect, denying any textual determinacy whatsoever.

This chapter seeks to recover a measure of textual determinacy in the social circulation of cultural meaning. It does not offer an entirely rounded analysis that would involve enquiry into production as well as audience research. Rather, it focuses specifically and more modestly on the text itself, obviously conditioned by the particular circumstances of its production and open to differential interpretation by viewers.

The rules of the game

In looking at any television programme, it is necessary to locate it in relation to genre, identifying general features that it shares with other texts in the flow of television and also registering its distinctive and quite possibly peculiar characteristics. Like mass popular cinema, the television institution must categorise its programmes in a manner that is instantly intelligible to audiences. This is especially important for television since it is such a voracious medium, producing huge volumes of output, much of which quickly becomes as dated as news.

One-off programmes are not favoured by the commercial imperatives of the industry; the series form and, better still, the serial are widely considered crucial to the pragmatics of both production and consumption. *The Apprentice* is an occasional series/serial in that it has limited seasons of several episodes, each of which tells a discrete story – the completion of that week's task and ejection of a loser – whilst also serving as an instalment in a longer story, unfolding over a season.

Like a great many television programmes today, the genre category of *The Apprentice* is a hybrid, drawing most particularly on game show conventions and those of 'reality TV'. The 'reality' of *The Apprentice*, as in the reality effect of any such programme, is contrived. In this case, it is manifestly so since it is an artificially constructed game for which there are definite rules to be observed. It dose not purport to be 'a slice of life' in the raw. In addition to representation of the game, however – task setting, team organisation, frantic activity and the resultant reward of winners and firing of a loser every week – the viewer is given some access to spaces and conversations 'behind the scenes', particularly the suite in Trump Tower where the candidates retreat to rest and recuperate from the rigours of the game, though the game continues to be played there in subtle ways as they are on camera during these moments of relaxation.

As in all social situations, there are both formal and informal rules, the game's regulations and the less formal conventions of conduct that are not only deemed appropriate to the game but also to life in general. The whole person is, in some sense, on the line, each individual's private emotions and back story subjected potentially to voyeuristic scrutiny. Such information is either willingly proffered or concealed from view by the game's players. They present themselves in specific and individuating ways: self-made, highly educated, spouse and parent, single mother, 'metrosexual' and so forth. Their self-definitions are projected, confirmed and put into question by the game. They are exposed to the other candidates, their judges and the viewing public. In this particular reality game show, though, it is not a voting public as in, most notably, *Big Brother*, which is more expressly a popularity contest. The participants represent models of conduct, to be approved or disapproved according to extant ideological criteria of 'the American dream', which involves the prospect of individual ascent to the top, irrespective of social background, and correct – 'enterprising' – business practices under neoliberal conditions. It is no accident that these shows owe at least part of their origin to social psychological 'experiments'. The situation is, in effect, laboratorial.

The programme is formally a competition between carefully selected 'candidates' – 18 in 2005, culled from a million applicants – to work with the great Donald Trump, the ultimate reward being to serve as his apprentice with the prospect of becoming as rich and famous as him. It is effectively a long and arduous job interview.

Although essentially an individualistic competition – there can be only one winner in the end – the game requires collaboration, formally and informally, between members of each of the two contending teams, which seek to complete tasks more successfully than the other team. The tasks usually though not always involve making more money. The essential balance between competition and collaboration, which includes occasional per-formances of team leadership – 'stepping up to the plate' – in addition to mere membership (after all, the show is about business management), is a delicate process that some candidates, of necessity according to the rules of the game, are better at feeling for and satisfying than others.

There has to be a winner, the fittest survivor of a gruelling ordeal, so there must be losers – one in each episode, condemned by the fatal, 'You're fired!' The stakes are high, the prize glittering and the cost of failure quite possibly very severe since candidates have usually given up their jobs in order to strive for the top job, to be the apprentice to Trump in the USA (Martha Stewart, on release from imprisonment for insider trading, substituted for Trump in the fourth series) and Alan Sugar in Britain.

The Apprentice is educative in Gramsci's sense of mundane political education for the masses as well as cadres (Hoare and Nowell-Smith, 1971), albeit accomplished through the mechanisms of sporting entertainment. The candidates are learning, and so are the audience supposed to be. This may be fun, but it is serious fun.

In the American version and third series considered here, Trump literally teaches a lesson every week in the time-honoured tradition of entrepreneurial didacticism, testified by innumerable management advice books, the words of which appear on the TV screen: 'Perseverence' in the first week, followed in subsequent weeks by 'Respect Comes From Winning'. 'Never Settle', 'Instinct', 'Play Golf' (Trump's favourite game, at which he considers himself to be rather good), 'Go Big Or Go Home', 'Sell Your Ideas', 'Let Nothing Get In Your Way', 'Pulling All-Nighters' and so on. Each invocation is followed up with a little speech from Trump and, where possible, a practical demonstration of the lesson in that episode. Kendra's lone all-nighter in the episode that involved having to design a brochure for a Pontiac car was probably the turning point in the whole game, the nodal moment in resolving the narrative when it became likely that she would win the 2005 competition.

It is important to notice the differential times of transmission and production. The programme's weekly episodes create the illusion of concise reports of the previous week's pro-televisual events, an ongoing reality. It is evident from the programme text itself, however, that the whole series is shot and edited before transmission. This can be inferred by the ordinary viewer from, for instance, the weather and times of dawn and dusk. This matters because, although each episode tells a story, the series as a whole tells an overarching narrative – in effect, a meta-narrative, a grand story about stories.

The late Jean-François Lyotard would never have seen *The Apprentice*. Had he witnessed the instructive story it tells about the hegemony of cool capitalism in the 2000s, however, he (1984 [1979]) might even have revised his claim that meta-narrative no longer elicits credulity. This is not merely a comment on the serial/series structure of a TV show but on the way in which *The Apprentice* represents in condensed form the grandest narrative of all today: capitalism rules without serious questioning and that's 'cool' since any conceivable question, however awkward, can be answered by business and logged into the greater scheme of things in a credible manner.

In studying genre, it is vital to note typical iconography, mise en scène and the characterisation of participants as players in the game in addition to selectively edited narrative and tempo. Certain settings and their contents are repeated throughout a series of *The Apprentice*: aerial shots of the Manhattan skyline with its skyscrapers, especially Trump Tower; the darkened boardroom with faces lit up, where Trump makes his judgements; admiring crowds when Trump occasionally issues his instructions to the contending teams on the street, supplemented most spectacularly by the applauding audience at the denouement in a theatre in the final episode; the various locales for each week's task, such as fast-food joints, department stores, offices, industrial plants, design studios, shops, leisure centres; luxury venues for the weekly reward to a winning team (restaurants, yachts and the like) and so on. There are bright mornings and dark nights, city lights, highways and byways. Everything happens at speed under tight time constraints, accompanied by popular music, the opening of each episode announced by 'Money, Money, Money'. This is a pressure-cooker environment.

The candidates are introduced at the beginning, with their characters, educational and occupational backgrounds sketched in and subsequently developed in action, their survival skills put to the test at every turn of events. They are a cross-section of young Americans: some hailing from Ivy League colleges; some from the wrong side of the tracks; men and women; whites and blacks; Northerners and Southerners; Western and Eastern; urban and rural. The variety of social distinctions and typical identities are recognisable features of American culture and society – 'the melting pot'

Cultural Analysis

that is familiar in more or less detail throughout the whole world, which has been schooled in Americana through Hollywood movies, TV shows and a rocking soundscape.

The third series

The opening episode of the third series establishes the format. Trump swoops into Manhattan in his personal helicopter and is whisked off to Trump Tower by stretch limo. He poses the programme's enticing question with the words printed on the TV screen: 'What if you could have it all?' The Stars and Stripes flutter; Trump issues his paean to New York's 'energy'. 'I'm looking for someone who can handle the pressure. I'm looking for someone who's a creative thinker. I'm looking for THE APPRENTICE.' The candidates also fly in. There are 18 of them, all of whom are introduced deftly in this opening episode by their own words and moving portraits, by which time you might already decide who you will love and who you will hate. They are more or less pushy young Americans, mostly from the business world. They have to appreciate that in the ordeal they are about to face, 'It's nothing personal. It's just business.'

Personality, though, does matter. For example, guitar-playing Danny, nominated as a 'Marketing Technology Firm Owner', is instantly presented as a problematic personality: 'the other candidates wouldn't see me as a CEO'. When he and the others gather together out of view and earshot of 'Mr Trump', he puts himself forward as 'the CMO – chief morale officer' and recommends a slogan to his team – 'Unbelievable!' After all, he is a self-styled 'out-of-a-box kind of a guy' in 'a leisure suit', who makes up a ditty for his team, 'Team Magna'. Danny is like a throwback to sixties hippydom, which immediately divides opinion among the contenders and elicits scepticism from Trump. His attempt to drum up custom by singing and playing guitar outside Burger King is a dismal failure, but, in spite of the clownishness, he is not the one to be fired as a result of his team's failure in the first task.

The loser is preppy Todd, the project manager who plans badly and does not get stuck into customer service. After all, Danny is amusing, albeit an extreme and over-the-top avatar of cool capitalism, destined to be toppled before long in any case.

In the first episode, the candidates are divided into two teams, according to whether they are college-educated or only high-school-educated – in Trump's words, 'Book Smarts' versus 'Street Smarts' – exemplifying the way in which class appears but is transcoded typically in what is supposed to be a classless society.

The teams name themselves. The high-schoolers called themselves 'Net Worth' because their combined earnings are three times that of the college-educated – straight away undercutting the educational advantages and disadvantages that might otherwise be associated with class. Even if they have never read a book, the Street Smarts know what counts – how to make money.

The college-educated graduates call themselves 'Magna', from 'Magna cum Laude' on their college diplomas.

The enigma of this particular series is to do with the value of a university education compared to that of 'street' knowledge. The Net Worth team starts off well in the series but is later overtaken by Magna and the eventual winner of the whole game turns out to be a university graduate from 'a good school', in the American sense. So, education counts for something – Trump himself is a college graduate – but a mixture of both book and street learning is probably best. Tana, who came second, dropped out of college and had been something of a front runner earlier in the game, but slipped up when she lost her knack for leadership in the final task.

The sixth episode is especially significant since the college-educated beat the 'Street Smarts' at their own game and demonstrated that 'cool' is all very well and, indeed, necessary so long as it maintains a business focus and does not get drawn too much into artiness. After all, it is a question of balancing college knowledge with street wisdom, culture with commerce. It is worth recounting the narrative of episode six in order to see how the discourse of *The Apprentice* achieves such a balance and, at a deeper level, resolves ideological tensions that erupt on the edge of the programme.

This episode is about advertising the Sony PlayStation's *Gran Turismo 4* video game. Trump outlines the task facing Magna and Net Worth this week: 'Nowadays, there's a new form of urban advertising. It's called graffiti. I'm not thrilled with graffiti but some of it is truly amazing. What you're going to be doing is creating a billboard using graffiti for PlayStation's newest product.' The teams will have to hire an artist to design the billboard for a wall in Harlem.

Some members of Net Worth go off to try out the game while Tara, project manager for the task, speaks directly to camera: 'I was project manager for this task because I understand Harlem. I wanted to tie the ad to that community. The city is a metaphor for the new game, the transition from the mean streets to, like, the new, more revitalised city.'

Tara is black and 'streetwise'. In the first episode she was nominated as a 'Senior Government Manager', so she is the only candidate of the 18 to work in the public sector. This may have something to do with her community awareness and regeneration rhetoric.

Another member of Net Worth, John, voices doubts about linking a video game to what he calls 'social consciousness'. This task, however, like all tasks in the game, is commercially driven. Concerned to display her marketing nous as well as 'street cred', Tara sums up the target demographic: 'urban, hip, 18–34 males'. Alex, the 'metrosexual' and smart-arsed project manager for Magna, talks about the artistic 'concept' of the project that must conform to 'the Sony message'.

On arrival in Harlem, we see 'the mean streets' decorated with graffiti. In turn, the teams meet artists in Marcus Garvey Park where Magna recruit Lady Pink, whose creative aspirations run to, 'What does the person who's going to buy the GT4 want?' Net Worth sign up Ernie, a black artist who 'can execute our vision [of] the mean streets of New York' (Tara). Tara wants to show 'some respect to the people here because this neighbourhood is undergoing a major renaissance, as you can see … grittiness … the underlying theme, that's how things work'.

Craig, another black member of Tara's team, warns her about keeping an eye on 'your client, your customer'. Alex of Magna, however, is worried about the social inappropriateness of his team members for this 'street' task. So, he conducts 'market research' by interviewing some young black men hanging around in the street (Trump's lesson for that week was 'Shut Up and Listen'). Informed by the research, Alex comes to the conclusion that 'bling, bling, it is … piles of cash raining down'.

As presented in the programme, the narrative of the contest is very clear indeed, edited precisely to make the point. Quite simply it is this: Tara, better qualified with 'street cred', allows the discourse of 'cool' art to obscure the commercial goal of the task, whereas Alex, sensible to his deficiencies in terms of local knowledge, asks the people and discovers that they are more interested in money than outlaw art with the slogan 'tear it up'. Although Net Worth's graffiti billboard is better artistically, it is judged to be less effective in terms of selling the product. Alex wins and Tara is fired. As Trump says, 'This was a marketing task and you didn't get it'.

This example – in some ways similar to the problem of Danny – illustrates a significant feature of cool capitalism. Signs of cultural difference and even rebellion are embraced and incorporated by business but not to the detriment of business, which some might otherwise insouciantly assume to be so. The bottom line remains the bottom line however 'funky' the consumerist façade.

The winners of the sixth episode, Magna, are rewarded by a 'legendary' advertising photographer shooting their portraits in downtown Manhattan. As Alex remarks, this 'taste of Mr Trump's lifestyle' has taken them from the mean streets of Harlem to 'the top of the world'.

All the candidates crave the great man's approval and they are always deeply impressed by the reward he gives them for winning a task. In episode 11, the teams have to invent and sell a new Domino's pizza. The reward for Magna Corp's winning 'Manga' pizza is breakfast in Trump's apartment at the top of the tower block. Kendra, the eventual winner, enthuses, 'Trump's pad was bling, bling. Trump must have been a rapper in a former life because I've never seen so much gold trim in my entire life.' The place is covered in gold leaf – Trump as King Midas. Trump is especially proud of his extremely long and gold-painted dining table, which goes nicely with his bleached-blond quiff of hair, rumoured to be a toupé. The table is so big that it had to be hoisted up the side of the skyscraper and passed into the apartment through an opened plate-glass window. 'We needed to erect a special crane to lift it up.' This is truly the high life in the eyes of the surviving candidates, dazzled by the ostentatious shine of it all.

The final episode, when the winner was eventually revealed, was transmitted live in the USA. This turns out to be, it is tempting to observe, a cross between the Nuremberg Rally and a Moscow show trial. Everyone already anticipates the probable winner, Book Smart Kendra, who handled her reconstituted team of troublesome losers better than Tana handled hers on the final task, but this is theatre.

It is relevant here to recall the spectacular denouement to the previous season of *The Apprentice*, the second series. The final two candidates, Jenna and Kelly, the eventual winner, wind up in the boardroom to be grilled by Trump. Following a period of stern questioning, Trump asks them to leave the room so that he can consult with his advisers – right-hand man George and left-hand woman Carolyn. He remains undecided, then turns to address the camera: 'I want your opinion. What do you think, right now?' Thanks to the magic of television, the boardroom, which is supposed to be several storeys up in the sky, suddenly swivels round and appears on the stage of a theatre in front of a large invited audience, applauding wildly on cue, adoring Trump. Leni Riefenstahl could not have stage-managed the event better and filmed it to more startling, though cheap, effect. This is Trump's stage and he will call on his trusted employees in the audience to help him reach the final solution.

That stunt is not repeated in the third series. It is announced straight away that the venue is the arts centre at New York University and the audience is present from the beginning for the show trial of Kendra and Tana. They are interrogated in the presence of the gathered losers, who criticise and praise as is their wont. Kendra, as was fated, inevitably wins. Although she was quiet at the beginning of the contest, her record has been exemplary: three straight wins as a project leader and obtaining the successful cooperation of her reconstituted team in completing the final task. The journey has been Herculean and this young, highly educated woman with a keen and qualifying sense of cool culture and feel for the game is revealed as the natural winner, or so it seems, at the end of a seamless process in which Book Smart and Street Smart skills have been combined felicitously.

The British version

The British version of *The Apprentice* is presented by Sir Alan Sugar, who is, by British standards, a reasonably large-scale entrepreneur, but certainly not in the same league as Trump. Unlike Trump, Sugar's headquarters, for instance, are not actually in a smart office block so have to be mocked up for television and represented in a City of London office building that is quite like Trump Tower in New York. His company's actual headquarters are in East London.

Although knighted (the candidates are always careful to call him 'Sir Alan', which in the usually elided speech of contestants becomes 'Suralan'), Sugar is from 'a humble background'. The winners of the first two series were a young black man of modest origins, working in the public sector, and a young white woman from a poor, socially disorganised background.

At the beginning of the third series, televised in spring 2007, Sugar insists, presumably with the preceding results in mind, that he is not socially biased, in order perhaps to reassure those among the 16 candidates from a more privileged background than himself of fair play – most notably the private school and Oxbridge-educated – saying, 'I don't care where you come from, whether you started in a council flat or born with a silver spoon. All I'm looking for is somebody who is drop-dead shrewd'. On this occasion, he will – perhaps inevitably – choose someone from a comparatively privileged background with a public – that is, private – school and Oxbridge education. He announces his dislike of 'schmoozers, bullshitters or liars', whatever their origins.

Sugar is instantly recognisable in Britain as the type of the East End barrow boy made good. He is also evidently of Jewish extraction and known to support the ostensibly socialist New Labour government, traits that may in the past – but hardly now – have been construed as representing outsiderness in the British economic and power elite.

In the 2007 series, Sugar managed to square the circle and select a winner who actually shared quite a similar background to himself but one that had been complicated by social mobility over a number of generations, though this was not at all made explicit in the programme, nor was it commented on in the news media.

According to conventional yet dubious wisdom, fine distinctions of class difference are said to be more pronounced in British culture than in the 'classless' USA. Nowadays, though, increasingly like America, class is not supposed to matter in Britain and the reverse of class prejudice is often decried as being just as discriminating as the old top-down kind. The British are still sensitive to signs of class, however tortuously so, but quite possibly no more than Americans. Still, social class is more markedly on the surface, so to speak, in the British version than it is in the American version of *The Apprentice*. Also, questions of 'race' and ethnicity are addressed with some sensitivity and they have acquired greater prominence than in the past in British culture and society – similar to the American preoccupation with 'identity'.

The persona of Sugar himself is especially notable, satirised brilliantly in Comic Relief's *Celebrity Apprentice* parody in March 2007, just before the commencement of that year's series.

Rather like the American prototype, Sugar also likes to fly about in a helicopter and boast of his own entrepreneurial achievements, though he is somewhat less ostentatious and brash than Trump. His speech is much more vulgar than that of Trump, illustrating the comparative permissiveness of British television's language code in comparison with the restrictions of American network television. He swears and enunciates what are generally regarded as rude yet witty similes to put down underperforming candidates. Generally, the tone of the British version is much more ironic and, indeed, tongue-in-cheek than the American original.

There is an autopsy programme, *You're Fired!*, on BBC Two immediately following each weekly episode shown on BBC One. It invites that week's loser to face a studio audience, the members of which get to vote 'hired' or 'fired', to reverse or confirm, in their opinion, Sugar's decision. There are also three invited, 'expert' guests who comment on that week's proceedings.

Mostly, discussion is about the character of the contestants and who is doing well and who is doing badly.

As with all successful reality shows on British television, there is constant coverage of the current show in the tabloid press, though generally, during the course of a season, the back story is kept firmly under wraps, necessitated by the delay between production and transmission. That the previous year's winner, Michelle Dewberry, had left Sugar's employment, pregnant, after only six months in the apprentice's job, however, was a major talking point in spring 2007. Dewberry said that the position she had been given was unrewarding and she could make more money as a freelance, though she also insisted she was still on good terms with 'Suralan'.

Here, I shall comment on just one episode from the third series that is particularly germane to the argument concerning apprenticeship to cool capitalism. It is from Week 8 of the season and was first televised on 16 May 2007.

In the episode, the two teams, Eclipse (originally the male team but in this episode with one female member, Jadine) and Stealth (originally female and exclusively so again), are given the task of branding and advertising a new pair of trainers ('sneakers' in the USA).

Sugar greets them in Piccadilly Circus, 'the most famous advertising arena in the world' where 'brands fight for position'. Sir Alan makes it clear what he wants: 'an advert that sells kit. I do not want an advert that wins the Montreux award for advertising tossers.'

Tre, a marketing and design consultant who mixes what appear to be 'fundamentalist' Islamic views – especially regarding the representation of women – with Sugar's own kind of arrogance, sardonic wit and vulgarity, is Eclipe's project manager for this task.

Ghasal, also Asian but with a Scottish accent, in contrast to Tre's cockney one, and very close to being fired, is given the chance to redeem herself as project manager for Stealth.

The teams are advised that 'the world doesn't need another trainer' so they had better come up with a really good 'big idea'. Tre instantly hit on the winning formula for his team:

All the street culture has been taken over by the big brands, yeah? So, what we're doing is we're reclaiming the streets. We're taking it back to the streets. We're giving them a [sic] underground alternative to the mass-produced representation of their culture.

The Eclipse team has already been out cool hunting on the street, speaking with 'the crucial youth market'. They decided to name their trainer 'Street'. This strategy is supposed to be non-conformist and rebellious, yet, in the trainer business, pace Nike, it is scarcely novel. It is, to all intents and purposes, thoroughly conformist, adopting signs of rebellion to accomplish the exact opposite: integration into the all-consuming culture of cool capitalism.

Stealth, unsurprisingly, also know that a 'cool' image matters but they are in trouble as a team due to the inexperience of their project manager, Ghasal, lacking street wisdom despite her youthfulness, and the constant bickering between the posh Katie and Irish Kristina (these characteristics of the two women are accentuated repeatedly in the programme). They call their trainer 'Jam', which some wag says might sell well to the Women's Institute, and try, unsuccessfully in Sugar's judgement, to link its 'solefulness' to music.

Eclipse have trouble hiring actors who can 'bump'n'grind' convincingly on their video. It transpires, however, that Simon Ambrose, from the select and expensive London suburb of Hampstead Garden, is a song-and-dance man who can get down on the street. Tre is sceptical: 'There's a fine line between good dancers and totally shite, bollocks dancers', referring to his mate, Simon. On this one, though, Tre eventually has to give in and acknowledge his earlier remark that Simon is 'a very talented boy'. Simon composes and delivers, in a passably 'street' hip-hop accent, a rap to accompany street moves on the video that convinces the team and, eventually, Sugar, too. Not bad for a white, middle-class Cambridge graduate from Hampstead Garden suburb. Incidentally, Sacha Baron Cohen, a graduate of Cambridge, too – who plays Ali G and the world-famous Borat – also hails from this area of London. Simon's rap went as follows:

> Street is not about corporate branding, high-street fashions and rip-off pricing. It's not about country walks and village fêtes. Street is about giving back, revolutionising the system, taking back control. It's about knowing yourself, knowing your style and representing your culture, representing the street. Reclaim the street!

Having borrowed the slogan 'reclaim the street' from the anti-capitalist movement, Simon is called urgently away from the recording studio where he has been laying down the track to breakdance on the video, which he also does with some panache. One of Sugar's advisers, Margaret, describes Simon as 'a rapping acrobat': if that is what 'Suralan' wants, so be it. Since Simon was eventually appointed 'the Apprentice' she was not proven wrong.

There is a problem, however, with the 'Street' campaign. The team agrees, at Tre's behest, that a percentage of the take should be donated to 'street youth centres'. There is some disagreement over whether this should be from the £39.99 price or the profit. In the end, the billboard ad says, '10 per cent of every sale will go to street youth centres'. Tre himself had wanted the 10 per cent to come from the more nebulous profit. In the brightly lit boardroom setting of the British version, Sugar thinks likewise:

> You're forcing the consumer to pay four pounds. They won't like that. I can promise you, they won't like that. What it should have been is that you are gonna give away some of your profits. That way the customer doesn't know what you're actually gonna give away but the sentiment is there.

Still, Eclipse win and the team members are rewarded by learning to make cocktails at the Ritz – very street. Ghasal is fired, after a fierce denunciation from Sugar of her talents and negative forecast of her long-term prospects. Katie now also looks to be on borrowed time, though she later made a comeback and was selected by Sugar for the final round in the competition. That she declined the offer confirmed his suspicion that Katie was after the publicity but not the job all along. In her words, she was then cast by Sugar as 'the pantomime villain'.

Conclusion

When analysing a television programme such as *The Apprentice*, it is important to not just impose the abstract terms of a linguistic model on the object in question. There is a texture to the text that is not reducible to words: images and sounds also matter and have a logic of their own that complicates the meaning of the words. It is difficult to convey such a highly textured discourse solely in words, and still images are inadequate in conveying the flow of the text.

Moreover, the present chapter treats of a complex cultural phenomenon in relation to ideology – namely, what I have called 'cool capitalism', the articulation of which within the programme is illustrated most sharply with reference to the episode on graffiti advertising in the 2005 season of the US *Apprentice* and the episode on designing and marketing a pair of trainers in the 2007 season on the British version. The articulation of cool capitalism in the two series is not reducible to these two episodes, though, but they best exemplify it by illustrating the focal point of the argument.

While this chapter is dedicated to an enquiry into the ideological legitimisation of capitalism today – especially its appropriation of 'cool' signs and symbols, thereby potentially neutralising opposition – there is, no guarantee that the lessons taught are effectively learnt by the viewing public. The appeal of the programme is, first and foremost, that of a game show and a kind of soap-operatic play of character and story over several weeks. That *The Apprentice* is imbued with market values and seeks to validate the absolute worth of capitalist business at whatever the human cost – most obviously the arduous testing of candidates in the show in order to reveal the fittest – though much more serious than that in terms of the complex structures of exploitation perpetuated by global capitalism, is no secret. It can be enjoyed without succumbing to the message.

I enjoy it – admittedly from an anthropological point of view, not simply as a matter of educative entertainment. There is little doubt, however, that such popular fare contributes to the articulation of a capitalist reality as the only reality and it does so by appealing to people, in a sense, on their own ground – hence, the significant differences between national versions of the show.

From a business point of view, it is probably a joke, an artificial and trivialising entertainment that bears no real relation to a real reality. That evaluation, though, rather misses the point that it is an evocation of a fantasy business world which marks out the boundaries of the social world itself.

10 CULTURAL STUDIES AND COOL CAPITALISM

Introduction

This chapter traces various trajectories of development in the field of Cultural Studies, identifying five in particular: theoreticism, methodism, pragmatism, subjectivism and consumerism.

The chapter concentrates on the consumerist trajectory as it emerged in Britain. While the phrases 'the Birmingham School' and 'British Cultural Studies' have been used to label this trajectory, it is more accurately named 'Hallian Cultural Studies' since Stuart Hall was its leading exponent and inspiration. Hall himself, however, is not necessarily responsible for the problems associated with the consumerist trajectory in the work of his followers.

There is a discernible homology and, indeed, to an extent, a convergence between consumerist Cultural Studies and the neoliberal ideology of consumer sovereignty, which incorporates signs of disaffection into capitalism itself, named here as 'cool capitalism' (see McGuigan, 2010). The genealogy of 'cool' is traced and its incorporation into capitalism examined. In effect, this strand of academic work – consumerist and one-dimensional Cultural Studies – which started out critical of prevailing forms of cultural, economic and political power, has ceased, in many respects, to be so. In conclusion, it is argued that Cultural Studies should renew its commitment to critique in the public interest and in a multidimensional framework of analysis.

In academia, Cultural Studies used to be regarded as politically suspect, as too political by half and decidedly left wing in its politics. Is that still so? To seek an answer to this question, first, it is necessary to consider where Cultural Studies has come from and, second, where it (they) is (are) going. In previous work, the origins and subsequent development of Cultural

Studies have been traced (McGuigan, 1992, 1997a and 1999). It is important to stress that it is an interdisciplinary field, not a discipline in its own right, though perhaps, as some have argued, to be understood as a post- or trans-discipline (Johnson et al., 2004). In consequence, Cultural Studies is inherently open to all sorts of borrowings and offerings, which makes it difficult to pin down, and, anyway, it is not necessarily desirable to treat it like a dead butterfly in a display case.

At one time, it was assumed that Cultural Studies originated in Britain, with the work of Richard Hoggart (1957), E.P. Thompson (1968 [1963]) and Raymond Williams (1958 and 1961). It can be traced back further, though – at least as far as George Orwell's essays on popular culture and Mass Observation's anthropological research on everyday cultures in mid-twentieth-century Britain (see Stanton, 1996). Williams (1989) himself attributed the emergence of Cultural Studies to the adult education movement, university extension classes and the Workers' Educational Association (Steele, 1997). Graeme Turner (2003 [1990]) has summarised this history with precision and identified its main lines of theoretical and methodological development.

The British origins of Cultural Studies have been contested. James Carey (1997) claimed that it was American even before British Cultural Studies was actually absorbed into and overtaken by American Cultural Studies. Possibly with tongue in cheek, in the launch issue of the *European Journal of Cultural Studies*, Handel K. Wright (1998) claimed an African origin for Cultural Studies. This startling claim was taken seriously enough for it to be disputed in the very same issue of the journal (McNeil, 1998). Significantly, a more recent anthology of writings from Cultural Studies, *Internationalizing Cultural Studies* (Abbas and Nguyet Erni, 2004) comes close to excluding British work entirely from the field of Cultural Studies as it stands at present.

Whatever the origins of Cultural Studies, quite clearly the field has developed in many different ways. Some of the most pronounced trajectories are identified briefly in this chapter, mainly in order to register that the subject is much more diverse than the tradition of 'British' Cultural Studies, which is the principal focus of attention here.

Over its formative years, this tradition proceeded through the nodal work of the Birmingham Centre for Contemporary Cultural Studies (CCCS), led by Stuart Hall in the 1970s, a school of thought that sought to critique prevailing social and cultural arrangements and inform action in cultural politics. Like any tradition, it changed over the years. Commitments were modified, realistic adaptations were made, participants educated in the 1970s matured and so did the field. Iconoclasm diminished and British Cultural Studies came to terms with a transformed historical condition in which older rationales for critique were made apparently irrelevant by events (the collapse of soviet communism, for instance). Most noticeably, the grounds for questioning capitalism and its culture were undercut, which coincided with greater acceptance of Cultural Studies as a respectable subject on the curriculum and of legitimate research, no longer a notorious enfant terrible or bête noir.

Specifically, then, has the radical tradition of Cultural Studies become complicit with latter-day cool capitalism and ceased to be a key site for theorising cultural politics?

Multiple trajectories

Cultural Studies is a controversial field that has been the object of hostile dismissal. The late Pierre Bourdieu held such a dismissive view, in collaboration with Loïc Wacquant. In their opinion, Cultural Studies was academically disreputable and merely an international publishing plot. To quote them: 'Cultural Studies, this mongrel domain, born in England in the 1970s, ... owes its international dissemination (which is the whole of its existence) to a successful publishing policy' (Bourdieu and Wacquant,1999: 47).

This judgement is far too polemical and fails to register the value of an interdisciplinarity that crosses over between the humanities and the social sciences. Still, Cultural Studies is not a unified field; there are several different perspectives and trajectories that do not always seem to bear a family resemblance to one another.

Generally speaking, all the various trajectories of Cultural Studies identified here have something going for them. Each has strengths and weaknesses. The weaknesses are exacerbated where there is no dialogue between the alternative trajectories of Cultural Studies; each of these may have resources that make up for deficiencies in other trajectories. This is not a call for a loose eclecticism but, rather, for more interactions between different perspectives in the field of Cultural Studies as this might enhance its political usefulness. Incidentally, the following list of salient trajectories does not include the post-colonial aspect of Cultural Studies since post-colonialism is, arguably, best considered as a separate field of study, albeit representing a similarly interdisciplinary space with distinct affinities to and connections with Cultural Studies.

Among the various trajectories of Cultural Studies, five 'isms' can be named:

- theoreticism
- methodism
- pragmatism
- subjectivism
- consumerism.

While these five isms do not exhaust the range of pedagogy and research to be found in Cultural Studies, each refers to a discernible trajectory and illustrates the competing logics that are active in an admittedly amorphous field. Each trajectory will now be considered in turn.

Theoreticism

The short history of Cultural Studies has featured a rapid succession and turnover of favoured theories and theorists. The theories (or 'paradigms') have included: culturalism, structuralism, Althusserian and Gramscian Marxism, as well as various strands of poststructuralism and postmodernism. The theorists have included Raymond Williams (whose cultural materialism has been a perpetual ghost at the feast), Stuart Hall, Roland Barthes, Michel Foucault and Gilles Deleuze, to name just a few.

Much of the theory has come from France. British scholarship's subservience to French theory is not a peculiarly national phenomenon in an otherwise distinctly empiricist culture since it is also evident in North America, Oceania, other European countries and around the world generally.

The rapid succession and turnover of theories and theorists is a problem because there has been a tendency for the latest theoretical fad or fashion to be deemed automatically superior to the previous one, often with scant justification. There is also a professional dynamic to all this, on which academic careers are built. That is particularly so of the journal *Theory, Culture & Society*, promoting mainly European continental theorists for consumption by anglophone Cultural Studies and sociology, rather like the *New Left Review* did in the 1960s and 1970s.

The credibility of theoreticism was dealt a severe blow by the Sokal affair in 1996. Left-wing physicist Alan Sokal (1996) had an article accepted for a special edition of the journal *Social Text* that was focused on 'the science wars'. It was entitled 'Transgressing the boundaries: toward a transformative hermeneutics of quantum gravity'. The title of the article alone should have alerted the editors of *Social Text* to the possibility that they were the intended victims of a hoax, quite apart from the ludicrous argument developed in the article itself.

Sokal declared the non-existence of an external world and, hence, its inaccessibility to the scientific method. Superficially, the article read like fashionable cultural theory *à la* Baudrillard. The editors of what had hitherto been a highly respected journal of social and cultural theory were taken in by Sokal's clever hoax.

Although Sokal was severely criticised for the hoax, perhaps justifiably so, nevertheless, he did point up some serious problems with contemporary social and cultural theory (see Sokal and Bricmont, 1998). These include the spurious and metaphorical use of natural-scientific terminology by the likes of Jean Baudrillard, the obscurantism of much theoretical writing and the careless attitude prevailing in Cultural Studies towards empirical evidence and validation of research (see Tallis, 1997, for similar criticisms).

Methodism

It is unclear how much this stems from the Sokal affair, but, since then, there have been strong indications of a turning away from high theory to practical questions of method.

It is true that Cultural Studies has been weak regarding method – that is, the development of specialist techniques for actually doing research. It has been much stronger on methodology, the formulation of theoretical principles for framing research and analysis.

A few years ago, I edited a book and had to change the title to *Cultural Methodologies* (McGuigan, 1997b) just before publication. That was because nearly all my contributors had chosen to write about theoretical methodologies instead of what I had asked them to do, which was to write about practical research methods. Part of the reason for this, it would seem likely, is to do with the interdisciplinary character of Cultural Studies. Researchers in the field have drawn liberally on methods developed in the disciplines of anthropology, art history, geography, linguistics, literary criticism, social history, sociology and others. There seemed to be no distinctive Cultural Studies method. Now, that presents difficulties when you are seeking funds for research projects.

More recently, a flurry of methods textbooks for Cultural Studies have been published (for instance, Gray, 2003, Johnson et al., 2004 and Saukko, 2003). They are serving a definite need for instruction in how to do it. The publishers have quite rightly seen a gap in the market and sought to fill it. None of these manuals will satisfy everyone in the field, though the book written by Richard Johnson and his former colleagues at Nottingham Trent University comes closest to a catholic and even-handed approach to the range of methods on offer. Yet, this book and the others mentioned here tend to overemphasise the subjectivist strand of Cultural Studies, which is treated separately below because of its growing significance.

More generally, an emphasis on methods, when taken too far, can lead to what may be termed 'methodism'. By this I mean the development of scientific technique virtually for its own sake. Such a tendency might lose sight of the critical reasons for studying culture in the first place in all its respects. This is likely to happen more if and when Cultural Studies becomes truly respectable and turns into a conventional discipline, thereby resulting in an ossification of the antidisciplinary project. The whole point of interdisciplinary study could thus be obscured by an empty professionalism lacking theoretical insight and imaginative flair.

The history of empiricist sociology and its administrative rather than critical use in practice at various times and in various places should be a warning to Cultural Studies to avoid going down that route.

Pragmatism

If the turn towards methods exemplifies a more realistic Cultural Studies, at least in terms of academic legitimacy, then the pragmatic strand is yet more realistic with regard to 'the real world'.

Obviously, there are pragmatic considerations for Cultural Studies. Research has to be funded and graduates of Cultural Studies want jobs. For a long time, however, nobody of any standing in the field actually argued explicitly for educating Cultural Studies students in the magical arts and protean powers of the market as preparation for 'cool hunting'.

Such an argument, once it has been made, in effect amounts to an acknowledgement of the convergence of consumerist Cultural Studies with 'cool capitalism' – a trend that is discussed at length later in this article. That terminal argument has now been put definitively by the theory and practice of 'creative industries' being said to be the prime object of latter-day Cultural Studies (Hartley, 2003; Hartley, 2005). Cultural Studies has finally set out on its journey from the humanities and social sciences faculties all the way over to its resting place in the business school.

In any earlier phase of development, the explicitly pragmatic case was made for bending Cultural Studies towards governmental uses, as in Foucauldian 'cultural policy studies'. Some years ago, Tony Bennett (1992) attacked the political pretensions and impracticality of Cultural Studies as a counter-hegemonic project. In spite of all the political rhetoric – most notably Stuart Hall's Gramscian programme for the field – Cultural Studies seldom addressed 'the real world' of power and actually existing political arrangements. Bennett advocated, instead, an instrumental relation to the specific tasks of cultural management, particularly in the public sector. This statist position, preceding a wholesale switch to the market position, had some success, especially in Australia in relation to the then (early 1990s) 'creative nation' agenda of the Labour government. It fared less well there in later years under a Liberal (that is, conservative) government.

In effect, the logic of Bennett's position was to turn Cultural Studies into a kind of management consultancy for neoliberal social democracy – not entirely different, as it turned out, from Hartley's subsequent alignment of the field with cool capitalism. With regard to policy-orientated Cultural Studies, the counter-argument still has to be made against pragmatic complicity with neoliberalism in favour of an independent, reflexive and critical approach to practical questions (McGuigan, 1996 and 2004) and this has to be put into operation in concrete research projects (as I hope I have demonstrated in the case study described in Chapter 3). That Cultural Studies should have something to say about cultural and other policy questions is incontestable, but it is unfortunate if *all* it can do is supplement already well-established administrative and instrumental agendas for research.

Subjectivism

Another notable trend in Cultural Studies is a retreat into subjectivism that probably has its roots in psychoanalysis and has been combined, fairly recently, with identity politics and queer theory. The methods books tend to recommend an ethnographic approach to the exploration of subjectivity, including in-depth interviews and life stories. Much of this work is focused on the task of 'enabling the subaltern to speak'. It is unquestionably so that Cultural Studies should aid individuals in their own self-understanding and the appreciation of different forms of life. Multiculturalism is an obviously related hot topic, though not just a matter of subjectivity. Without doubt, identity and difference are very important themes in Cultural Studies.

The danger of this trajectory, however, is that it may slide into solipsism, which is indifferent to an understanding of the wider social world and macro-power dynamics. There is such a fascination with interpersonal micro-power relations in this strand of work that the connections to macro-power slip off the agenda.

Subjectivism is showing signs of becoming a significant trend in Cultural Studies. This may not yet be full-blown in terms of publishing, but a great deal of research at the postgraduate level is focused on subjectivity, identity and difference, at least in Britain. Much of this work is very individualistic, admitting, for instance, not only biographical evidence but also autobiographical evidence.

If the pragmatic trajectory in both its statist and market forms is the worldliest branch of Cultural Studies, then subjectivism is the least worldly and open to the criticism of self-indulgence. Generally, the discipline of psychology, in its excessively scientific mode, outlaws the self-understanding of the psychologist as a legitimate object of enquiry, denounced long ago as 'introspection'. Is Cultural Studies of the subjectivist kind veering towards a more indulgent kind of psychology?

The retreat into subjectivism is an interesting social phenomenon in its own right for Cultural Studies to theorise and research. It fits in with recent theoretical arguments about 'individualisation' (Beck and Beck-Gernsheim, 2002) in contemporary society, a trend that dovetails so neatly with neoliberal 'consumer sovereignty'. It should be recalled that, in some dim and distant past, the proponents of Cultural Studies saw themselves contributing to progressive social transformation, reformist and/or revolutionary. Is it political disappointment, then, that leads to a subjectivist retreat in Cultural Studies scholarship?

Consumerism

Because there is so much to say about 'consumerism' in Cultural Studies, it occupies the whole of the next section.

The moment of consumption

Talking about political disappointment ... The University of Birmingham's Centre for Contemporary Cultural Studies (CCCS) was founded in 1963 by a professor in the English department, Richard Hoggart. Following Hoggart's departure for UNESCO in the late 1960s, Stuart Hall succeeded him as Director of the Centre. Hall had already been working there on a fellowship financed partly by Sir Allen Lane of Penguin.

The Birmingham Centre reached its peak in the 1970s, under the inspiring leadership of Hall, when a group of talented research students in Cultural Studies were trained, several of whom became major figures in the field. Hall left for a post at the Open University in 1979.

Subsequently, the Centre had a chequered history. What was originally a research and postgraduate centre operating on a modest scale and in an institutionally embattled environment burgeoned into a fully fledged department in the form of the Faculty of Social Sciences, incorporating Sociology. The department of Cultural Studies and Sociology taught undergraduates as well as postgraduates in large numbers. Staff membership expanded too.

In its later years, the department's research suffered, possibly due to the pressures of teaching brought about by the sudden massification of British higher education in the 1990s rather than the loss of Hall's leadership and the succession crisis that dragged on for over 20 years. It was closed down in 2002 by a draconian university management in rapid response to a comparatively low research rating for the department – and, therefore, reduced funding for research – calculated by the Higher Education Funding Council England (HEFCE). To appreciate the significance of the CCCS, it is important to register this rise and fall narrative and complex institutional history, which is far too intricate to unravel in detail here.

The Centre's extraordinary influence at its height was out of all proportion to its size – it had only three or four staff members in the 1970s and into the 1980s. Its demise, shortly after hosting an international conference that attracted scholars from around the world, came as a shock and was extremely controversial.

By the beginning of the twenty-first century, then, Cultural Studies had emerged as an internationally extended field that was inspired to a widely acknowledged extent by the pioneering work of Birmingam's CCCS. Back in the 1960s, when Hoggart and Hall fashioned their innovative research centre, they could only have imagined such eventual success in their wildest dreams. In effect, the Centre did not hold as Cultural Studies spiralled into a new era, if not necessarily out of control.

'The Birmingham School' is often equated with 'British Cultural Studies'. In situ, neither label made much sense. In fact, these labels came from elsewhere, mainly Australia and the USA, and were a construction from outside of illusory unity that masked over internal differences and obscured the porousness of boundaries.

A more accurate label might be 'Hallian Cultural Studies' because Stuart Hall was indeed the presiding genius over 'the Birmingham School' and 'British Cultural Studies'. His formal association with the Birmingham CCCS ended over a quarter of a century ago, but Hall is now the subject of book-length studies about his thought and practice (for instance, Procter, 2004, and Rojek, 2003).

Hall's brilliance was primarily to do with his role as a teacher, both in education and politics. That he was the first editor of *New Left Review* is relevant to understanding his long-term task as both an intellectual mediator and charismatic guide. Hall performed a leading role in teaching the British Left about Western Marxism and European continental theory. When he succeeded Hoggart as Director of the Birmingham Centre, there was a sharp turn towards theory, which entailed the appropriation of ideas from the Western Marxist tradition (rather than Marxism-Leninism), French semiology and structuralism, with a smattering of American symbolic interactionism thrown in for good measure. In an interview recalling the heydays of the Centre, Hall (1997: 39) remarked particularly on its way of working:

> there was a connection between the intellectual productivity of the Centre and its attempt to transform its way of working. And both were connected with, on the one hand, its relative marginality in relation to the university, and, on the other, the political context in which it was operating: 1968 and after. We were very involved in the sit-in in 1968 in Birmingham, for example, and in student politics generally. In relation to the democratization of knowledge, this was a very creative moment. We had a genuinely collective way of producing knowledge, based on a critique of the established disciplines, a critique of the university as a structural power, and a critique of the institutionalization of knowledge as an ideological operation.

Hall and his acolytes were politically motivated – notoriously so at the University of Birmingham – and with a subversive reputation throughout British academia. At the time, this was not an isolated neo-Marxist intervention in the academy but it was unusually effective, or so it seemed.

Like the comparable Frankfurt School of an earlier period, cultural analysis at Birmingham was committed to a non-reductionist, non-economistic Marxism. In his political writings, Hall (1988) analysed the shift to the Right in Britain at large with his formulations of 'Thatcherism' and 'authoritarian populism', derived from a particular reading of Antonio Gramsci on hegemony, culture and power in Italy during the 1920s and 1930s (Forgacs and Nowell-Smith, 1985; Hoare and Nowell-Smith, 1971). Hegemony theory was also supposed to reconcile the theoretical differences between contending paradigms in Cultural Studies, particularly 'culturalism' and 'structuralism', while deliberately excluding classically Marxian political economy from the analytical framework (Hall, 1980).

Alongside his academic work, Hall wrote for the British Communist Party journal *Marxism Today* but was not a member of the party and never called himself a communist. *Marxism Today* represented the views of a revisionist current in the party during the 1980s, inspired very much by Hall, which eventually broke with communism and, some would argue, Marxism tout court. In fact, *Marxism Today* closed down when the Soviet Union collapsed in 1991, as much for financial as political reasons. The final phase of the *Marxism Today* tendency, for which Hall was theorist-in-chief, was the 'New Times' agenda (Hall and Jacques, 1989), which, curiously enough, announced not only a fundamental break into a post-Marxist political arena of post-Fordism and postmodernism but also a rapprochement with political economy.

In the 1980s, cultural theory and analysis were inextricably linked to Left politics of one kind or another. While Cultural Studies would, of course, be castigated for intruding politics into scholarship, participants in the field insisted on the political nature of education and research. Nevertheless, scholarly precision was by no means neglected.

In turning away from economic determinacy and the base–superstructure model of classical Marxism, enormous attention was lavished on the politics of consumption and popular culture. Orthodox Marxist and Frankfurt School critiques of mass consumerism and manipulation were rejected in favour of a nuanced understanding of the contradictions and pleasures of consuming practices.

Birmingham scholars discovered that consumption under capitalism was not too bad after all; actually, it was really rather good. Among other things, consumption provided a site for escape from and 'resistance' to enslavement by the capitalist system.

This case was argued most strenuously at first with regard to spectacular youth subcultures (Jefferson, 1975). Young people were especially adept at appropriating capitalist commodities for their own uses and issuing messages of resistance through style, deportment and ritualistic behaviour, as exemplified by mods, rockers, punks and so on.

There was a persistent accent placed on the activity of consumption, and not only in youth culture. As time went by, consumption practices generally were considered active, not passive, including television viewing and shopping. Feminism impacted powerfully on the Centre's work from the mid-1970s (WSGCCCS, 1978). Questions of 'race' also became increasingly important (CCCS, 1982).

Hall's (1974) own 'encoding/decoding model' – formulated for research on television audiences – had already concentrated on the moment of decoding meaning as being an active and socially motivated process. Initially just class but, later, discourses of gender, generation and ethnicity were thought to be as crucially involved in decoding cultural texts. Theories of reading, subject positioning and so forth were incorporated into cultural research at Birmingham. All this contributed to the CCCS's shared interest in the moment of consumption as the cardinal moment for cultural analysis – the most distinctive feature of this whole school of thought and its great influence on the development of Cultural Studies in general.

There were controversial issues at stake in turning away from a Marxist critique of capitalist culture and towards scholarly research and appreciation of active consumption, which came to a head in the mid-1980s. The debate ensuing from that moment raised questions about the specificity of the historical conjuncture and appropriate political strategy in addition to analytical questions concerning the political meanings of consumption.

In 1984, Stuart Hall published an article entitled 'The culture gap' in an issue of *Marxism Today* that was devoted to reflecting on George Orwell's *Nineteen Eighty-Four*, now that the fatal year had been reached (the article is included in Hall, 1988). Hall (1988: 211) remarked at the outset, 'Orwell was wrong about many things. But one thing he did get right was the general relationship between culture and social change.' Then, Hall went on to criticise the Left for not fully understanding this relation.

Referring back to the debate over Labour's third general election defeat to the Conservatives in a row in 1959, Hall discussed the changing class structure of British society and the experience of everyday life. The Tory prime minister Harold Macmillan had told the British electorate in the late 1950s, 'You've never had it so good'. This was when the issue of 'the affluent worker' had arisen for politics and sociology. Was Labour still electable when it could no longer rely on the traditionally socialist appeal to workers' poverty?

The conditions of working-class life had changed largely for the better since the Second World War. Hall (1988: 212) remarked, 'as we all know, the slow, uneven, contradictory impact of consumer capitalism *did* refashion social relations and cultural attitudes quite widely and irrevocably'. 'Mass consumption' had modified 'everyday life-patterns'.

Linked to this was a popular resistance to the statist features of welfare socialism, already captured presciently by Ralph Miliband's (1978) notion of 'de-subordination'. Authority was no longer deferred to, including that of the welfare state, the historical achievement of post-war social democracy. In comparison, the market seemed to offer freedom and greater prospects for self-realisation. In a key passage in 'The culture gap', Hall (1988: 215) declared:

Consumer capitalism works by working the markets: but it cannot entirely determine what alternative uses people are able to make of the diversity of choices and the real advances in mass production which it also always brings. If 'people's capitalism' did not liberate the people, it nevertheless 'loosed' many individuals into a life somewhat less constrained, less puritanically regulated, less strictly imposed than it had been three or four decades before. Of course the market has not remained buoyant and expansive in this manner. But the contradictory capacity, for a time, of the system to pioneer expansion, to drive and develop new products and maximize new choices, while at the same time creaming off its profit margins, was seriously underestimated. Thus the Left has never understood the capacity of the market to become identified in the minds of the mass of ordinary people, not as fair and decent and socially responsible (that it never was), but as an expansive popular system.

We can see here the Marxist sense of contradiction giving rise to an ambivalent attitude towards 'people's capitalism' and grasping its positive as well as negative sides. When that sense of dialectical tension breaks in lesser hands, one way out is historic reconciliation with prevailing arrangements and a sale's rush into a headlong hedonism that dispenses with the miserabilism of Marxism.

Another essay from 1984 – this one by a then young research student at the Birmingham Centre, Erica Carter – is entitled 'Alice in the consumer wonderland'. This essay is consistent with Hall's dialectical ambivalence and it exemplifies the impact of feminism on Cultural Studies. Thus, there is the obligatory auto-critique of Cultural Studies for its masculine bias, particularly in youth cultural research. Carter wanted to revalue the subordinate, feminine term 'consumption', with its string of associations, in the binary system commanded by masculine dominance. Gender is crucial to consumption.

Moreover, the construction of 'an impassive monolith – the Market' must be rejected if feminised consumption is to be properly understood. Carter goes on to do exactly that.

It is important to appreciate that Carter (1984: 191) maintained the dialectical tension that characterised Hall's argument: 'Passive manipulation or active appropriation, escapist delusion or utopian fantasy, consumerism can be all of these.'

Such argumentation opened up a rich vein of research orientated primarily at consumption as the privileged moment of cultural analysis. What were considered the unacceptably masculine connotations of 'production' added to this turn away from it and towards consumption.

These essays by Hall and Carter from 1984 have been selected for closer consideration because they are good, analytically complex and still thought-provoking examples from the genre of consumerist Cultural Studies, which became the main trajectory for much subsequent work. It is not surprising, however, that the arguments they put forward had alarming implications for critics of capitalist culture and society, such as Judith Williamson.

Writing in the Bennite journal on the Left of the Labour Party, the *New Socialist*, Williamson attacked a slide into what was later called 'cultural populism' (McGuigan, 1992 and 1997a). Williamson did not deny for one moment that the politics of consumption mattered, but the wholesale embrace of consumerism that had apparently captured cultural analysis in the Birmingham tradition was not a way forward intellectually and politically. She (1985: 20) also recognised the appeal of such an upbeat trend for disillusioned critics associated with Cultural Studies:

> the great irony is that it is precisely the illusion of autonomy which makes consumerism such an effective diversion in people's lives. At a time when such power in the economic and political spheres seems very distant, the realm of the 'superstructure' is, for consumers and Marxists alike, a much more fun place to be. Certainly it offers more fun than try-ing to deal with the frustrations channelled into it but created, predom-inantly, by the economic realities which are still the major constrictions on most people's lives. And also more fun than trying to envisage new ways in which some of the needs and desires appropriated by consumer goods can be met.

The developed critique of consumptionist – or, indeed, consumerist – Cultural Studies now consists essentially of two general propositions. First, that consumption is only one moment within a circuit of production, dis-tribution and exchange. To isolate consumption from these other moments is one-dimensional and does not grasp the ontological complexity of cul-ture in circulation. Second, the active consumers, readers, subjects, listeners, viewers, spectators, cybersurfers and so on of Cultural Studies have an affin-ity with the sovereign consumers of free-market ideology – the idea that customers' choices in the market wholly determine what is produced and made available. It is quite unnecessary to claim that this was a self-conscious choice of affiliation made by erstwhile cultural critics but it is instead enough to note a discernible homology between the active subject of Cultural Studies and the sovereign consumer of free-market capitalism. This was clearly evident early on in the work of John Fiske (1989a and 1989b), the prolific writer who was responsible for taking such a one-dimensional and consumptionist orientation to a logical and absurd extreme. Successive cohorts of Cultural Studies students have been taught roughly this story. It is a story that has considerable resonance with the young consumer in our neoliberal age.

The culture of cool capitalism

Let's face it, Birmingham was cool. Anyone who has ever met an avatar of the CCCS will know that they have been in the presence of a seriously cool customer. Moreover, the cool stance of Cultural Studies, as represented by 'the Birmingham School' and its affinity with cool in the vernacular is not a superficial matter just for teasing about. As Cultural Studies is said to have originated in Africa, somewhat implausibly by Handel K. Wright (1998), rather more plausibly did certain 'cool' features of Western consumerism, it would seem – and long before Norman Mailer's (1970 [1957]) 'white negro' of the 1950s. There is also an interesting homology and a curiously tangled convergence of attitudes to be traced between a field of study devoted to understanding culture in the raw and the paradoxical development of a substantive culture to be excavated here.

Scholars of the topic generally agree that cool came out of Africa (MacAdams, 2002: 14). In their survey of the meanings of 'cool', past and present, *Cool Rules*, Dick Pountain and David Robins (2000) cite the work of the art historian Robert Farris Thompson on the ancient African notion of 'itutu', which he translates as 'cool composure'. It refers to composure in battle, heat and life generally, especially for young males. 'Cool' in this sense has been highly valued by the West African Yoruba and also in other parts of Africa, such as among Bantu-speakers in the South. When Africans were forced into slavery in the Americas, itutu became a means of maintaining a sense of dignity in oppressive conditions.

There is an obvious line here that travels from slavery, through mid-twentieth century hipster and jazz culture to present-day street style, hip-hop and rap. Cool in its diverse manifestations, historically, in different places and among white people, is an appropriation from black warrior culture, originating in Africa and marked by a predominantly masculine expression of dignity, though not confined exclusively to men nor the young, certainly not now. Yet, rebellious young men have, indeed, been strongly attracted to cool.

There have been innumerable subcultural manifestations since the Second World War, such as the Parisian existentialists of the 1940s, the New York beats of the 1950s, the San Francisco hippies of the 1960s, the London punks of the 1970s and the city traders from the 1980s onwards in New York and

London. It has also been much more widely articulated since, if only in speech. Now, the word 'cool' seems to be on the lips of nearly every youngster in Western culture, a term of commonplace approval, meaning little else than 'good' or 'okay', and adopted insouciantly by their parents. Of that trajectory, Pountain and Robins (2000: 12) say, 'this attitude, which originally expressed resistance to subjugation and humiliation, has been expropriated by the mass media and the advertising industry since the '80s and '90s, and used as the way into the hearts and wallets of young consumers'.

In light of the trajectory of cool over the past 50 years, ostensibly from one side of a cultural divide to the exact opposite side, it is reasonable to ask, is there any essence to cool at all? Albeit aware of the reversal of cool's social valence, Pountain and Robins (2000: 26) claim that the cool attitude does have essential features, 'recognizable in all its manifestations as a particular combination of three core personality traits, namely narcissism, ironic detachment and hedonism'. Strangely enough, they continue (2000: 28), the cool attitude has become 'the dominant ethic of late consumer capitalism'.

Consider each of the three features. First, there is narcissism. In rebel cultures, self-regard, individual style and offensive deportment characterised the dissident who perhaps had precious little else to show off about. In this respect, the Parisian existentialist, dressed all in black, puffing elegantly on a Gauloise cigarette, obliged to act out anti-bourgeois non-conformity in every free choice, was a perfect example of cool, condemned to freedom in an inauthentic world, as Sartre would put it.

It is not very cool, however, to become too heated about the issues like some decidedly uncool revolutionary Marxist. So, ironic detachment – the second principal feature of cool – is the appropriate stance. There is a don't care attitude in conjunction with disgust at the system: 'whatever', with its sneer and feigned indifference. Punks and their progeny represented an extreme branch of the ironic tendency.

Third, since nothing much can be done about it, you might just as well have a good time. Alternative and hedonistic lifestyles, taking illegal drugs and the rest of it, used to be reliable means of upsetting the 'straights'. Some dropped out but, in the main, the hippies of the 1970s were weekenders, which were the harbinger of the present-day hedonistic mainstream – a notable constituent being extravagant unruliness and binge-drinking among teenage girls and young women. That's cool, too.

Pountain and Robins (2000) discussed the history and debates around the incorporation of cool into the mainstream. They concluded (2000: 178): 'Cool may have been an expression of rebellion but it is surely not any longer.'

The most profound thesis on contemporary cool is journalist Thomas Frank's book-length study *The Conquest of Cool* (1997), derived from his doctoral research in Cultural Studies. Frank is especially interesting because he knows his way around Cultural Studies as well as 'the real world'. His *One Market Under God* (2001) further develops the thesis on cool and examines what he regards as Cultural Studies' complicity with neoliberal, 'free-market' ideology. At the beginning of *The Conquest of Cool*, Frank (1997: x) had already announced:

> While my subject is arguably one of considerable current interest, my approach will seem antiquated to many. The Conquest of Cool is a study of cultural production rather than reception, of power rather than resistance; it does not address the subject of consumer evasiveness except as it is addressed by advertising executives and menswear manufacturers; it has little to say about the effectiveness of particular modes of popular resistance to mass culture, how this or that symbol was negotiated, detoured, or subverted. While cultural reception is a fascinating subject, I hope the reader will forgive me for leaving it to others. Not only has it been overdone, but our concentration on it, it seems to me, has led us to overlook and even minimize the equally fascinating doings of the creators of mass culture, a group as playful and even as subversive in their own way as the heroic consumers who are the focus of much of Cultural Studies today.

Writing in the context of 'culture wars' in the USA – rather than British Cultural Studies – Frank focuses his attention specifically on management theory and the 'consumer revolution' of the 1960s. By so doing, he indicates that complicity between Cultural Studies and consumer capitalism goes back, in effect, to *before* Cultural Studies really got going. This argument is especially devastating since it does not even give Cultural Studies credit for influencing marketing with its novel ideas. Instead, consumerist Cultural Studies has merely absorbed marketing ideas and sold them back to the marketing industry.

Frank challenges the conservative myth of 'the sixties' as the source of all evil, moral degeneracy and social decay. Instead, the legacy of that disputed decade has contributed to the flourishing of corporate America, if not necessarily to old-fashioned 'family values', except as a reaction formation. There is undoubtedly a cultural difference between 'conservatives' and 'liberals' but no great gulf need exist between them in terms of material interest, assuming that corporate power is of mutual interest. The division between rich and poor is starker than the division between conservative and liberal attitudes.

When seen in retrospect, the young rebels of sixties' counterculture were saviours rather than gravediggers of corporate America. As Frank (1997: 4) remarks, 'rebel youth remains the cultural mode of the corporate moment, used to promote not only specific products but also the general idea of life in the cyber-revolution'.

Incidentally, Peter Biskind (1998) has put forward a similar argument regarding the role of the 'movie brats' who came to prominence in the 1970s, an offshoot of the sixties, in saving Hollywood. The Francis Ford Coppolas, Peter Fondas, Dennis Hoppers, Bob Rafelsons and Bert Schneiders presented themselves as dangerous rebels, but they succeeded in giving Hollywood a cool makeover and, hence, boosted its long-term profitability. It is interesting to note that, around the turn of the millennium, Hopper appeared in a TV ad as a corporate executive of middle years driving a sleek motorcar that burns off his younger self on a 'born to be wild' motorbike from the 1969 counterculture movie *Easy Rider.*

Plenty of other examples can be given of the inversion of oppositional meaning derived from the counterculture to at least tacit support for the prevailing hegemony, which, in effect, is consent to the ravages of neoliberal globalisation. In fact, the signs of what were hitherto regarded as rebel culture have even been recruited by governments of a neoliberal persuasion – most typically by governments that still claim to be, in some sense, social democratic.

This was noticeable during saxophone-playing Bill Clinton's Democratic presidency of the USA in the 1990s. At the Democratic convention that adopted the hapless Al Gore as Clinton's successor in the presidential race in the year 2000, Clinton was represented as a seasoned rock star, which contrasted sharply with Gore's technocratic stiffness.

The New Labour government of Tony Blair in Britain, originally elected in 1997, sought to associate itself with the notion of 'cool Britannia' and wooed celebrity and reputedly radical figures from the entertainment industry, especially popular music. Many of them went along with the charade for a few months, but, when the government decided to cut entitlement to benefits for those only bureaucratically defined as 'unemployed', such as struggling young musicians, support for the rhetoric of 'cool Britannia' soon evaporated. The very idea became an embarrassment for the government and was not heard of again. John Harris (2003) has told the story of this symptomatic episode in detail and with considerable insight.

So it seems that business and its political allies eventually won the battle with the countercultural rebels through incorporation. According to Frank, however, it is not quite that simple. Business itself was already going through dramatic transformations in the 1950s and 1960s alongside the emergence of rebel youth culture in the USA. It was necessary for that counterculture to paint business as 'the monolithic bad guy' – 'the standard binary narrative' – but, in fact, business proved to be responsive to progressive ideas, including those of the counterculture, which it was eager to co-opt to its cause. Business was only too willing to integrate rebel ideology into its corporate practices, to 'revolutionise' management. In sum, Frank (1997: 8) tells 'the story of the bohemian cultural style's trajectory from adversarial to hegemonic; the story of hip's mutation from native language of the alienated to that of advertising'.

The notion that business merely incorporated countercultural signs to sell its products is too simplistic, however. Business leaders welcomed the cultural challenge since it accorded with their own thinking on the needs of capital. This involved breaking with 1950s' conformity, the robotic American way of life, which critics, both humanistic and social scientific, attacked endlessly – 'organisation man', 'one-dimensional man' and so on. In fact, 'By the middle of the 1950s, talk of conformity, of consumerism, and of the banality of mass-produced culture were routine elements of middle-class American life' (Frank, 1997: 11). Furthermore he noted (1997: 13),

'The meaning of "the sixties" cannot be considered apart from the enthusiasm of ordinary, suburban Americans for cultural revolution'. The consensus was already forming for the great shift into cool capitalism, the marriage of counterculture and corporate business, which has survived the high divorce rate ever since.

Frank (1997: 18–19) argues that Cultural Studies, in its American form but strongly influenced by the British, slipped into the trap of taking the advent of cool capitalism at face value:

> Today corporate ideologues routinely declare that business has supplanted the state, the church, and all independent culture in our national life. Curiously enough, at the same time many scholars have decided it is folly to study business. For all of cultural studies' subtle readings and forceful advocacy, its practitioners often tend to limit their inquiries so rigorously to the consumption of culture-products that the equally important process of cultural production is virtually ignored.

This is precisely the direction in which Birmingham-style Cultural Studies went – towards the struggle at the point of consumption, expressions of 'resistance' and 'difference' solely on the terrain of consumption, 'a strategic blunder of enormous proportions', in Frank's estimation.

Frank is unusual among cultural analysts in that he reads management literature to discern the ideological principles of corporate America and cool capitalism. During the 1950s and 1960s, there was increasing disquiet in business circles about 'organisation man's' lack of imagination and creativity. A key tool of the newer management was 'market segmentation', finely differentiating tastes and lifestyle categories, taking difference seriously, seeing heterogeneity instead of mass homogeneity. Consumer subjectivity became the focus of attention for this school of management, as it did for a great deal of Cultural Studies. The customer had become 'hip' to what was going on – a quaint term now, even uncool despite being the forerunner of cool discourse in business.

Although such language made an early appearance in the story related by Frank, for stretches of time it lay fairly dormant, until it returned louder and more insistent than ever in the 1990s. In the longer historical view, the counterculture turns out to have been a moment in the development of middle-class and corporate America. To cap it all, the 1990s saw 'the consolidation of a new species of hip consumerism, a cultural perpetual motion machine in which disgust with the falseness, shoddiness, and everyday oppressions of consumer society could be enlisted to drive the ever-accelerating wheel of consumption' (Frank, 1997: 31).

Today, business is said to be 'funky' (Ridderstråle and Nordström, 2002 [2000]). The longing for another world has diminished for the young, replaced by the longing for cool commodities at the expense of self-exploitation by youthful consumers, such as young girls recruited to the complex ruses of viral marketing (Quart, 2003). In such circumstances, culture jammers such as Kalle Lasn (1999) call desperately for 'the uncooling of America'.

Conclusion – multidimensional analysis and critique in the public interest

There is little doubt that Cultural Studies is a product of its time, reflecting shifts in culture and society over the past 40 or 50 years. Its task, however, is to not only reflect but also analyse the times. Stuart Hall sought to do that, often with great insight. His followers have generally been less successful at conjunctural analysis, especially those who focused their attention exclusively on consuming practices. Production has been neglected, though there are recent indications of a renewed interest in the politics of production, particularly with regard to the dire working conditions of many young people in 'the creative industries' (McRobbie, 2002).

More generally, multidimensional analysis is to be recommended in Cultural Studies (Kellner, 1997). To grasp the ontological complexity of culture in circulation, it is necessary to examine different points in the circuit. The Open University model for 'doing Cultural Studies' identifies five nodal points in this cultural circuit: consumption, identity, production, representation and regulation – all of which interact with each other (du Gay et al., 1997). Such a model is essential yet, in practice, it is difficult to address *every* connection in the circuit. Inevitably in a complex field of study there must be a division of labour and a range of specialisations that, in principle, are ideally in some relationship of mutuality.

Finally, what should impel research? Why not opt for critique in the public interest? It is an abrogation of responsibility for Cultural Studies not to be critical. There is plenty of need for it. In its politicised forms, Cultural Studies has engaged in advocacy on behalf of subordinate and marginalised groups and quite rightly so. It needs a broader concept of 'the public interest' to frame these concerns, however, which is, admittedly, a slippery notion. Greg Philo and David Miller (2001) have questioned the purposes of cultural and Media Studies, particularly what they see as its astonishing political quietism and virtual irrelevance to cultural politics of a critical kind in recent years.

It is unfortunate that the dominant ideology thesis and its more sophisticated version in hegemony theory have fallen out of vogue since Cultural Studies itself has fallen so much under the sway of neoliberalism and its 'cool' representation. Cultural Studies should, instead, contribute critically to debates on issues of public interest, however defined, rather than allow the agenda to be set for it by cool capitalism. This is a reasonable proposition, I believe, on which to conclude.

REFERENCES

Abbas, A. and Nguyet Erni, J. (eds) (2004) *Internationalizing Cultural Studies: An anthology*. Oxford: Basil Blackwell.

Abercrombie, N., Hill, S. and Turner, B. (2000) *The Penguin Dictionary of Sociology* (4th edn). London: Penguin.

Adam, B. (1998) *Timescapes of Modernity: The environment and invisible hazards*. London: Routledge.

Adorno, T. and Horkheimer, M. (1979 [1944]) *Dialectic of Enlightenment*. London: Verso.

Agar, J. (2003) *Constant Touch: A global history of the mobile phone*. Cambridge: Icon Books.

Ali, T. (2005) *Rough Music: Blair/Bombs/Baghdad/London/Terror*. London: Verso.

Allan, S., Adam, B. and Carter, C. (eds) (2000) *Environmental Risks and the Media*. London: Routledge.

Anderson, B. (2006 [1983]) *Imagined Communities: Reflections on the origin and spread of nationalism*. London: Verso.

Anderson, P. (1976) *Considerations on Western Marxism*. London: New Left Books.

Anderson, P. (2000) 'Renewals', *New Left Review*, 1 (2): 5–24.

Arthurs, J. (1994) 'Women and television', in S. Hood (ed.) *Behind the Screens: The structure of British television in the nineties*. London: Lawrence & Wishart. pp. 82–101.

Bach, S. (1985) *Final Cut: Dreams and disasters in the making of* Heaven's Gate. London: Faber and Faber.

Baehr, P. and Wells, G. (eds) (2002) *The Protestant Ethic and the 'Spirit' of Capitalism and Other Writings of Max Weber*. London: Penguin.

Bakhtin, M. (1984 [1965]) *Rabelais and His World*. Bloomington, IN: Indiana University Press.

Banham, M. and Hillier, B. (eds) (1976) *A Tonic to the Nation: The festival of Britain 1951*. London: Thames & Hudson.

Barber, B. (1996 [1995]) *Jihad vs. McWorld: How globalism and tribalism are reshaping the world*. New York: Ballantine Books.

Barrell, T. (2006) 'The battle of Little Britain', *Sunday Times* Magazine, 5 November: 14–23.

Barry, B. (2001) 'Muddles of multiculturalism', *New Left Review*, 8 (2): 49–71.

Barthes, R. (1979) *The Eiffel Tower and Other Mythologies*. Berkeley, CA: University of California Press.

Baudrillard, J. (1983) *In the Shadow of Silent Majorities, or, the End of the Social*. New York: Semiotext(e).

Bauman, Z. (1991) *Modernity and Ambivalence*. Cambridge: Polity Press.

Bauman, Z. (2000) *Liquid Modernity*. Cambridge: Polity Press.

Bayley, S. (1999) *Labour Camp: The failure of style over substance*. London: B.T. Batsford.

BBC DVD (2005) *Little Britain: The Complete First Series*. London: BBC Worldwide.

BBC Four (2003) *Upwardly Mobile*. London, 1 March.

Beale, A. (1999) 'From "Sophie's choice" to consumer choice: framing gender in cultural policy', *Media, Culture & Society*, 21: 435–58.

Beck, U. (1992 [1986]) *Risk Society: Towards a new modernity*. London: Sage.

Beck, U. (1992) 'From industrial society to risk society: questions of survival, social structure and ecological enlightenment', *Theory, Culture & Society*, 9: 97–123.

Beck, U. (1995 [1988]) *Ecological Politics in an Age of Risk*. Cambridge: Polity Press.

Beck, U. (1998) 'Politics of risky society', in J. Franklin (ed.), *The Politics of Risk Society*. Cambridge: Polity Press.

Beck, U. (2000) 'Foreword' in S. Allan, B. Adam and C. Carter (eds), *Environmental Risks and the Media*. London: Routledge. pp. xii–xiv.

Beck, U. and Beck-Gernsheim, E. (1995 [1990]) *The Normal Chaos of Love*. Cambridge: Polity Press.

Beck, U. and Beck-Gernsheim, E. (2002 [2001]) *Individualization*. London: Sage.

Benjamin, W. (1970 [1955]) *Illuminations*. London: Jonathan Cape.

Bennett, T. (1992) 'Putting policy into cultural studies', in L. Grossberg, C. Nelson and P. Treichler (eds), *Cultural Studies*. London: Routledge. pp. 23–37.

Bianchini, F. and Parkinson, M. (eds) (1993) *Cultural Policy and Urban Regeneration: The West European experience*. Manchester: Manchester University Press.

Billig, M. (1992) *Talking of the Royal Family*. London and New York: Routledge.

Billig, Michael (1995) *Banal Nationalism*. London: Sage.

Birnbaum, N. (1955) 'Monarchs, and sociologists: a reply to Professor Shils and Mr Young', *The Sociological Review*, 3 (1): 5–23.

Biskind, P. (1988) *Easy Riders, Raging Bulls*. London: Bloomsbury.

Björkegren, D. (1996) *The Culture Business: Management strategies for the arts-related business*. London: Routledge.

Blair, T. (1998) 'Why the Dome is good for Britain', People's Palace Speech, Royal Festival Hall, 24 February: 1–5.

Bloch, E., Lukacs, G., Brecht, B., Benjamin, W. and Adorno, T. (1977) *Aesthetics and Politics*. London: New Left Books.

Boltanski, L. and E. Chiapello (2005 [1999]) *The New Spirit of Capitalism*. London: Verso.

Bourdieu, P. and Wacquant, L. (1999) 'The cunning of imperialist reason', *Theory, Culture & Society*, 16 (1): 41–58.

Bourdieu, P. and Wacquant, L. (2001) 'NewLiberalSpeak: notes on the new planetary vulgate', *Radical Philosophy*, 105: 1–5.

Bragg, B. (2006) *The Progressive Patriot: A search for belonging*. London: Transworld.

Brenner, N. and Theodor, N. (2002) 'Cities and "actually existing neo-liberalism"', *Antipode*, 34 (3): 349–79.

Burgess, A. (2004) *Cellular Phones, Public Fears, and a Culture of Precaution*. Cambridge: Cambridge University Press.

Calhoun, C. (ed.) (1992) *Habermas and the Public Sphere*. Cambridge, MA: MIT Press.

Calhoun, C. (1995) *Critical Social Theory*. Cambridge, MA and Oxford: Basil Blackwell.

Cameron, D. (2000) *Good to Talk: Living and working in a communcation culture*. London: Sage.

Campbell, B. (1998) *Diana, Princess of Wales: How sexual politics shook the monarchy*. London: Women's Press.

Carey, J. (1997) 'Reflections on the project of (American) cultural studies', in M. Ferguson and P. Golding (eds), *Cultural Studies in Question*. London: Sage. pp. 1–24.

Carter, E. (1984) 'Alice in the consumer wonderland', in A. McRobbie and M. Nava (eds), *Gender and Generation*. London: Routledge. pp. 185–214.

Castells, M. (1997) 'An introduction to the information age', *City*, 7: 6–16.

Castells, M. (2000 [1996]) *The Rise of the Network Society*. Malden, MA and Oxford: Basil Blackwell.

Castells, M. (2004a [1997]) *The Power of Identity*. Malden MA and Oxford: Basil Blackwell.

Castells, M. (2004b [1998]) *End of Millennium*. Malden, MA and Oxford: Basil Blackwell.

Castells, M., Fernandez-Ardevol, M., Qiu, J.L. and Sey, A. (2007) *Mobile Communication and Society: A global perspective*. Cambridge, MA: MIT Press.

CCCS (Centre for Contemporary Cultural Studies) (1982) *The Empire Strikes Back: Race and Racism in 70s Britain*. London: Hutchison.

Chandran, R. (2000) 'An insult to all our countrymen', *Daily Mail*, 11 October: 7.

CITF (Creative Industries Task Force) (1998) *The Creative Industries: Mapping document*. London: Department for Culture, Media and Sport.

Cockburn, A., St. Clair, J. and Sekula, A. (2000) *5 Days That Shook the World: Seattle and beyond*. London: Verso.

Cohen, R. (1994) *Frontiers of Identity: The British and others*. London: Longman.

Cohen, S. (2001) *States of Denial: Knowing about atrocities and suffering*. Cambridge: Polity Press.

Colley, L. (1992) *Britons: Forging the nation 1707–1837*. London: Yale University Press.

Colls, R. (2002) *Identity of England*. Oxford: Oxford University Press.

Connolly, M. (2008) 'Capital and culture: an investigation into New Labour cultural policy and the european Capital of Culture 2008'. PhD disertation, University of Wales, Cardiff.

Corner, J. (2003) 'Debate: the model in question: A response to Klaehn on Herman and Chomsky', *European Journal of Communication*, 18 (3): 367–75.

Cottle, S. (1998) 'Ulrich Beck, risk society and the media: a catastrophic view?', *European Journal of Communication*, 13 (1): 5–32.

Couldry, N., (1999) 'Remembering Diana: the geography of celebrity and the politics of lack', 'Diana and Democracy', *New Formations*, 36: 77–91.

Coward, R. (1984) *Female Desire: Women's sexuality today*. London: Paladin.

Coward, R. (1998) 'Birthday soap', *Guardian*, 14 November: 23.

Crabtree, J., Nathan, M. and Roberts, S. (2003) *Mobile UK: Mobile phones and everyday life*. London: Work Foundation/iSociety.

Crystal, D. (2004) *The Stories of English*. London: Allen Lane.

Crystal, D. (2008) '2b or not 2b?', *Guardian* Review, 5 July: 2–4.

Curtis, M. (2003) *Web of Deceit: Britain's real role in the world*. London: Vintage.

Dahlgren, P. (1995) *Television and the Public Sphere: Citizenship, democracy and the media*. London: Sage.

Davidson, N. (2000) *The Origins of Scottish Nationhood*. London: Pluto Press.

Davis, M. (2004) 'Planet of slums – urban involution and the informal proletariat', *New Left Review*, 26 (2): 5–34.

Davis, M. (2006) *Planet of Slums*. London: Verso.

Davis, S. (1997) *Spectacular Nature: Corporate culture and the Sea World experience*. Berkeley, CA and London: University of California Press.

Debord, G. (1994 [1967]) *The Society of the Spectacle*. New York: Zone Books.

Douglas, M. and Wildavsky, A. (1982) *Rick and Culture: An essay on the selection of technological and environmental dangers*. Berkeley, CA: University of California Press.

Driver, S. and Martell, L. (1998) *New Labour: Politics after Thatcherism*. Cambridge: Polity Press.

Du Gay, P., Hall, S., Janes, L., Mackay, H. and Negus, K. (1997) *Doing Cultural Studies: The story of the Sony Walkman*. London: Sage.

Du Noyer, P. (2004 [2002]) *Liverpool: Wondrous place – from the Cavern to the Coral*. London: Virgin.

Duffy, R. (2002) *A Trip Too Far: Ecotourism, politics and exploitation*. London: Earthscan.

Dyer, R., Lovell, T. and McCrindle, J. (1997 [1977]) 'Women and soap opera', in A. Gray and J. McGuigan (eds), *Studying Culture*. London: Arnold. pp. 35–41.

Eagleton, T. (1984) *The Function of Criticism: From* The Spectator *to post-structuralism*. London: Verso.

Eco, U. (1987 [1967]) 'Towards a semiological guerilla warfare', in U. Eco, *Travels in Hyperreality*. London: Picador. pp. 135–44.

EFTCD (European Task Force on Culture and Development) (1997) *In From the Margins: A contribution to the debate on culture and development in Europe*. Strasbourg: Council of Europe.

ERM Economics (May 2003) *European Capital of Culture: Socio-economic impact assessment of Liverpool's bid*. Manchester: ERM Economics.

Fairclough, N. (2000) *New Labour, New Language*. London: Routledge.

Fiske, J. (1989a) *Reading the Popular*. London: Unwin Hyman.

Fiske, J. (1989b) *Understanding Popular Culture*. London: Unwyn Hyman.

Florida, R. (2003 [2002]) *The Rise of the Creative Class: And how it's transforming work, leisure, community and everyday life*. Melbourne: Pluto.

Forgacs, D. and Nowell-Smith, G. (eds) (1985) *Antonio Gramsci: Selections from cultural writings*. London: Lawrence & Wishart.

Frank, T. (1997) *The Conquest of Cool: Business culture, counterculture, and the rise of hip consumerism*. Chicago, IL: University of Chicago Press.

Frank, T. (2001) *One Market Under God: Extreme capitalism, market populism and the end of economic democracy*. London: Secker & Warburg.

Fraser, N. (1992) 'Rethinking the public sphere – a contribution to the critique of actually existing democracy', in C. Calhoun (ed.), *Habermas and the Public Sphere*. Cambridge, MA: MIT Press. pp. 109–42.

Fukuyama, F. (1989) 'The end of history?', *National Interest*, 16: 3–18.

Fukuyama, F. (1992) *The End of History and the Last Man*. Harmondsworth: Penguin.

Furedi, F. (2002 [1997]) *Culture of Fear: Risk-taking and the morality of low expectation*. London: Cassell.

Gamble, Andrew (2001) 'Neo-liberalism', *Capital and Class*, 75: 127–34.

Garnham, N. (1990) *Capitalism and Communication: Global culture and the economics of information*. London: Sage.

Garnham, N. (1992) 'The media and the public sphere', C. Calhoun (ed.), *Habermas and the Public Sphere*. Cambridge, MA: MIT Press.

Garnham, N. (1995) 'The media and narratives of the intellectual', *Media, Culture & Society*, 17: 359–84.

Garnham, N. and Epstein, J. (1985) 'The cultural industries, cultural consumption and cultural policy', *The State of the Art or the Art of the State? Strategies for the cultural industries in London*. London: Industry and Employment Branch, Department for Recreation and the Arts, Greater London Council. pp. 145–65.

Gerbner, G. (1995) 'Television violence – the power and the peril', in G. Dines and J. Humez (eds), *Gender, Race and Class in Media*. London: Sage.

Geser, H. (2003) 'Towards a sociological theory of the mobile phone', available online at: www.socio.ch/mobile/t_geser1.htm

Giddens, A. (1992) *The Transformation of Intimacy: Sexuality, love and eroticism in modern societies*. Cambridge: Polity Press.

Gilligan, C. (1993 [1982]) *In a Different Voice: Psychological theory and women's development*. Cambridge, MA: Harvard University Press.

Gilroy, P. (1987) *There Ain't No Black in the Union Jack: The cultural politics of race and nation*. London: Hutchinson.

Gittings, J. (2005) *The Changing Face of China: From Mao to market*. Oxford: Oxford University Press.

Glancey, J. (2001) *London: Bread and circuses*. London: Verso.

Goffman, E. (1971 [1959]) *The Presentation of Self in Everyday Life*. London: Penguin.

Goldberger, P. (1998) 'The big top', *The New Yorker*, 27 April and 4 May: 152–9.

Gray, A. (2003) *Research Practice for Cultural Studies*. London: Sage.

Gray, J. (1992) *Men are from Mars, Women are from Venus*. New York: HarperCollins.

Greenhalgh, P. (1988) *Ephemeral Vistas: The expositions universelles, great exhibitions and world's fairs, 1851–1939*. Manchester: Manchester University Press.

Gripsrud, J. (1992) 'The aesthetics and politics of melodrama', in P. Dahlgren and C. Sparks (eds), *Journalism and Popular Culture*. London: Sage. pp. 84–95.

Grosshans, H. (1983) *Hitler and the Artists*. New York: Holmes & Meier.

Habermas, J. (1972 [1968]) *Knowledge and Human Interests*. London: Heinemann.

Habermas, J. (1987 [1981]) *The Theory of Communicative Action:* Volume 2: *Lifeworld and System: A critique of functionalist reason*. Cambridge: Polity Press.

Habermas, J. (1989 [1962]) *The Structural Transformation of the Public Sphere: An inquiry into a category of bourgeois society*. Cambridge: Polity Press.

Habermas, J. (1992) 'Further reflections on the public sphere' and 'Concluding remarks', in C. Calhoun (ed.), *Habermas and the Public Sphere*. Cambridge, MA: MIT Press. pp. 421–79.

Habermas, J. (1996 [1992]) 'Civil society and the political public sphere', in J. Habermas, *Between Facts and Norms: Contributions to a discourse theory of law and democracy*. Cambridge: Polity Press. pp. 329–87.

Habermas, J. (1999 [1996]) *The Inclusion of the Other: Studies in political theory*. Cambridge: Polity Press.

Hall, J. (2006) *The Rough Guide to British Cult Comedy*. London: Penguin.

Hall, S. (1974) 'The television discourse – encoding and decoding', in A. Gray and J. McGuigan (eds), (1997 [1993]) *Studying Culture: An introductory reader*. London: Arnold. pp. 28–34. Originally published in *Education and Culture*, 25, Paris: UNESCO.

Hall, S. (1980) 'Cultural studies – two paradigms', *Media, Culture & Society*, 2: 57–72.

Hall, S. (1982) 'The rediscovery of "ideology" – return of the repressed in media studies', in M. Gurevitch, T. Bennett, J. Curran and J. Woollacott (eds), *Culture, Society and the Media*. London: Methuen. pp. 56–90.

Hall, S. (1988) *The Hard Road to Renewal: Thatcherism and the crisis of the left*. London: Verso.

Hall, S. (1997) 'Culture and power', *Radical Philosophy*, 86: 24–41.

Hall, S. (2000) 'A question of identity', *Observer*, 15 October: 27.

Hall, S. and Jacques, M. (eds) (1989) *New Times: The changing face of politics in the 1990s*. London: Lawrence & Wishart.

Hames, T. and Leonard, M. (1998) *Modernising the Monarchy*. London: Demos.

Harding, L. (1997) 'Lift-off for £750m Dome', *Guardian*, 27 June: 3.

Hari, J. (2005) 'Why I hate "Little Britain"', *Independent*, 22 November: 35.

Harkin, J. (2003) *Mobilisation: The growing public interest in mobile technology*. London: O_2/Demos.

Harris, J. (2003) *The Last Party: Britpop, Blair and the demise of British rock*. London: Fourth Estate.

Hartley, J. (2003) *A Short History of Cultural Studies*. London: Sage.

Hartley, J. (ed.) (2005) *Creative Industries*. Malden, MA and Oxford: Blackwell.

Harvey, D. (1989) 'Flexible accumulation through urbanization reflections on "post-modernism" in the city', in D. Harvey, *The Urban Experience*. Oxford: Blackwell. pp. 256–78.

Harvey, D. (2005) *A Brief History of Neoliberalism*. Oxford: Oxford University Press.

Hatton, R. and Walker, J.A. (2005 [2000]) *Supercollector: A critique of Charles Saatchi*. London: Ellipsis.

Hayek, F. (1944) *The Road to Serfdom*. London: Routledge & Kegan Paul.

Heathcoat Amory, E. and Rayner, G. (2000) 'Racism slur on the word "British"', *Daily Mail*, 11 October: 6–7.

Herman, E. and Chomsky, N. (1988) *Manufacturing Consent: The political economy of the mass media*. New York: Pantheon Books.

Heseltine, M. (2000) *Life in the Jungle: My autobiography*. London: Hodder & Stoughton.

Hesmondhalgh, D. (2007 [2002]) *The Cultural Industries*. London: Sage.

Hitchens, C. (1993) *For the Sake of Argument*. London: Verso.

Hitchens, C. (1995) *The Missionary Position: Mother Theresa in theory and practice*. London: Verso.

Hitchens, C. (1999) *No One Left to Lie To: The triangulations of William Jefferson Clinton*. London: Verso.

Hoare, Q. and Nowell-Smith, G. (eds) (1971) *Selections from the Prison Notebooks of Antonio Gramsci*. London: Lawrence & Wishart.

Hobsbawm, E. (1994) *Age of Extremes: The short twentieth century 1914– 1991*. London: Michael Joseph.

Hochschild, A.R.(2003 [1983]) *The Managed Heart: Commercialization of human feeling*. Berkeley, CA: University of California Press.

Hochschild, A.R. (2003) *The Commercialization of Intimate Life: Notes from home and work*. Berkeley, CA: University of California Press.

Hoggart, R. (1957) *The Uses of Literacy*. London: Chatto & Windus.

Huntington, S. (1993) 'The clash of civilizations?', *Foreign Affairs*, 72 (3): 22–49.

Huntington, S. (1996) *The Clash of Civilizations and the Remaking of World Order*. New York: Simon & Schuster.

Huntington, S. (1997) 'The West and the rest', *Prospect*, February: 34–9.

Huntington, S. (2004) *Who Are We? America's great debate*. London: Free Press.

Hutton, W. (2000) 'Never mind facts, let's have a scandal', *Observer*, 15 October: 30.

IEGMP (Independent Expert Group on Mobile Phones, The Stewart Report) (2000) *Mobile Phones and Health*. Didcot: NRPB.

Irvine, A. (1999) *The Battle for the Dome*. London: Irvine News Agency.

Jefferson, T. (ed.) (1975) *Resistance Through Rituals*. Birmingham: Centre for Contemporary Cultural Studies.

Johnson, P. (2000) 'In praise of being British', *Daily Mail*, 11 October: 12–13.

Johnson, R., Chambers, D., Raghuram, P. and Ticknell, E. (2004) *The Practice of Cultural Studies*. London: Sage.

Johnston, P. (2000a) 'Straw wants to rewrite our history – British is a racist word, says report', *Daily Telegraph*, 10 October: 1.

Johnston, P. (2000b) 'Thinkers who want to consign our island story to history', *Daily Telegraph*, 10 October: 6.

Johnston, P. (2000c) 'Straw beats a very British retreat over race report', *Daily Telegraph*, 14 October: 1.

Junor, P. (1998) *Charles: Victim or Villain?* London: HarperCollins.

Jones, J. (1998) 'Passion and commitment – the difficulties faced by working mothers in the British television industry', in S. Ralph, J. Langham Brown and T. Lees (eds), *What Price Creativity?* Luton: John Libbey. pp. 221–8.

Katz, J. and Aakhus, M. (eds) (2002) *Perpetual Contact: Mobile communication, private talk, public performance*. Cambridge: Cambridge University Press.

Keane, J. (1998) *Civil Society: Old images, new visions*. Cambridge: Polity Press.

Kellner, D. (1997) 'Critical theory and cultural studies – the missed articulation', in J. McGuigan (ed.), *Cultural Methodologies*. London: Sage. pp. 12–41.

Klaehn, J. (2002) 'A critical review and assessment of Herman and Chomsky's "propaganda model"', *European Journal of Communication*, 17 (2): 147–82.

Klaehn, J. (2003) 'Debate: model monstruction: various other epistemological concerns – a reply to John Corner's commentary on the propaganda model', *European Journal of Communication*, 18 (3): 377–83.

Klein, N. (2000) *No Logo: Taking aim at the brand bullies*. London: HarperCollins.

Kumar, K. (2003) *The Making of English National Identity*. Cambridge: Cambridge University Press.

Lasn, K. (1999) *Culture Jam: The uncooling of America*. New York: Eagle Brook.

LECC (Liverpool European Capital of Culture) (2002) *Bid Document*. Liverpool: Culture Company.

Leonard, M. (1997) *BritainTM: Renewing our identity*. London: Demos.

Lewis, B. (1999) *Looking for Mandy's Place: An epic millennium poem*. Loughborough University School of Art and Design.

Lewis, J. and Miller, T. (eds) (2003) *Critical Cultural Policy Studies*. Malden, MA and Oxford: Blackwell.

Lewis, P., Richardson, V. and Woudhuysen, J. (1998) *In Defence of the Dome*. London: Adam Smith Institute.

Liverpool Vision (2003) *Development Update 9: Liverpool City Centre*: Liverpool Vision.

Livingstone, S. and Lunt, P. (1994) *Talk on Television: Audience participation and public debate*. London: Routledge.

Lomborg, B. (2001 [1998]) *The Skeptical Environmentalist: Measuring the real state of the world*. Cambridge: Cambridge University Press.

Lovell, T. (1980) *Pictures of Reality: Aesthetics, politics and pleasure*. London: British Film Institute.

Lupton, Deborah (1999) *Risk*. London: Routledge.

Lyotard, Jean-François (1984 [1979]), *The Postmodern Condition: A report on knowledge*. Manchester: Manchester University Press.

Lyotard, J.-F. (1991 [1988]) *The Inhuman: Reflections on time*. Cambridge: Polity Press.

MacAdams, L. (2002) *Birth of the Cool: Beat, bebop & the American avant-garde*. London: Scribner.

MacPherson, W. (1999) *The Stephen Lawrence Inquiry: Report of an inquiry by Sir William McPherson of Cluny*. London: Her Majesty's Stationery Office.

Mailer, N. (1970 [1957]) *The White Negro*. San Francisco, CA: City Lights.

Maitland, S. (1998) 'The secular saint', in M. Merck (ed.), *After Diana: Irreverent elegies*. London: Verso.

Martin, P. (2000) 'Dome and gloom', *Sunday Times* Magazine, 9 July: 40–6.

Marx, K. (1976 [1867]) *Capital: Volume 1*. London: Penguin.

McGuigan, J. (1992) *Cultural Populism*. London: Routledge.

References

McGuigan, J. (1996) *Culture and the Public Sphere*. London: Routledge.

McGuigan, J. (1997a) 'Cultural populism revisited', in M. Ferguson and P. Golding (eds), *Cultural Studies in Question*. London: Sage. pp. 138–54.

McGuigan, J. (ed.) (1997b) *Cultural Methodologies*. London: Sage.

McGuigan, J. (1998a) 'What price the public sphere?', in D.K. Thussu (ed.), *Electronic Empires: Global media and local resistance*. London: Arnold.

McGuigan, J. (1998b), 'National government and the cultural public sphere', *Media International Australia incorporating Culture and Policy*, 87: 68–83.

McGuigan, J. (1999) 'Whither cultural studies?', in N. Aldred and M. Ryle (eds), *Teaching Culture: The long revolution in cultural studies*. Leicester: National Institute of Adult Continuing Education. pp. 79–91.

McGuigan, J. (2002) 'The public sphere', in P. Hamilton and K. Thompson (eds), *The Uses of Sociology*. Oxford: Blackwell. pp. 81–128.

McGuigan, J. (2004a) 'A shell for neoliberalism – New Labour Britain and the Millennium Dome', S. Burnett, E. Caunes, E. Mazierska and J. Walton (eds), *Relocating Britishness*. Manchester: Manchester University Press. pp. 38–52.

McGuigan, J. (2004b) *Rethinking Cultural Policy*. Maidenhead: Open University Press.

McGuigan, J. (2005a) 'The power of nightmares', *Flow: A Critical Forum on Television and Media Culture*, 2.1.

McGuigan, J. (2005b) 'Neo-liberalism, culture and policy', *International Journal of Cultural Policy*, 11 (3): 229–41.

McGuigan, J. (2006 [1999]) *Modernity and Postmodern Culture*. Maidenhead: Open University Press.

McGuigan, J. (2006) 'Richard Hoggart – public intellectual', *International Journal of Cultural Policy*, 12 (2): 199–208.

McGuigan, J. (2010) *Cool Capitalism*. London: Pluto Press.

McGuigan, J. and Gilmore, A. (2001) 'Figuring out the Dome', *Cultural Trends*, 39: 41–83.

McGuigan, J. and Gilmore, A. (2002) 'The Millennium Dome – sponsoring, meaning and visiting', *International Journal of Cultural Policy*, 8 (1): 1–20.

McKay, G. (1996) *Senseless Acts of Beauty: Cultures of resistance since the sixties*. London: Verso.

McKay, G. (1998) *DIY Culture: Party & protest in nineties Britain*. London: Verso.

McNaghten, P. and Urry, J. (1998) *Contested Natures*. London: Sage.

McNeil, M. (1998) 'De-centreing or re-focusing cultural studies?', *European Journal of Cultural Studies*, 1 (1): 57–64.

McRobbie, A. (2002) 'Clubs to companies – notes on the decline of political culture in speeded up creative worlds', *Cultural Studies*, 16 (4): 516–32.

Mellor, A. (1991) 'Enterprise and heritage in the dock', in J. Corner and S. Harvey (eds), *Enterprise and Heritage: Crosscurrents of national culture*. London: Routledge.

Mestrovic, S. (1997) *Postemotional Society*. London: Sage.

MFME (Movement for Middle England) (1992) *Race, Culture and Identity: The view from Middle England.* Leicester: The Movement for Middle England.

Miège, B. (1989) *The Capitalization of Cultural Production.* New York: International General.

Miliband, R. (1978) 'A state of de-subordination', *British Journal of Sociology*, 29 (4): pp. 399–409.

Miller, D. (ed.) (2003) *Tell Me Lies: Propaganda and distortion in the attack on Iraq.* London: Pluto Press.

Miller, T., Govil, N., McMurria, J., Maxwell, R. and Wang, T. (2005 [2001]) *Global Hollywood 2.* London: British Film Institute.

Monbiot, G. (2005) 'Junk science', *Guardian*, 10 May: 23.

Morrison, B. (2000) 'That was the Dome that was', *Independent on Sunday – Sunday Review*, 3 December: 14–16.

Morton, A. (1997 [1992]) *Diana: Her true story in her own words.* London: O'Mara Books.

Myerson, G. (2001) *Heidegger, Habermas and the Mobile Phone.* Cambridge: Icon.

Mythen, G. (2004) *Ulrich Beck: A critical introduction to risk society.* London: Pluto Press.

Nairn, T. (1981 [1977]) *The Break-Up of Britain: Crisis and neo-nationalism.* London: Verso.

Negus, K. and Pickering, M. (2004) *Creativity, Communication and Cultural Value.* London: Sage.

Nicolson, A. (1999) *Regeneration: The story of the Millennium Dome.* London: HarperCollins.

NMEC (New Millennium Experience Company) (2000) *Millennium Experience: The Guide.* London: New Millennium Experience Company.

Orbach, S. (1998), 'A crying shame', *Marxism Today*, Nov./Dec. 61–2.

Page, J. (2000) 'The Millennium Dome', *RSA Journal*, 3–4: 1–8.

Palast, G. (2001) 'Ask no questions...', *Observer – Business*, 25 March: 6.

Paredes, M.C. (2003) 'Television set production at the US–Mexican border: trade policy and advanced electronics for the global market', in J. Lewis and T. Miller (eds), *Critical Cultural Policy Studies: A Reader*, Malden, MA and Oxford: Blackwell. pp. 272–81.

Parekh, B. (1997) 'National culture and multiculturalism', in K. Thompson (ed.), *Media and Cultural Regulation.* London: Sage. pp. 163–205.

Parekh, B. (1999) 'Political theory and the multicultural society', *Radical Philosophy*, 95: 27–32.

Parekh, B. (2000a) 'A Britain we all belong to', *Guardian*, 11 October: 19.

Parekh, B. (2000b) 'Why it is vital to change what it means to be British – Bhikhu Parekh, author of the controversial report on Britishness, defends its recommendations and calls for the UK to be declared multicultural', *Daily Telegraph*, 18 October: 26.

Parekh, B. (2000c) *Rethinking Multiculturalism: Cultural diversity and political theory*. Basingstoke: Macmillan.

Parton, J. (1999) 'My doomsday at the Dome', *Mail on Sunday* Review, 5 September: 58–9.

Patterson, R. (2002) 'Work histories in television', *Media, Culture & Society*, 23: 495–520.

Pauwels, C. and Loisen, J. (2003) 'The WTO and the audio-visual sector – economic free trade vs. cultural horse trading?', *European Journal of Communication*, 18 (3): 291–313.

Perin, C. (1992) 'The communicative circle – museums as communities', in I. Karp, C. Mullen. Kramer and S.D. Lavine (eds), *Museums as Communities: The politics of public culture*. Washington, DC: Smithsonian Institution. pp. 182–220.

Perryman, M. (2005) 'Keep the flags flying – World Cup 2002, football and the remaking of Englishness', in J. Littler and R. Naidoo (eds), *The Politics of Heritage: The legacies of 'Race'*. London: Routledge. pp. 202–15.

Perryman, M. (2006) *Ingerland: Travels with a football nation*. London: Simon & Schuster.

Petropoulis, J. (2000) *The Faustian Bargain: The art world in Nazi Germany*. London: Allen Lane.

Philo, G. and Miller, D. (eds) (2001) *Market Killing: What the free market does and what social scientists can do about it*. Harlow: Longman.

Pines, J. (2001) 'Rituals and representations of black "Britishness"', in D. Morley and K. Robins (eds), *British Cultural Studies: Geography, nationality, and identity*. Oxford: Oxford University Press. pp. 57–66.

Plant, S. (2002) *On the Mobile*, available online at: www.motorola.com/mot/doc/0/234_MotDocpdf

Pountain, D. and Robins, D. (2000) *Cool Rules: Anatomy of an attitude*. London: Reaktion.

Private Eye (2000) 1013: 19.

Procter, J. (2004) *Stuart Hall*. London: Routledge.

Puro, Jukka-Pekka (2002) 'Finland – a mobile culture', in J. Katz and M. Aakhus (eds), *Perpetual Contact: Mobile communication, private talk, public performance*. Cambridge: Cambridge University Press. pp. 19–29.

Quart, A. (2003) *Branded: The buying and selling of teenagers*. London: Arrow.

Rampton, S. and Stauber, J. (2003) *Weapons of Mass Deception: The uses of propaganda in Bush's war on Iraq*. London: Robinson.

Rheingold, H. (2002) *Smart Mobs: The next social revolution*. Cambridge, MA: Perseus Books/Basic Books.

Richards, G. (2000) 'The European cultural capital event – strategic weapon in the cultural arms race?', *International Journal of Cultural Policy*, 6 (2): 159–81.

Richards, S. (1997) 'Interview: Peter Mandelson – I used to be a sceptic, but now I'm a true believer, says Millennium dollar man: The alternative would be spam, spam and more spam', *New Statesman*, 4 July: 16–17.

Ridderstråle, J. and Nordström, K. (2002 [2000]) *Funky Business*. London: Prentice Hall.

Riesman, D., Glazer, N. and Denny, R. (1989 [1961]) *The Lonely Crowd: A study of the changing American character*. New Haven, CT: Yale University Press.

Rifkin, J. (2000) *The Age of Access: How the shift from ownership to access is transforming capitalism*. London: Penguin.

Rocco, F. (1995) 'The great millennium lottery', *Independent on Sunday – Sunday Review*, 1 January: 8–12.

Rojek, C. (2001) *Celebrity*. London: Reaktion.

Rojek, C. (2003) *Stuart Hall*. Cambridge: Polity Press.

Runnymede Trust (2000) *The Future of Multi-Ethnic Britain: The Parekh Report*. London: Profile.

Rustin, M. (1994) 'Incomplete modernity – Ulrich Beck's *Risk Society*', *Radical Philosophy*, 67: 3–12.

Samuel, R. (1998) *Island Stories: Unravelling Britain: Theatres of Memory Volume II*. London: Verso.

Saukko, P. (2003) *Doing Research in Cultural Studies: An introduction to classical and new methodological approaches*. London: Sage.

Schegloff, E. (2002) 'Beginnings in the telephone', in J. Katz and M. Aakhus (eds), *Perpetual Contact: Mobile communication, private talk, public performance*. Cambridge: Cambridge University Press. pp. 284–300.

Schiller, D. (1999) *Digital Capitalism: Networking the global market system*. Cambridge, MA: MIT Press.

Seaford, H. (2001) 'The future of multi-ethnic Britain – an opportunity missed', *Political Quarterly*, 72 (1): 107–13.

Sennett, R. (2006) *The Culture of the New Capitalism*. New Haven: Yale University Press.

Shaw, R. (ed.) (1993) *The Spread of Sponsorship – In the Arts, Sport, Education, the Health Service and Broadcasting*. Newcastle: Bloodaxe Books.

Shils, E. and Young, M. (1953) 'The meaning of the Coronation', *Sociological Review*, 1 (2): 63–81.

Sim, S. (2001) *Lyotard and the Inhuman*. Cambridge: Icon Books.

Simmonds, D. (1984) *Princess Di: The national dish*. London: Pluto Press.

Sinclair, S. (1999) *Sorry Meniscus: Excursions to the Millennium Dome*. London: Profile.

Sklair, L. (2002) *Globalization: Capitalism and its alternatives*. Oxford: Blackwell.

Sokal, A. (1996) 'Transgressing the boundaries: toward a transformative hermeneutics of quantum gravity', *Social Text*, 46–47: 217–52.

Sokal, A. and Bricmont, J. (1998 [1997]) *Intellectual Impostures*. London: Profile.

Sparks, C. (1994) 'Independent production', in S. Hood (ed.), *Behind the Screens: The structure of British television in the nineties*. London: Lawrence & Wishart. pp. 133–54.

Stallabrass, J. (2006 [1999]) *High Art Lite: British art in the 1990s*. London: Verso.

Stanton, G. (1996) 'Ethnography, anthropology and cultural studies - links and connections', in J. Curran, D. Morley and V. Walkerdine (eds), *Cultural Studies and Communications*. London: Arnold.

Steele, T. (1997) *The Emergence of Cultural Studies: Cultural politics, adult education and the English question*. London: Lawrence & Wishart.

Steinert, H. (2003 [1998]) *Culture Industry*. Cambridge: Polity Press.

Straw, J. (2000) 'Blame the Left not the British', *Observer*, 15 October: 27.

Tallis, R. (1997) *The Enemies of Hope: A critique of contemporary pessimism*. New York: St Martin's Press.

Thompson, E.P. (1968 [1963)] *The Making of the English Working Class*. Harmondsworth: Penguin.

Thompson, J.B. (1990) *Ideology and Modern Culture: Critical social theory in the era of mass communication*. Cambridge: Polity Press.

Thompson, J.B. (1997) 'Scandal and social theory', in J. Lull and S. Hinerman (eds), *Media Scandals*. Cambridge: Polity Press.

Toynbee, P. (2000a) 'I paid up, I queued up, and now I'm thoroughly fed up', *Guardian*, 5 January: 20.

Toynbee, P. (2000b) 'The £758 million disaster zone', *Daily Mail*, 6 January: 6–7.

Turner, G. (2003 [1990]) *British Cultural Studies: An introduction*. London: Routledge.

Urry, J. (2000) *Sociology Beyond Societies: Mobilities for the twenty-first century*. London: Routledge.

Ursell, G. (1998) 'Labour flexibility in the UK commercial television sector', *Media, Culture & Society*, 20: 129–53.

Vargas Llosa, M. (2006) 'The fence of lies', *New Statesman*, 6 November: 34–7.

Voltaire, F. M. A. de (1947 [1759]) *Candide – or Optimism*, trans. J. Butt. Harmondsworth: Penguin.

Walden, G. (2000) *The New Elites: Making a career in the masses*. London: Allen Lane.

Walter, N. (2004) 'What's love got to do with it?', *Guardian*, 14 January: 25.

Ward, D. (2003) 'How the DIY sounds of skiffle still inspire today', *Guardian*, 6 September: 13. Quoting A. Lowry.

Ward, D. (2006) 'City of tattered dreams', *Guardian G2*, 9 March: 10–11.

WCCD (World Commission on Cultural Development) (1996 [1995]) *Our Creative Diversity*. Paris: UNESCO.

Wilde, J. and de Haan, E. (2006) *The High Cost of Calling: Critical issues in the mobile phone industry*. Amsterdam: SOMO Centre for Research on Multinational Corporations.

Wilhide, E. (1999) *The Millennium Dome*. London: HarperCollins.

Wilks-Heeg, S. (2004) 'Capitalising culture – Liverpool 2008', *Local Economy*, 19 (4): 341–60.

Williams, R. (1958) *Culture and Society*. London: Chatto & Windus.

Williams, R. (1961) *The Long Revolution*. London: Chatto & Windus.

Williams, Raymond (1974) *Television: Technology and cultural form*. London: Fontana.

Williams, R. (1977) 'A lecture on realism', *Screen*, 18 (1): 61–74.

Williams, R. (1980 [1960/1969]) 'Advertising – the magic system', in R. Williams, *Problems in Materialism and Culture: Selected essays*. London: Verso. pp. 170–95.

Williams, R. (1984) 'State culture and beyond', in L. Apignanesi (ed.), *Culture and the State*. London: Institute of Contemporary Arts. pp. 3–5.

Williams, R. (1985 [1983]) *Towards 2000*. Harmondsworth: Penguin.

Williams, R. (1989) *The Politics of Modernism: Against the new conformists*. London: Verso.

Williamson, J. (1985) 'Consuming passions', *New Socialist*, February: 19–20.

Wilson, E. (1998) 'The unbearable lightness of Diana', in M. Merck (ed.), *After Diana: Irreverent elegies*. London: Verso.

Winston, B. (1996) *Technologies of Seeing: Photography, cinema and television*. London: British Film Institute.

Wright, H.K. (1998) 'Dare we de-centre Birmingham?: Troubling the "origin" and trajectories of cultural studies', *European Journal of Cultural Studies*, 1 (1): 33–56.

WSGCCCS (Women's Studies Group Centre for Contemporary Cultural Studies) (1978) *Women Take Issue: Aspects of women's subordination*. London: Hutchinson.

Yergen, D. and Stanislaw, J. (2002 [1998]) *The Commanding Heights: The battle for the world economy*. New York: Touchstone.

INDEX

Research Methods Books from SAGE

www.sagepub.co.uk

SAGE

The Qualitative Research Kit

Edited by Uwe Flick

Read sample chapters online now!

Doing Ethnographic and Observational Research — Michael Angrosino
The SAGE Qualitative Research Kit — Edited by Uwe Flick

Using Visual Data in Qualitative Research — Marcus Banks
The SAGE Qualitative Research Kit — Edited by Uwe Flick

Doing Focus Groups — Rosaline Barbour
The SAGE Qualitative Research Kit

Designing Qualitative Research — Uwe Flick
The SAGE Qualitative Research Kit — Edited by Uwe Flick

Managing Quality in Qualitative Research — Uwe Flick
The SAGE Qualitative Research Kit — Edited by Uwe Flick

Analyzing Qualitative Data — Graham Gibbs
The SAGE Qualitative Research Kit — Edited by Uwe Flick

Doing Interviews — Steinar Kvale
The SAGE Qualitative Research Kit — Edited by Uwe Flick

Doing Conversation, Discourse and Document Analysis — Tim Rapley
The SAGE Qualitative Research Kit — Edited by Uwe Flick

www.sagepub.co.uk

Supporting researchers for more than forty years

Research methods have always been at the core of SAGE's publishing. Sara Miller McCune founded SAGE in 1965 and soon after, she published SAGE's first methods book, *Public Policy Evaluation*. A few years later, she launched the Quantitative Applications in the Social Sciences series – affectionately known as the 'little green books'.

Always at the forefront of developing and supporting new approaches in methods, SAGE published early groundbreaking texts and journals in the fields of qualitative methods and evaluation.

Today, more than forty years and two million little green books later, SAGE continues to push the boundaries with a growing list of more than 1,200 research methods books, journals, and reference works across the social, behavioural, and health sciences.

From qualitative, quantitative and mixed methods to evaluation, SAGE is the essential resource for academics and practitioners looking for the latest in methods by leading scholars.

www.sagepublications.com